The Segregated Hour

The Segregated Hour

*A Layman's Guide
to the History of Black Liberation Theology*

JEREMY LUCAS

WIPF & STOCK · Eugene, Oregon

THE SEGREGATED HOUR
A Layman's Guide to the History of Black Liberation Theology

Wipf & Stock
A Division of Wipf and Stock Publishers
199 W. 8th Ave., Suite 3
Eugene, OR 97401
www.wipfandstock.com

ISBN 13: 978-1-60608-396-3

Manufactured in the U.S.A.

Contents

Introduction

WITH REGARD to the most prominent content of this book, I must confess that my age and the color of my skin are both reasonable limitations to understanding, much less explaining, one of the most controversial subjects in American history. For many years, I was the silent product of an integrated society now reaping the benefits and challenges of a movement long gone. I have never been a victim of social injustice or an affiliate of white oppression. You will not find me among the ashes of a broken family or the riches of an affluent minority. I am, if anything, a common man of faith who loves his Lord, his family, and his imperfect country.

While there are no rules that can prevent one man from telling another man's story, I fully accept the strong possibility that I am insufficient to the task at hand. Over the years, it has become socially inappropriate for a white man to speak of black history with any racial discernment because he himself is not the subject of his own account. Let the record show that I am willing to risk a violation of this order but will make every effort to be objective in the pages that follow.

∿ ∿ ∿

For most Americans of the present day, our national history as a people is only appreciated through the lens of the generations we represent. Baby boomers cherish the victories of a war their parents fought, Generation X-ers still wonder why they ever had to hide in the cellar, and millennial kids can't imagine what life was like before the Internet. Trying to communicate any level of comprehensive American history often requires a different approach for each audience.

The eldest generation has, dare I say, the greatest attention span for information, so long as the history within which they lived is not redefined. While they have little tolerance for loose interpretations of the past, their attentive nature will hear out the vast majority of arguments if the information is reliable. However, for many the study of history still remains a sacrilegious activity if their own memories are made to appear incompatible with the new picture of history being introduced.

For those who make up what is known as Generation X, history has become a critical practice where no topic is off limits. These are the young people who grew up in homes where the terrors of a Cold War merged from what *might* have happened to what *never* happened. They learned that history is made up of imperfect people and imperfect nations all vying for their own right to succeed. More often than not, this is a generation of Americans who are open to seeing our national past with a critical lens of historical curiosity.

Millennials are, perhaps, the most difficult to comprehend because no dominant, mature voice has emerged to represent them. Unlike either of the previous generations, this group has learned through technological means that yesterday, quite literally, is old news. (The seventh winner of "American Idol" is far more relevant than the third or fourth.) Almost all of history, for them, represents a completely different world from anything they know today. As a result, their generation tends to be somewhat indifferent toward the events of our national past.

Depending on the generation, discussions of our racially divided history can produce a very different set of opinions. American slavery has become an abstract institution that we acknowledge, but with great difficulty imagining how it was ever justified. There are no living defenders of its practice. A little closer but no less abstract is public segregation. Children might still poke fun at one another's skin color, but they would never consider it serious enough to require separate facilities. We simply live in a different world than the one we so often read. The farther we get from our past, the more diverse we become in our convictions about what matters and what does not.

Black Liberation, for many Americans, is an irrational ideology that has no political purpose for the present day. From a distance, it seems incredibly out of touch with the way most people have evolved in their racial maturity. For the boomers who saw it emerge, Black Liberation represents the violent thinking of an era they wish to forget. For others, it seems curiously opposed, in theory, to the ideals of a postmodern culture. And yet, for causes rarely understood, Black Liberation has continued to thrive for decades in some of the most desolate neighborhoods of American society.

Residents of the inner city have a long history of fighting for survival during the week and turning to the steeple at the end of the road on Sunday morning. Fiery sermons and lively worship have established the Black Church as a traditional place of hope for those who have few or no tangible blessings when the service has ended. Their message, for the most part, has always been simple: when the world breaks your spirit, the Lord will build it back up with the help of the church.

Toward the end of the civil rights movement, these two institutions of African American history, the Black Liberation movement and the Black Church, were merged together in what became known as Black Liberation Theology.[1] Their progress to that point is the subject of this book. But before I begin, it seems only fair to explain briefly why someone such as myself would have ever become so engaged with the issue.

∾ ∾ ∾

1. It should be noted that there are many, many black churches operating independently from the views of Black Liberation and/or the teachings of Black Theology.

Several years ago, my wife and I moved to a quiet little town in Virginia where we both intended to work for a few years at the local university. Although I had lived in cities all over the United States and felt prepared for our new adventure, we soon discovered a culture shock like none we could have expected. Much to our surprise, racial segregation was very much alive and well.

I could recall watching the Grisham-inspired film "A Time to Kill" just before the turn of the century from a living room in the Pacific Northwest and thinking that the distant Mississippi setting was anything but realistic. Nowhere in the country, it seemed, could so much racial tension persist underneath the surface. And while it is true that the town of Canton had been fictionalized, it never truly occurred to me that racism was still so prevalent in the nation that I loved. Nor did I imagine that there could be a town quite so hampered by a past that many Americans now considered ancient history.

Our new small town home in Virginia had been the site of strikes and school closures that occurred as a result of enforcing *Brown v. the Board of Education* more than half a century before. Many of the children who lost their opportunity at an education during those years were now mothers, fathers, and grandparents living in the same town. Not much had changed in the community since the civil rights movement, and racial segregation was far more obvious than one might otherwise expect. The town was out of date, the jobs were sparse, and yes, the schools were still heavily segregated by the court of public opinion.

I worked as an assistant catering director for the university, and most of our salaried management shared the same story: we were well paid and we were white. Most of our employees who worked in the preparation and serving of each meal on campus shared their own story: they were underpaid and they were black. The racial contrast between staff and management was staggering.

Cheyenne was a mother of three who worked in my department. She had no husband, no car, no phone, and no prospects for the future. Across the street from our campus was a McDonald's restaurant offering $7.00/hr to all new hires, but Cheyenne insisted on staying with our staff at a pay of less than $6.00/hr because she simply could not risk a shift in the pay period. Her home had been built by Habitat for Humanity, but she was in danger of defaulting on an already low mortgage. Between her full time service at the school and her full time care of children at home, she was a classic example of an economic depression most noticeable in the black community.

Each year, it fell on me to evaluate Cheyenne as a candidate for higher wages, but it wasn't long before I realized that this was just an illusory task I had given myself. No matter how hard she worked or how much I felt she deserved, the corporate powers that be would only permit a five cent pay raise. Some in our office had whispered rumors of the decade before my arrival when this same woman had been given a two cent raise.

From time to time, whether from frustration with life or income, Cheyenne would break down into tears in my office. Almost without knowing, I had become her advocate as well as her enemy. The notion of paying people for the value of their labor was common sense as far as I was concerned, but when I approached my superiors, the road blocks were far beyond my reach. As I soon discovered, Cheyenne was not the only one on the dining staff who faced an uphill climb. The challenges were widespread and troubling. Even if I cared deeply about their misfortune, they knew that I wouldn't be there forever.

My title and social condition were a gateway of personal opportunity. At some point, my wife and I would be leaving town for a life of our independent choosing. For Cheyenne and the many other African American citizens of small-town Virginia, the fight to earn a decent living would continue in our absence.

Throughout our tenure, we visited several churches in the area and discovered a remarkable divide between the Black Church and the white church. On one particular Sunday morning, we were stunned to hear a white preacher compare the actions of the Good Samaritan to a white man providing necessary charity to a black man. It was then that we looked around to discover there was not a black face in the crowd. Across town and nearer to the face of poverty, my wife and I spent a Sunday morning worshipping with an all black congregation. We were openly welcomed, but received curious stares. There, in the middle of Virginia, we encountered a most sacred and segregated hour of American life on both sides of the aisle.

For several years after we left, I simply never made a connection between the Black Church and the concerns of a struggling black community. One seemed easily independent of the other. It never occurred to me that there was a reason segregation had managed to survive in the church. That is, until the presidential campaign of 2008.

In March of 2007 thousands of eyes were glued to the confrontational interview between Sean Hannity of Fox News and the Reverend Jeremiah Wright of Trinity United Church of Christ in Chicago (an interview now widely available on YouTube). Senator Barack Obama, an emerging candidate for president, was a long time friend of Wright as well as a member of his church. Their relationship had even inspired Obama to write a New York Times bestseller called *The Audacity of Hope*. Clearly, Wright was caught off guard when Hannity began challenging the teachings of Black Liberation Theology for the first time on a national stage. Their conversation became rather awkward and unsettling for many of the same reasons that I opened with in this introduction. A white man was openly challenging a black man on matters of racial theology.

Diehard Republicans and curious liberals began spreading word that Obama was potentially in league with a racist cult from

Chicago. And as the year progressed, few thought that a man with questionable affiliations would surpass the Democratic popularity of Hillary Clinton as the nominee of his party. But when he won the Iowa caucus in January of 2008, all eyes turned back to the junior senator from Illinois. Within just a few weeks, he would have to publically address his views of Reverend Wright, the Black Church, and race relations in America.

Voters from California to New Hampshire soon became witness to a cycle of videos within which Wright was seen cursing America for its oppressive history. The voting electorate, including those who had already cast their ballots in Obama's favor, were beginning to wonder about the relationship between these two men. Popular news commentators like Bill O'Reilly of Fox News, Glenn Beck of CNN, and radioman Rush Limbaugh stirred up controversy on the subject, but I began to wonder if there was a valuable history getting lost in the shuffle of politics. Few analysts seemed willing or able to offer a balanced assessment of Wright's theology without using the subject as a partisan wedge.

For most of the summer before that historic November election, I managed to turn off the news and immerse myself in the study and research of Black Liberation Theology. I have written this book to share that research, but I have no illusions that my work will in any way cover all that needs to be said.

1

Anything But Civil

SOON AFTER the sun rose on the morning of April 15, 1865, Abraham Lincoln left a room of grown men in tears. Edwin Stanton, the Secretary of War, had been by his side through the night, and following Lincoln's dying breath, Stanton paused before rising to say what everyone in the room had already concluded: "Now he belongs to the Ages."[1] Sorrow seemed to engulf the country, regardless of locality. The bloodiest fighting in American history had taken such a toll on the Union and Confederate soldiers that few took any pleasure in the death of their president. Just six days earlier, a worn and muddy General Robert E. Lee had entered Appomattox Courthouse to stand before General Ulysses S. Grant and offer the full surrender of his Southern armies. Grant would recall their encounter with sadness:

> I felt like anything rather than rejoicing at the downfall of a foe who had fought so long and valiantly, and had suffered so much for a cause, though that cause was, I believe, one of the worst for which a people ever fought, and one for which there was the least excuse. I do not question, however, the sincerity of the great mass of those who were opposed to us.[2]

The "cause" that Grant spoke of is frequently debated among historians, but generally accepted by modern Americans. Most

1. Bennett, *America*, 389.
2. Quoted in Bennett, *America,* 389.

believe that the Civil War was a war to end slavery. But slavery was not the primary cause for a war between the states. Shortly after the votes had been tallied in favor of President-elect Lincoln in November of 1860, prominent figures in South Carolina gathered together in a "secession convention," where they agreed to remove their state from the Union by December 20. As other states followed, President Buchanan was "paralyzed" by the divisive actions of his countrymen.[3] The limbo of a lame duck president allowed seven states to remove themselves from the *United* States of America before Lincoln arrived in Washington to do anything about it. Restoring the Union was, without question, Lincoln's foremost objective in going to war.

President Lincoln saw the immoral nature of American slavery and wanted nothing more than to see it removed from the nation he loved, but he was a man of law. The new president knew that ending slavery would require the federal government to interfere with a constitutional privilege—the right of the states to govern themselves in the manner of their own choosing without the imposition of a higher body. Immorality was not sufficient grounds for ending slavery. Lincoln was incredibly cautious about setting any precedent for dictating moral behavior from the White House.

As Lincoln and the Union debated how best to restore the country, slaves were seen as a crutch to the Southern economy that, if emancipated, would create a ripple effect in the war. Rather than ending slavery based on moral outrage, the federal government did so as a strategic maneuver. They resolved to end slavery as a means for restoring the Union. "If the rebels did not stop fighting and return to the Union by January 1, 1863, the president would free 'thenceforward and forever' all slaves in the rebel states."[4]

3. Bennett, *America*, 308.

4. Oates, *Malice toward None*, 319.

The end of slavery in rebel states, however, was not a forbidding of slavery everywhere. This would require congressional action—an amendment to the Constitution. Two years after Lincoln's Emancipation Proclamation took effect, both the House of Representatives and the Senate approved legislation that would officially outlaw slavery in the whole of the United States. And on February 1, 1865, the president signed a "Joint Resolution submitting the proposed 13th Amendment to the states."[5]

With just twenty-seven amendments passed in the history of the U.S., none has been more difficult to sell to the American people than the thirteenth. Members of Congress who pushed it through Washington channels had little opposition, and almost every opponent of abolition was now serving in the Confederacy, thus making Congress a mostly northern institution. But in order to pass, it still had to face the states.

> The Congress . . . shall propose Amendments to this Constitution . . . which . . . shall be valid to all Intents and Purposes, as part of this Constitution, when ratified by the Legislatures of three fourths of the several States.[6]

More than 30 percent of the nation's thirty-six states were officially aligned with the Confederacy, a body whose infrastructure demanded slavery as the basis of its economic success. Passing an amendment abolishing slavery everywhere would require a heavy hand of persuasion in the South by a federal government rooted in the philosophy of northern lawmakers. This was a tall order for a nation still at war.

For years slavery had been justified among southern divines (pastors and bishops) through an interpretation of Genesis 9 that assumed far more than the text would either literally or figuratively allow.

---

5. U.S. Constitution, amend. 13.
6. U.S. Constitution, art. 5.

> And Ham, the father of Canaan, saw the nakedness of his father, and told his two brethren without. And Shem and Japheth took a garment, and laid it upon both their shoulders, and went backward, and covered the nakedness of their father; and their faces were backward, and they saw not their father's nakedness. And Noah awoke from his wine, and knew what his younger son had done unto him. And he said, "Cursed be Canaan; a servant of servants shall he be unto his brethren."[7]

Known today as racial prophecy, a belief was born among slave owners that this was a text separating white men from black men, making the latter more apt for labor and the former more fit to lead. Shem, in the text, was to become the "servant of servants" to his brothers and the generations that would follow. This is a tough passage to process for most Christians, regardless of any slave-based implications. But the separation of Ham from his brothers was a national divide rather than a racial one.

> These are the families of the sons of Noah, after their generations, in their nations: and by these were the nations divided in the earth after the flood.[8]

Still, many of these southern "divines" would cite the Old Testament "to show that the Israelites, including Abraham and other favored patriarchs, held slaves without drawing God's censure. They cited the New Testament to demonstrate that neither Jesus nor the apostles ever preached against slavery and used the Noahic curse to provide a racial justification for the specific enslavement of blacks."[9] The Reverend James A. Lyon of Columbus, Mississippi, himself a slave owner, declared from the pulpit, "As to the lawfulness of the institution slavery in itself considered,

7. Genesis 9:22–26. Note: All Scripture references are from the King James Version.

8. Gen 10:32.

9. Genovese, *Consuming Fire*, 4.

disconnected from its abuses, we scarcely deem it necessary to discuss it."[10] With the racial argument based on obscure passages in the Old Testament, the New Testament became sufficient grounds for demanding the obedience of a slave without his own individual right.

> Servants, be obedient to them that are your masters according to the flesh, with fear and trembling, in singleness of your heart, as unto Christ.[11]
>
> Servants, obey in all things your masters according to the flesh; not with eyeservice, as menpleasers; but in singleness of heart, fearing God.[12]
>
> Exhort servants to be obedient unto their own masters, and to please them well in all things; not answering again.[13]

To tamper with the traditionally Christian view on American slavery in the South was to negotiate a new balance between Scripture and the sacred rights of man embraced in the words of Jefferson's Declaration of Independence:

> We hold these Truths to be self-evident, that all Men are created equal, that they are endowed, by their Creator, with certain unalienable Rights, that among these are Life, Liberty, and the Pursuit of Happiness.

Christian slave owners faced a conflict of written authority. They believed firmly that Scripture was its own constitution between God and humankind but conceded that the founding documents were a purely human constitution. Much of Jefferson's Declaration had been based on the political theory of

---

10. Quoted in Genovese, *Consuming Fire*, 59.

11. Ephesians 6:5.

12. Colossians 3:22.

13. Titus 2:9.

a late seventeenth century English philosopher, John Locke, who testified of this equality among men.

> The state has a law of nature to govern it, which obliges every one: and reason, which is that law, teaches all mankind, who will but consult it, that being all equal and independent, no one ought to harm another in his life, health, liberty, or possessions.[14]

Even for a good student of Scripture, it can be difficult to reconcile Pauline scriptures that refer to this relationship between master and servant. Our social environment no longer includes any such categories. We have employers rather than masters. We have employees rather than servants. And in most cases, Americans work with one another of their own free will. Nonetheless, Lincoln and his administration were forced to make a decision about slavery for what they saw as the greater good of the nation. Since there was no explicit condemnation of slavery from Genesis to Revelation, this became the greatest challenge in selling the Thirteenth Amendment to southern divines and confederate spokesmen.

In his earliest years, Lincoln had witnessed the inhumane treatment of slaves and "brooded over their condition." Sailing down the Ohio River with a friend during their early twenties, the future president witnessed "a coffle of twelve slaves on board, all chained together" like fish on a line. Lincoln's observations of slavery during that trip would torment his heart and mind for years to come.[15] But Lincoln was a man who respected the laws of his country. He knew that the Founders had set in place a very difficult path for change. The Constitution had been written for the purpose of restricting the federal government from meddling in the affairs of the states or altering laws at the whim of a presi-

---

14. Locke, *Second Treatise*, chap. 2, sec. 6.
15. Quoted in Oates, *Malice toward None*, 59–60.

dent. To end slavery in the United States of America would require crossing that boundary for the first time in his nation's history.

As Grant closed in on the vulnerable flank of Lee's army in April of 1865, Lincoln had already begun working to persuade the southern states to accept the Thirteenth Amendment as an appropriate means to an end. In between the surrender of Lee on April 9 and the president's death on April 15, two southern states, Tennessee and Arkansas, approved the amendment. Over the course of several months, more southern states would follow, but with great apprehension. It wasn't until the end of 1865, with the signature of Georgia, that this complicated amendment was officially ratified.

Of the deeply southern states that rejected the amendment, only Mississippi stood in defiance. Symbolic though it was, their disapproval set a tone for the future of southern reconstruction. Knowing that they made up an important part of the remaining quarter of states not required for ratification, Mississippi remained silent for almost 130 years, finally ratifying the abolition of slavery in 1995.[16] An intentional refusal to accept the end of slavery was the backdrop upon which all of postwar Reconstruction would fall. While Mississippi verbally opposed a change, several other states only approved the amendment in order to gain postwar security under the federal government.

Before his death, Lincoln had been at odds with Congress over how to bring "rebellious states back into the fold." Understandably, many in Congress were concerned that a lenient return to the Union after so bloody a war would perpetuate the conflicts that divided the nation. Lincoln, however, proposed a Ten Percent Plan providing that "once 10 percent or more of the voting population of any occupied state had taken the oath [of allegiance to the Union], they were authorized to set up a loyal government." Not everyone had agreed with the president's proposal, but with Andrew Johnson suddenly at the helm of a

16. Silverman, *You Can't Air That,* 119.

new administration, the Thirteenth Amendment would become a tool for pressuring southern states to give up far more than they were prepared to concede. In order for members of the broken Confederacy to regain equal statehood with "full rights under the Constitution," Johnson insisted that they approve the Thirteenth Amendment as a prerequisite for their redemption.[17]

With few exceptions, the end of slavery meant that southern state leaders had to find new ways of continuing their deeply held views. Each state reconvened a constitutional convention and discussed laws unto which they could continue in much the same way as they had before the war. If slavery was to be abolished amidst their collective disapproval, then it would have to be reborn under another name and another system. Racism would soon become the new institution of slavery through the introduction of Black Code legislation.

The codes were intended to "subject former slaves to a variety of special regulations and restrictions on their freedom."[18] Not surprisingly, in November of 1865, Mississippi enacted the most explicit of these codes.

> Be it further enacted . . . that all freedmen, free negroes and mulattoes in this State, over the age of eighteen years, found on the second Monday in January, 1866, or thereafter, with no lawful employment or business, or found unlawfully assembling themselves together either in the day or night time . . . shall be fined in the sum of not exceeding, in the case of a freedman, free negro or mulatto, fifty dollars . . . and imprisoned at the discretion of the court.[19]

Essentially, if a black man was found with no work, he could be fined and imprisoned as though unemployment were

---

17. Divine, *America*, 453–55.

18. Ibid., 455.

19. Quoted in Johnson, *American Past*, 3.

his crime. Under this and other Black Codes across the south, the black community was once again enslaved through labor laws.

❧ ❧ ❧

For many Americans, it has become almost commonplace to disregard the challenges of modern racism by declaring that the Civil War brought an official end to slavery and thus gave black people every opportunity to be as free as anyone else. "Any failure to succeed is their own fault," they say.

Certainly there is truth in expecting people from all walks of life to stand up for their own freedoms, but the Supreme Court had previously ruled that blacks were not to be considered citizens of the United States. Hence, the Thirteenth Amendment did not provide the necessary justice that the black community required. They could neither vote in elections nor have their testimony accepted in a court of law. With Black Codes now firmly in place among southern states, slavery by its new name had become just as bitter. And after enduring a war that brought an end to the former institution of slavery, the new conflict between black and white was *anything but civil*.

The First Movement for Civil Rights

A T A gathering in 1867 in New York City, Sojourner Truth, an American abolitionist who had been born into northern slavery, spoke on the post-war situation:

> They have got their liberty—so much good luck to have
> slavery partly destroyed; not entirely. I want it[s] root
> and branch destroyed. Then we will all be free indeed.[1]

Her argument was simple. Slavery had been abolished by Lincoln in an effort to crush the lifeline of the southern economy, but the foundation of American slavery had been built on the immoral belief that blacks were less than human. Deeply felt racism was the "root and branch" of American genocide. Those who believed their laboring slaves were merely objects to possess and not fellow humans could just as easily treat them like dogs or horses trained only to serve their masters. Blood had been spilt in an effort to restore the Union, but little blood had been spilt in favor of civil equality.

Two days after the March 4, 1857, inauguration of President James Buchanan, Chief Justice Roger Brooke Taney had declared a landmark ruling in the case of *Dred Scott v. Sanford*. Under the laws of Missouri, Dred Scott was a slave. When his master moved to the free state of Illinois, Scott believed it was his right to file suit against those who were continuing to enslave him. Justice Taney's ruling, however, stole any hope that Scott and his family might

1. Quoted in Boyd, *Autobiography*, 144.

have held. In the words of historian William Bennett, the ruling was "truly breathtaking."[2] When Taney read the verdict of the court, a pin could have dropped in the chamber without notice:

> It is obvious that they [those of the enslaved African race] were not even in the minds of the framers of the Constitution when they were conferring special rights and privileges upon the citizens of a State in every other part of the Union. . . . Indeed, when we look to the conditions of this race in the several States at the time, it is impossible to believe that these rights and privileges were intended to be extended to them.
>
> It is the opinion of the court that . . . neither Dred Scott himself, nor any of his family, were made free by being carried into this territory; even if they had been carried there by the owner, with the intention of becoming a permanent resident . . . it is the judgment of this court, that it appears by the record before us that [Dred Scott] is not a citizen of Missouri, in the sense in which that word is used in the Constitution.[3]

Justice Taney and the Supreme Court had determined that Scott had no rights in the United States of America because he was black. Thus, when slavery was ended by the Thirteenth Amendment, no one could pretend that blacks were equal. On the contrary, a man freed from slavery who had no citizenship was not free, nor was he equal.

Over the years that gave rise to the Civil War, many Americans had toyed with the concept of emigration, or simply, the notion of sending blacks back to Africa. The American Colonization Society, established more than a half a century before, had been created for the sole purpose of "providing a way to resettle free blacks outside the United States."[4] It was believed

2. Bennett, *America*, 293.

3. U.S. Reports, *Dred Scott v. John F. A. Sanford*, par. 55, 56, 193, 202.

4. Yarema, *American Colonization Society*, 3.

by members of the ACS, both white and black, that there could be no unity between the races. Equal citizenship, it was thought, would be a danger to society. No one could imagine the black community co-existing with white Americans who had once enslaved their people.

Still, the ACS did not gain widespread popularity.

> Firebrand abolitionists insisted that the Society's propaganda, branding free blacks as inferior and incapable of citizenship, lowered rather than elevated blacks and served only to increase prejudice and hatred.[5]

The challenge of allowing black equality and the possibility of *African* American citizenship required members of Congress to address their conscious fears of an integrated society. No one could be sure how things would turn out, but congressional Reconstruction demanded more than just an amendment to end slavery. The very roots of racial discrimination had to be pulled. If the Founders meant to exclude slaves from their declaration of human equality, then their philosophy had to be seen as imperfect.

Within just five years of the Thirteenth's ratification, Congress passed the fourteenth and fifteenth amendments. The former provided "national citizenship" and equal rights for all persons born or naturalized on American soil. Under the Fourteenth Amendment, the federal government now had responsibility for ensuring the equal rights of all Americans, black or white. The Fifteenth Amendment took its predecessor just a step further, prohibiting "denial of franchise" because of race, color, or past servitude. In other words, no man could be denied the right to vote and thus lose his voice as a citizen of the United States.[6]

As both amendments began to pass through the ratification process, states and independent organizations were finding ways

5. Ibid., viii.
6. Divine, *America*, 456–57.

around the federal system. If a black man was to be given his federal right to vote, then white men would take it upon themselves to make voting and citizen participation that much more difficult. And almost a century before the existence of Black Power, newly titled African Americans were preyed upon by the awful vanity of white power. None became more memorable in their actions than the Ku Klux Klan.

By intimidating black voters, the KKK was able to break the will and spirit of liberated citizens and keep them from finding a voice. In South Carolina, Elias Hill, a crippled black preacher from York County, was violently harassed for encouraging his congregants to stand up for themselves.

> They came in a very rapid manner, and I could hardly tell whether it was the sound of horses or men. At last they came to my brother's door, which is in the same yard, and broke open the door and attacked his wife, and I heard her screaming and mourning. I could not understand what they said, for they were talking in an outlandish and unnatural tone, which I had heard they generally used at a negro's house.... She was crying and the Ku-Klux were whipping her to make her tell where I lived. ... Then I knew they would take me, and I answered, "I am here." ... They pointed pistols at me ... as if they were going to shoot me, telling me they were going to kill me.[7]

To the west of York County, Harriet Hernandes testified of the violence that she and her daughter had endured while her husband was out of the house.

> They came in; I was lying in bed.... They took me out of bed; they would not let me get out, but they took me up in their arms and toted me out—me and my daughter Lucy. He struck me on the forehead with a pistol ... he kicked

7. U.S. Congress, *Report,* Vol. 1.

> me over when I went to get over; and then he went on
> to a brush pile, and they laid us right down there, both
> together. They laid us down twenty yards apart, I reckon.
> They had dragged and beat us along. They struck me right
> on top of my head, and I thought they had killed me.

When asked how many other black citizens in her neighborhood faced the same violence, Hernandes replied, "It is all of them, might near."[8]

By 1875 the problems in Mississippi were such that Governor Adelbert Ames hoped to obtain assistance from President Grant.

> The "white liners" have gained their point – they have, by
> killing and wounding, so intimidated the poor Negroes
> that they can in all human probability prevail over them
> at the election. I shall at once try to get troops from the
> general government.[9]

The federal government certainly played a part in trying to suppress the violence, but by 1877, its efforts had ended and the constitutional amendments were no longer being enforced. Where the Thirteenth Amendment had ended slavery, white power mandated black labor. Where the Fourteenth Amendment had given citizenship to African *Americans*, white power lessened the potential for equality. And where the Fifteenth Amendment had given voting rights to all men regardless of color, white power crushed the voices of the black community for almost a century.

By the turn of the century, public segregation had been fully realized through the widely familiar "separate but equal" ruling of the Supreme Court known as *Plessy v. Ferguson.*

> If one race be inferior to the other socially, the Constitution
> of the United States cannot put them upon the same

8. U.S. Congress, *Report,* Vol. 5.

9. Perman, *Civil War and Reconstruction,* 387.

plane.... [Even] the question of the proportion of colored blood necessary to constitute a colored person, as distinguished from a white person ... these are questions to be determined under the laws of each state.[10]

ლ ლ ლ

With the end of Reconstruction came an end of government intervention on behalf of the black community. Without a continued hand of protection, years of uncontested violence opened the door to a new age of poverty. And while there have always been poor men of every race and nationality, the dominant face of poverty in America began to have just one face. The first movement for civil rights had failed.

10. U.S. Reports, *Plessy v. Ferguson,* par. 25–26.

3

Poor Man Out

BY WAR'S end, Philadelphia, the city of brotherly love, had long become a beacon of hope and opportunity for those in the black community. Thousands upon thousands of former slaves, now freedmen, were missing brothers and sisters, fathers and mothers, sons and daughters. Their search was recorded in the *Christian Recorder*, a weekly newspaper representing the African Methodist Episcopal Church (AME). Below are just a few examples of "advertisements" for lost family members.

September 22, 1866
Information Wanted

Information wanted of the whereabouts of my husband, Richard Jones, and my two sons, John and Thomas. We were separated in the woods, near a place called Alleywhite, in November, 1862. I was carried back to Suffolk by the Union troops. I have heard nothing of them since. We were owned by Birven Jones, of Smithfield, Suffolk County, Virginia. I am the grand-daughter of old Tom Peet Wilson. I am much in want at this time.

May 8, 1869
Information Wanted

Information wanted of my son Charles Blackwell. He was sold from me in Lancaster County, Virginia, ten years ago, when quite young. He was sold from the estate of Mr. Joseph Beacham to Mr. Lewis Dix, and

then taken to Mississippi. I am an old man and need
the companionship of my son. Any assistance in secur-
ing information of his whereabouts will be thankfully
received. Ministers in Mississippi and throughout the
entire country will please read in their churches.

April 2, 1870
Information Wanted

Information wanted of Sarah Williams, who I left at
Halifax Court House, VA, about 25 years ago. She be-
longed to a man whose name was William Early, who
kept a dry-goods store. Any information of her will be
thankfully received by her sister, Martha Ann Good,
who was taken away from Nathan Dexter, who kept a
hotel at Halifax, at 12 o'clock at night, when quite small,
and sold in Alabama, but who now lives at 225 Currant
Alley, Philadelphia, PA. Ministers in the South, please
read in your churches.[1]

Henry McNeal Turner, who had recruited blacks to serve in
the Union army, was an optimistic military chaplain who could
envision the end of discrimination. He believed, like many during the war, in the vision of Abraham Lincoln toward a more
perfect Union. However, after Lincoln's assassination, the rise of
white power, and the eventual failure of Reconstruction by 1877,
Turner emerged as an AME spokesman for emigration and black
nationalism.[2] His views were not held by everyone, but there was
an ever-increasing need to resolve the race issue in America.
More importantly, those at the bottom of the economic totem
pole—those with no money, no family, and no education—were
in need of someone to care for their plight.

From its very inception, the AME church quickly became an
institutional organization devoted to helping those who couldn't
help themselves. When the black community needed support,

1. Quoted in Johnson, *American Past*, 7–10.
2. Divine, *America*, 477–78.

they learned to lean on the shoulder of the Black Church. For too many years, members of the AME had witnessed the application of false doctrine to promote a biblical defense of slavery. As a result, their handling of Scripture became less about proving what they believed and more about living what they knew. Long before it was ever written down, they developed a theology of service based on social responsibility.

∾ ∾ ∾

By the end of the Civil War, the economic structure of the South had been almost entirely transformed. Nearly 40 percent of the cotton crop that had once been the apex of southern prosperity was now being grown west of the Mississippi. The rapidly progressing industrial revolution moved the postwar South into a "classic pattern of underdevelopment" that affected the lives of black and white Americans alike.[3] No assessment of radical Reconstruction would be complete without, at least, a partial acknowledgment that economic hardship was colorblind. Nonetheless, blacks were suffering from "dire poverty, and the old [white] ruling class remained largely intact." The result was an unshakable image of worthless blacks and superior whites.[4]

Success for an African American required a much steeper climb than the average citizen. With the public at large disregarding their potential at every turn, any achievement became heroic. For example, Hiram Rhodes Revels became the first black senator, filling a seat left vacant by the former president of the Confederacy, Jefferson Davis. Then there was P.B.S. Pinchback, who served briefly as the first black governor of Louisiana. And after the turn of the century, Jack Johnson defeated Tommy Burns, to become the first black heavyweight champion in the sport of professional boxing.[5] These accomplishments proved

3. Foner, *Short History*, 169.

4. Ibid., 179.

5. AfricanAmericans.com, "African American Firsts."

that nothing was impossible in the black community, but they failed to remove the impressions of the majority who saw blacks as collectively inferior.

As Revels, Pinchback, and Johnson were carving out a name for themselves in a predominantly white society, the vast majority of blacks were coming of age with little or no identity. By the 1890s, the rate of sickness among African Americans was 20 percent higher than it had been on the plantations. Many were being squeezed out of crafts and industries where they had once been successful under slavery. With the changing face of technology and the low rate of education among blacks, their plunge toward inevitable poverty became ever more obvious.[6] Even with prominent teachers like Booker T. Washington and W.E.B. Du Bois working in segregated universities, the likelihood that a black child would achieve anything resembling an American Dream was far less than that of his or her white counterpart. This was not for lack of desire but for lack of support. "Separate but equal" had proven almost immediately that there was no such thing.

∽ ∽ ∽

Contemporary Americans may wonder why the poor and disadvantaged citizens of their country do not simply rise up from their own ashes and find a way to succeed.

Surely, they say, it cannot fall on the rest of society to be responsible for what a few minor citizens failed to achieve. Some have called this a "social Darwinism" akin to Herbert Spencer's *survival of the fittest*: the belief that human survival does not depend on the assistance of others but, rather, is our own responsibility. Such conditional affection toward the poor is, perhaps, the most ignorant of all reasons to refuse lending a hand. Under this school of thought, people are far more inclined to help the rich who lose their wealth than the poor who never had it.

6. Fogel and Engerman, *Time on the Cross*, 261.

The period of post-Reconstruction signaled a philosophical and economic split between the struggles of the white community and the disproportional weight of poverty in the black community. While there were always exceptions to the rule, poor African Americans were left to fend for themselves at a time when they most needed the compassion of their countrymen. But a movement was coming and they knew it was only a matter of time.

4

Depression of the Darker Brother

A FTER THE case of *Plessy v. Ferguson*, almost thirty years passed in which the violence-prone Klan became relatively mild. Issues popped up from year to year, but it wasn't until after the First World War that an influx of Jews and Catholics on American soil stirred a "reincarnation of the KKK." By its own measure, there were nine million members in 1924 alone.[1] If their count was even remotely accurate, there were almost as many members in the Klan as there were African Americans in the country.[2] It takes little imagination to consider the racial tension that existed during the Roaring Twenties.

When the stock market crashed in 1929, depression emptied the pockets of middle and upper class Americans but created an "architecture of despair" among the poorer African American community. Many had "been at the bottom so long that it might have seemed that nothing could possibly get worse." Participants in the Great Migration, the departure of half a million blacks from the rural South during World War I, were now the heaviest hit victims of the Great Depression.[3]

Before he was elected to the United States House of Representatives in 1945, Adam Clayton Powell Jr. was a member of the inner-city Harlem community. The City of New York had no public welfare system to help residents deal with the problems cre-

1. Watkins, *Great Depression*, 33.
2. U.S. Census Bureau, "Race and Hispanic Origin."
3. Watkins, *Great Depression*, 71.

ated by the Depression. Recognizing the needs in his community, Powell organized a relief program headquartered in Abyssinian Baptist Church, thus continuing the ideal that a church existed to serve its community.[4] He later wrote of the circumstances that had led to the shortage of official services in Harlem:

> Harlem was a community that had been built to house about eighty thousand whites, mostly German and Irish. Within one decade it became the world's largest racial ghetto because three hundred thousand Negro people from the South and the Caribbean had poured into it. Despite the fact that Harlem had quadrupled its population, not a single new school or hospital had been built in the district; and to aggravate matters, the private hospitals in the Harlem area refused to accept Negro patients. And so, in this compact area, three hundred thousand Negro people were forced to live, serviced by institutions created for only eighty thousand.[5]

Under the watch of President Franklin Roosevelt, a great many programs were enacted to stimulate the economy and restore the basic freedoms of everyday Americans. The KKK had fallen in popularity after the Depression, but they continued to march, burn crosses, and engage in the lynching of African Americans. Even though the president's domestic agenda had been incredibly popular across the country, any effort by lawmakers to bring forward an anti-lynching bill uncovered the heartless prejudice that still existed in Congress.

Hoping to avoid even the slightest discussion, Senator Ellender of Louisiana implored his fellow senators to "at all cost preserve the white supremacy of America."[6] In the face of great

---

4. Boyd, *Autobiography,* 285.

5. Powell, *Adam by Adam,* 61–62.

6. Watkins, *Great Depression,* 323.

animosity in the South, no anti-lynching bill ever passed through Congress. And the violence continued.

By the 1940s several new spokesmen had begun to lecture the black community about their responsibility to take back the freedoms that had been stolen by the white community. Among them was A. Philip Randolph. Speaking from Detroit in 1942, he pressed his audience to fight for their God-given rights through whatever means were necessary.

> Slavery was not abolished because it was bad and unjust. It was abolished because men fought, bled and died on the battlefield. Therefore, if Negroes secure their goals, immediate and remote, they must win them and to win them they must fight, sacrifice, suffer, go to jail and, if need be, die for them. These rights will not be given. They must be taken.[7]

Randolph introduced a daunting and overlooked truth. Slavery was not itself removed from America because of its immorality. Neither the federal government nor the American people had ever cooperated for the purpose of bringing an end to human bondage. In other words, there had never been a collective recognition of slavery's stain on the canvas of American history. And in the absence of that recognition, blood had still been shed and lives had still been lost. He continued:

> As to the composition of our movement. Our policy is that it be all-Negro and pro-Negro, but not anti-white, or anti-Semitic or anti-labor, or anti-Catholic. The reason for this policy is that all oppressed people must assume the responsibility and take the initiative to free themselves.[8]

7. Quoted in Boyd, *Autobiography*, 310.
8. Ibid., 311.

Randolph was not looking for a reversal of power. His objective was not to destroy the majority but to equalize the rights of the minority. Randolph insisted that the black community had a "moral obligation to demand the right to enjoy and make use of [our] civil and political privileges." He ended the speech by saying:

> If we don't, we will lose the will to fight for our citizenship rights, and the public will consider that we don't want them and should not have them. This fight to break down these barriers in every city should be carefully and painstakingly organized. By fighting for these civil rights the Negro masses will be disciplined in struggle.[9]

For the first time in years, it seemed there were men and women in the black community who were prepared to rise up in a disciplined fight for their civil rights. Some might argue that the rest of the nation had it coming.

∾ ∾ ∾

The most eloquent interpretation of this period came from the hand of an African American poet named Langston Hughes. In his poem "I, Too," Hughes speaks of "the darker brother" who finds himself sent to the kitchen "when company comes." The darker brother is not asked whether he would prefer the kitchen or the table, but is expected to steer clear of any guests who might see him. While in the kitchen, he laughs, eats, and grows strong for a coming day when he will make his way to the table with or without an invitation.

The civil rights movement did not start because white Americans believed they were being unjust. It began when the black community found the strength to fight for their right to an equal seat at the table.

---

9. Ibid., 312.

5

Malcolm and Martin

A FTER YEARS of being in the back of the bus, when it was clear that at least some African Americans were ready to take action, two key men emerged with a resolve that could not have been more different. One, Malcolm X, believed in taking rights by force if and when the situation called for it. Whites, in his eyes, had been permitted to bear arms against blacks without reprimand (lynchings, burnings, shootings), so it only followed that in America, all blacks had a right, nay, a responsibility, to protect themselves against those who wished them harm. The other, Martin Luther King Jr., had matured in a world of theology, where peaceful solutions were a far more appropriate means to the same end. He reveled in the study of Henry David Thoreau and what he saw as a fitting call for the times: civil disobedience.

To understand Malcolm and Martin without bias, readers must set aside any individual preference for violent or non-violent problem-solving techniques. If someone illegally enters your home, do you reach for a gun or a phone? Some of us are more prone to violence than others. Some of us hold our anger deep within until rage consumes our otherwise peaceful exterior. The point is, all of us are torn between peace and war. The closer an enemy gets to the home of a peaceful individual, the more he or she may consider options that would never have been imaginable otherwise. In other words, a fair rendering of Malcolm and Martin requires realism and sensitivity.

In an effort to capture the widespread anger of his times, Malcolm wrote:

> The black man in North America was economically sick and that was evident in one simple fact: as a consumer, he got less than his share, and as a producer gave least. The black American today shows us the perfect parasite image—the black tick under the delusion that he is progressing because he rides on the udder of the fat, three-stomached cow that is white America.[1]

Ossie Davis, writing sometime after the death of Malcolm X, elevated the message with even harsher, more explicit terms.

> White folks do not need anybody to remind them that they are men. We do! This was his [Malcolm's] one incontrovertible benefit to his people. Protocol and common sense require that Negroes stand back and let the white man speak up for us, defend us, and lead us from behind the scene in our fight. But Malcolm said . . . Get up off your knees and fight your own battles. That's the way to win back your self-respect. He knew that every Negro who did not challenge on the spot every instance of racism, overt or covert, committed against him and his people, who chose instead to swallow his spit and go on smiling, was an Uncle Tom and a traitor, without . . . commonly accepted aspects of manhood.[2]

The lower people get on the social totem pole, the more they are oppressed by the weight of those above. Blacks were being told of their rights by whites who frequently hindered their liberties with a burning cross, a noose, or a pattern of slanderous threats. The federal government had long ago washed its hands of any responsibility for the well-being of its black citizenry. As a result, they were fed to the wolves of white supremacy and left to

1. Haley and Malcolm X, *Malcolm X*, 361.
2. Quoted in Haley and Malcolm, *Malcolm X*, 524–25.

fend for themselves, without a vocal warrior to remind them that they were full-fledged human beings with a will, with strength, and with the power to defend themselves. Furthermore, if whites were free to make threats against blacks, should blacks avoid a pre-emptive strike, even when whites had proven they were willing to act on their word? Under what ludicrous doctrine was one man able to beat his fellow man to a bloody pulp while that beaten man was denied the right to rise up and reciprocate? Naturally, these were not questions becoming a peaceful man. They were questions becoming a man of war.

Malcolm X was among those who were angered by oppression, and thus, his words became a battle cry for many in the black community.

> There's only one way to be independent. There's only one way to be free. It's not something someone gives to you. It's something that you take. Nobody can give you independence. Nobody can give you freedom. Nobody can give you equality or justice or anything. If you're a man, you take it. If you can't take it, you don't deserve it. Nobody can give it to you . . . Freedom comes to us either by ballots or by bullets.[3]

However harsh his words may have been, it is difficult to condemn them without also condemning the American Founders and their revolutionary resistance to British oppression. Blood was shed to force the issue of freedom. And in every case where people have been enslaved, whether physically or politically, violent revolution has been a natural and understandable progression. In many cases around the world, revolutionary efforts have not always provided people with the freedom they originally sought, but the fight goes on until the war has been exhausted and a truce can be established. This was Malcolm X: a man of war making efforts to build up an ideological army.

3. Boyd, *Autobiography*, 405.

His philosophical antithesis was King, who is still questioned by some in the black community for his commitment to words more than action.

> We must not return violence under any condition. I know this is difficult advice to follow.... But this is the way of Christ; it is the way of the cross. We must somehow believe that unearned suffering is redemptive ... We will match your capacity to inflict suffering with our capacity to endure suffering.[4]

Speaking to a gathering of students in California, King used a message about *agape* love, as found in the Greek New Testament, to teach what he believed was an appropriate response to racial brutality in America:

> Biblical theologians would say it [agape] is the love of God working in the minds of men. It is an overflowing love which seeks nothing in return. And when you come to love on this level you begin to love men not because they are likable, not because they do things that attract us, but because God loves them and here we love the person who does the evil deed while hating the deed that the person does.[5]

Peace-loving people of faith have often looked at this gentle approach and thought kindly of King. His life, for many people today, has become the legendary embodiment of peace for race relations in America. Most remembered for his "I Have a Dream" speech, Martin was a visionary orator who offered few practical suggestions for solving the kind of anger that still existed among men like Malcolm X. As King preached of an enduring patience, Malcolm insisted that patience had long been exhausted. Although both men wanted to achieve the same ends, they had begun with different theological roots.

4. Quoted in Cone, *Risks of Faith*, 58.
5. King, "Power," 31–32.

While enduring prison time, Malcolm X—born Malcolm Little—found his own version of "messiah" through the teachings of men like W. D. Fard and Elijah Muhammed, who he eventually came to believe were messengers "to the black people of North America."[6] His entire autobiographical chapter on salvation was a report on self-redemption through the Nation of Islam.

The Nation of Islam, anathema to the rest of the Muslim world, was founded in 1930 by a man of no consequence from Detroit whose followers eventually crowned him their incarnate god and declared that "white people are inherently evil." The Nation even went so far as to say that there was "no life after death," which flew in the face of the Islamic faith.[7] Malcolm was indoctrinated by the foremost leader of the Nation, Elijah Muhammed, and thus had little patience for the white community—even when they agreed with him on past and present injustices. He became "the national spokesperson" for the group and was a "symbol of young blacks' rage against white America's racism and also against middle-class blacks who [had] forgotten the plight of their poor brothers and sisters left behind in the ghetto."[8]

On the other side of the aisle was the biblical theology of King. He had learned much from the politics of the past but based his vision of hope on Christian cooperation and learned tolerance for those who do not look or act like everyone else. King believed in a future where "right there in Alabama, little black boys and black girls will be able to join hands with little white boys and white girls as sisters and brothers."[9] Asked about how long it would take to achieve his dream, he replied, "Not long, 'cause mine eyes have seen the glory of the coming of the

6. Haley and Malcolm X, *Malcolm X*, 218.

7. Armstrong, *Islam*, 150.

8. Cone, *Risks of Faith*, 98.

9. Washington, *I Have a Dream,* 105.

Lord, trampling out the vintage where the grapes of wrath are stored. . . . His truth is marching on."[10]

When forced to address the rising views of Malcolm X, King responded from a jail in Birmingham. His condemnation of their "bitterness and hatred" suggested that "black nationalism" was a fruitless endeavor of men who had lost their faith in anything good.

> This movement is nourished by the contemporary frustration over the continued existence of racial discrimination. It is made up of people who have lost faith in America, who have absolutely repudiated Christianity, and who have concluded that the white man is an incurable devil.[11]

King saw himself as standing "in the middle of two opposing forces in the Negro community," but he wasn't exactly in the middle. The fact that Malcolm had militarized his position meant that Martin had to de-militarize his own. And while the two men continued to take turns on the political stage in their movement for civil rights, a similar pot was bubbling in Washington over whether to wage a war against poverty in America and cure the long-term effects of slavery, discrimination, and racial hatred in the black community. Poverty, as it turned out, was a far more complex problem than the color of a man's skin. And while the impending birth of Black Liberation Theology would be rooted in salvation for the downtrodden poor, the debate wasn't quite so black and white.

10. Ibid., 124.
11. King, "Letter," 93.

6

The War on Poverty

IN ALMOST every dialogue regarding poverty, Americans face a strange paradox of speaking for those whose experience they have never shared. While many enter the discussion believing that poverty is the ultimate consequence of a lazy population, few intellectuals have ever been utterly reduced to an inadequate standard of living. Indeed, there are always those who choose to live in poverty out of rebellion or self pity, but their actions cast a shadow on the less prominent faces of those who suffer from involuntary poverty. This point, apart from race, deserves a good deal of our attention.

The many complications of poverty have not and never will be summarily defined as problems confined to the black community or resulting entirely from racial victimization. On the contrary, poverty must be understood for what it is: *any* human existence without the means to pursue one's own happiness. Such an existence can, by all means, be chosen. But more often than not, poverty is generated by gradual or sudden misfortunes, ranging from the unfortunate loss of work to unexpected illness, disabilities, or even old age. Since the late twentieth century, Americans have gradually come to believe that the poor in their communities are on a path of voluntary self-expression, as though poverty was and is the life that all poor choose in order to make a grand illustration on the social landscape. Richard Wagner, Harris Professor of Economics at George Mason University, once wrote:

> The distinction between involuntary poverty by chance and voluntary poverty through choice is simpler to make conceptually than it is to perceive empirically. Poverty is generally a mixture of choice and chance, with that mixture varying from case to case.[1]

He continued:

> It might seem reasonable that [public] policy should seek to aid cases where poverty is the result of chance, while refraining from aiding cases where poverty is the result of choice. The trouble with this prescription is that it cannot be implemented without knowledge of souls and minds. Nature does not generate birthmarks or other signals that allow such categorization. . . . The receipt of aid by those who are poor through choice will encourage more such choices. But to withhold aid to prevent such outcomes will imperil those who are poor through chance.[2]

Wagner was arguing that, although in theory one could be against helping those who haven't helped themselves, practically speaking, no one can truly know the heart and soul of the person whose poverty they so quickly condemn as voluntary. To avoid help for one is to avoid help for all on the basis of an unconfirmed and ignorant assumption.

As the fire of the civil rights movement was burning, conservatives and liberals entered a complex debate over the issue of poverty in America. Barry Goldwater, an Arizona Senator, made the political case in *The Conscience of a Conservative*:

> How easy is it to reach the voters with earnest importunities for helping the needy? And how difficult for Conservatives to resist these demands without appearing to be callous and contemptuous of the plight of less

1. Wagner, *American Conservatism*, 670.
2. Ibid., 671.

fortunate citizens. "Have you no sense of social obligation?" the Liberals ask.[3]

More than anything, Goldwater was standing up against
the idea of federal welfare programs that, he believed, "promote
the idea that the government owes the benefits it confers on the
individual, and that the individual is entitled, by right, to receive
them."[4] Believing he was right to suggest excessive government
intervention might produce more harm than good, a growing
block of newly impassioned conservatives began seeing any mention of welfare, whether on the federal or local level, as an almost
sinful concept. The unintended consequence of the Goldwater
Conscience was that Republicans were quickly painted with an
accusatory brush of elitism. It didn't matter that there were conservatives working in every public sector of social service.

In the absence of any visible compassion, another voice
emerged. Just two years later, Michael Harrington, whose writing of *The Other America* would soon inspire Lyndon Johnson
to begin a War on Poverty in 1964, helped to paint the picture of
"social blindness" in the conservative mind.

> Here is the most familiar version of social blindness: "The
> poor are that way because they are afraid to work. . . . If
> they were like me (or my father or my grandfather), they
> could pay their own way. But they prefer to live on the
> dole and cheat the taxpayers.[5]

His condemnation of the Goldwater *Conscience* is
striking:

> Those who could make the difference too often refuse
> to act because of their ignorant, smug moralisms. They
> view the effects of poverty—above all, the warping

3. Goldwater, *Conscience*, 57.

4. Ibid., 59.

5. Harrington, *Other America*, 14.

> of the will and spirit that is a consequence of being
> poor—as choices.[6]

Regardless of his socialized and atheistic tendencies, it was difficult for Conservatives to argue with Harrington's point: pursuit of the American dream among educated and working class Americans in a post-war society had created "a new kind of blindness about poverty."[7]

For the most part, the only poverty that middle and upper class citizens would admit to witnessing was that of a chosen departure from the norm. Like Christopher McCandless, who left the affluent suburbs of Washington to go "Into the Wild" and live without money by choice, successful Americans were beginning to see poverty through the lens of their sons and daughters who wandered into such a lifestyle as a means for adventure. In the case of McCandless, he believed that an affluent society was imprisoned by its own wealth and that wealth, into which he was born, was the root of all evil.[8] Many of America's children who disappeared into the world of poverty by choice were basing their decision on the same message that thousands of preachers have made clear in their pulpits: money can pollute the mind and divert the community from its spiritual responsibility.

Nevertheless, while some members of American society were choosing to live a life of poverty as a sign of rebellion, Harrington brought to life some of the unpopular yet far more widespread forms, such as case poverty and insular poverty.

> Case poverty is the plight of those who suffer from
> some physical or mental disability that is personal and
> individual and excludes them from the general advance.
> Insular poverty exists in areas like the Appalachians or

6. Ibid., 15–16.

7. Ibid., 4.

8. Penn, *Into the Wild*.

the West Virginia coal fields, where an entire section of
the country becomes economically obsolete.[9]

But the problem of poverty, according to Harrington, didn't
stop with these two forms. Unemployment, desperation, and old
age were among the many factors he identified in *The Other
America*.

It is bad enough for a worker to be laid off for a matter of weeks. When this becomes months, or even years,
it is not simply a setback. It is a basic threat to fundamental living standards, a menace to impoverishment.
... In short, the simple prescription of the comfortable
middle-class citizen, "I can't see why those people don't
just move, but I guess they're lazy," is spoken out of profound ignorance. There are many reasons why they can't
move; and in many cases it wouldn't make a difference
if they did. These are not people [who] are subject to a
temporary, cyclical kind of joblessness. They are more
often the ones who have had their very function in the
economy obliterated.[10]

A great number of human beings are required for
a brief period to do work that is too delicate for ma-
chines and too dirty for any but the dispossessed. So
the Southern Negroes, the Texas-Mexicans, and the
California Anglos are packed like cattle into trucks and
make their pilgrimage of misery ... [but not before they]
sell themselves in the marketplace. The various hiring
men chant out piece-work prices or hourly rates.[11]

Many states report that half their citizens over 65
have incomes too low to meet their basic needs ... Over
half of these people are covered by some kind of Federal
program (social security, old-age assistance, and so on).
Yet, the social security payments are, by Federal admis-

9. Harrington, *Other America*, 11.

10. Ibid, 32, 34.

11. Ibid, 40, 50.

sion, completely inadequate to a decent life.... The lonely aged poor are . . . the most impoverished single group in the subculture of poverty.... We have, as the Senate Committee well described it, a "storage bin" philosophy in America. We "maintain" the aged; we give them the gift of life, but we take away the possibility of dignity.[12]

Greatly ignored in the culture of poverty were the children who, whether their parents were poor by choice or chance, had become the most vulnerable. The "ghetto," in which so many children were being raised, was characterized by an "immoral maldistribution of wealth, high levels of unemployment, dilapidated housing, decrepit schools, inadequate health care, unavailable child care, and shattered familial and communal bonds."[13] Children forced to live in this environment "don't know of light beyond the tunnel of this darkness—they don't grow and they get stuck in this type of mentality."[14] Death in this world was becoming, ironically, a part of *life* for children who couldn't even begin to focus on education or the future. LeAlan Jones, a teenager from the South Side of Chicago would testify several years later of walking into a worn-down tenement building where five-year-old Eric Morse had been thrown from a fourteenth-floor window by two other children who taunted him for refusing to participate in a criminal theft.

No one around them appreciates life, so why should they? Look at the building—you walk in and it smells like urine, you walk up the stairs and it's dark, broken lights. When you live in filth, your mind takes in filth and you feel nothing.... These kids don't have the right ingredients to be good kids. . . . It's like you're in this

12. Ibid., 104–5, 108, 119.

13. Jones and Newman, *Our America*, 11.

14. Ibid., 95.

maze, and you either die in it or you escape.... I live here
not because I chose to, but because I have to.[15]

By the time President Johnson had begun his domestic
war, poverty was proving to be more than the absence of money
or the inability to support oneself. It was an entire sub-culture
that chewed on human life like quicksand. There was no way to
draw the line between chosen poverty and involuntary poverty.
Hence, when Harrington introduced an educated and comfortable America to the *other* America, the federal government,
under liberal leadership, took the message as an opportunity to
make a case for their political War on Poverty.

As Goldwater predicted, it wouldn't be a hard sell to the
easily broken hearts of a reflective American public who were
beginning to feel pressed by leaders of the civil rights movement
to address the guilt of racial discrimination, segregation, and
slavery. In a sense, one might argue that "white America" wanted
to make amends with "black America" and thus gave it their best
shot through the War on Poverty. After all, the most familiar face
of poverty was predominantly, though not exclusively, black.

∽ ∽ ∽

Sorrow filled the nation on November 22, 1963, when the first of
several infamous assassinations took the life of President John
F. Kennedy. In the wake of his death, as with 9/11 four decades
later, it would have been seen as unpatriotic and unsympathetic
to come out against the new president and his sobering State of
the Union address the following January. It was in that address,
however, that President Lyndon Johnson introduced the War on
Poverty and began a "creative federalism" in which the federal
government would gradually disregard states and their gover-
nors in order to eradicate poverty at the local level.[16] Many were
sympathetic to the cause, but most were ignorant of the prece-

15. Ibid., 97, 145, 159, 200.
16. Davidson, "War on Poverty," 2.

dent that Johnson was setting. If, in fact, he were to be successful in rooting out poverty through the means he was attempting to use, state governments would soon become nothing more than a nuisance and a hindrance to the greater good.

The Office of Economic Opportunity (OEO) was created to be the administrative leg of the War on Poverty. The agency quickly began passing over the states to fund and strengthen local communities, in spite of opposition from state leaders like California governor and future president Ronald Reagan.[8] Likely unaware of the changes they were making to a constitutional precedent, local officials became "wary of state involvement," seeing it as an unnecessary third party to their benevolent federal-local relationship.[17]

Nonetheless, these Community Action Agencies (CAA) that operated in conjunction with the federal government had little success. Ideas were always being proposed as a cure for the disease of poverty, but there were either too many or too few locals involved to be productive. Not to mention the fact that the greatest ingenuity was lost when men and women tried to implement their own concepts without cooperation. The OEO had been established to coordinate the War on Poverty, but the office was organizing more programs than it could possibly execute.[18]

In the latter months of 1966, Vice President Hubert Humphrey continued to make a case to the American people for fighting the president's domestic war. "A balanced attack on poverty must provide at least four somewhat distinct remedies: job creation, job preparation, transfer payments, and equal employment opportunity."[19]

Born in 1911 to the agricultural industry of South Dakota and raised to adulthood against the backdrop of the Great Depression, Humphrey knew first hand what it was to be out of

17. Ibid, 5.

18. Sundquist, "Co-ordinating the War on Poverty," 41.

19. Humphrey, "War on Poverty," 8.

work and without a home.[20] But even a casual observer of his four "remedies" could see that the Humphrey cure for poverty was primarily based on finding work for the unemployed, without concern for the culture that poverty had created. He was a well-spoken man of ideas, but neither Johnson nor his vice president could have been expected to usher in a perfect program. And in the absence of perfection, the followers of Martin and Malcolm soon found themselves vying for Black Power on the local level.

20. Senate Historical Office, "Hubert H. Humphrey," par. 6.

7

The Fight for Black Power

THIRTEEN WOUNDS from a sawed-off shotgun took the life of Malcolm X on February 21, 1965.[1] Few churches in Harlem were willing to facilitate a funeral service on his behalf for fear of violent recourse. When Bishop Childs of the Faith Temple made his church available through a complicated "humanitarian gesture," both he and his wife were tormented with bomb threats.

Coming to the bishop's defense, the Federation of Independent Political Action (FIPA) threatened every business in the city. Jesse Gray, spokesman for FIPA, had an organized plan to "picket all Harlem business establishments which would not close" on behalf of the service "in tribute to Malcolm X."[2] Understandably, tensions rose in the black community, but FIPA became a powerful example of well-organized black action committees on the local level.

The previous year, President Johnson had signed the Civil Rights Act of 1964, thus bringing an official end to segregation in every school and public place. Prior to such legislation, upper and middle class blacks were treated just as poorly as lower class blacks who had no education and no money. Segregated facilities gave the public image that all blacks, regardless of education or skill, were still among the bottom-feeders of American society. But now, with integration well underway, it became obvious that the ultimate beneficiaries of the civil rights movement were

1. Haley and Malcolm X, *Malcolm X*, 505.
2. Ibid., 508, 510.

"middle-class blacks—blacks who had competitive resources such as steady incomes, education and special talents."[3]

As the upper echelon of the black community was finally able to step back and realize their own unlimited potential for success, a new question arose. "Should we, as a community, seek out our own happiness or continue the fight for civil rights as they remain nonexistent for the impoverished of society?" Some, to be sure, went their own way. Others, moved by the leadership of Malcolm and Martin, focused their attention on trying to solve the problem of inner city poverty.

The Office of Economic Opportunity, waging its own War on Poverty, established Community Action Programs (CAPs) in each major locality to be "developed, conducted, and administered with the maximum feasible participation of residents of the areas and members of the groups served." Communities were now integrating more than their facilities. They were being told to integrate their ideas. And with freedom to exercise their civil rights, black leaders began fighting for control of their local CAPs. What was intended to be an effort of racial cooperation turned into a battleground for Black Power. White officials from each locality were sensing the 'potential threat to their authority' by the conflicts that were happening right in front of them.[4]

Integration of water fountains, restaurants, and restrooms was quite different from forcing blacks and whites to work together on solutions for the inner city. What might seem easy enough in retrospect was much more complicated at the time. In many communities, officials and legislators had "long-standing commitments to local industry to maintain a large supply of surplus, unskilled labor."[5] Any solutions to poverty that might lower the supply of unskilled labor were a threat to the *status quo*. Hence, one of the key problems on the local level was that

3. Wilson, *Truly Disadvantaged*, 125.

4. Davidson, "War on Poverty," 7.

5. Wheeler, "Civil Rights Groups," 155.

white officials talked of compassion but did little to rock the boat. And the black community took notice.

> The Black power movement and the anti-poverty program shared the same social space and developed a complex interactive relationship. Their association in time and social location led some observers to argue that a causal relationship existed, i.e., that the War on Poverty in some way caused the growth of the Black power movement and its increasing militancy.[6]
>
> The conflict between moderate civil rights organizations and militant Black power groups was nurtured in the struggles for CAP control.[7]

Black Power was an ideology born out of self-preservation as well as a defense of the inner city. But those who aligned themselves to such thinking were being linked to the teachings of Malcolm X and his controversial slander of white America. They saw their most vulnerable communities being excluded from the great hope of an American dream and therefore made themselves the vocal heroes of a weaker population. American poverty soon evolved into a primarily black issue resting on the hope of black solutions.

Where the civil rights movement had pushed for integration and assimilation, Black Power was now demanding "control over ghetto institutions" and the right to "build Black pride and consciousness." As they gradually achieved their demands, some in this new movement had become "advocates of violence as a means of defending ghetto residents against police brutality." And by fighting back, they believed that two things were being accomplished. First, violence in response to violence was a means to necessary empowerment. The man who allowed a government officer to knock him down, in the ideology of Black Power, was

6. Benson, "Militant Ideologies," 328.
7. Ibid., 333.

a man deprived of his manhood. Second, this constituted "an effective strategy for bringing attention of authorities [both locally and federally] to Negro problems."[8]

Among the many blacks who were consistently frustrated by the system were Huey P. Newton and Bobby Seale in Oakland, California. In the fall of 1966 they formed what was known as the Black Panther Party for Self-Defense. They chose the panther as their emblem because it was "known to be an animal that never makes an unprovoked attack, but will defend itself vehemently when attacked." They considered themselves a necessary and often symbolic organization for standing against oppression by local authorities.[9] For example, upon the arrival in San Francisco of Betty Shabazz, the widow of Malcolm X, she was "escorted and guarded by the Black Panthers." And as the Panthers earned credibility in the black community, their aims expanded. Rather than just fighting police brutality and protecting notable citizens, they began to implement "free breakfast" programs for needy school children, while organizing anti-war rallies to encourage "black people and other minorities to resist the military draft and to resist fighting in Vietnam."[10]

The 1968 assassinations of Martin Luther King Jr. (April 4) and Bobby Kennedy (June 6) made this a pivotal year in the political and racial struggle. The first assassination signified an end to the most prominent voice of non-violent action in the black community. The second signaled an unofficial end to the fight against poverty by leaders in Washington. Richard Nixon, who inherited the social programs of the Johnson administration, was unlikely to encourage any further support for the War on Poverty. For most of his administration, he was either fully engrossed in the conflicts and costs of Vietnam or battling his own demons of internal conspiracy.

8. Ibid, 330.

9. Harris, "Black Nationalism," 412.

10. Ibid., 414.

In the eyes of many Americans—both black and white—the battle for civil rights had finally been exhausted. All that could be done had been done. But contrary to popular opinion, the fight wasn't over. Black Power was now a rising anti-poverty force to be reckoned with in American society.

It should be noted with empathy that the Black Power movement and its extended organizations were not created for the *purpose* of hatred and violence. On the contrary, they were extremists by the necessity of self defense and social empowerment for those who couldn't help themselves. Shelby Steele, most known for his writings on the subject of peaceful race relations, described this as "reaching back from a moving train to lift on board those who have no tickets."[11] In other words, when the movement for civil rights stopped, a significant part of the black community began moving forward, but a great many were left standing on the curb. The latter group just needed the aid of American compassion. Johnson had intended that charity would be colorblind, but even in 1965 he had to acknowledge that poverty had its own kind of segregation:

> Negro poverty is not white poverty. Many of its causes and many of its cures are the same. But there are differences—deep, corrosive, obstinate differences—radiating painful roots into the community, into the family, and the nature of the individual.... These differences are not racial differences. They are solely and simply the consequence of ancient brutality, past injustice, and present prejudice. They are anguishing to observe. For the Negro they are a constant reminder of oppression.[12]

> The Negro, like these others [in poverty], will have to rely mostly upon his own efforts. But he just cannot do it alone.... Much of the Negro community is buried under a blanket of history and circumstances. It is not a lasting

11. Steele, *Content of Our Character*, 108.
12. Schulman, *Lyndon B. Johnson*, 227.

> solution to lift just one corner of that blanket. We must
> stand on all sides and we must raise the entire cover if
> we are to liberate our fellow citizens.[13]

Johnson was suggesting that the racial divide would not be cured by lawmakers in Washington but by the everyday citizens of present and future generations. It would require the black community to forgive past offenses and the white community to acknowledge their imperfect history. Furthermore, those suffering in poverty—whether black or otherwise—would need to "rely mostly" on their own efforts, with the compassionate aid of the American middle and upper class. In Johnson's eyes, even with the Civil Rights Act of 1964 that passed under his watchful administration, the "blanket of history and circumstances" was still covering most of the black community. Only a corner had been lifted.

Before his untimely death in 1968, King had already begun to acknowledge the possibility of a violent explosion in the inner city in the days and years ahead. Speaking to a government that had failed its impoverished citizens, he said, "If you do not begin to use your vast resources of wealth to lift God's children from the dungeons of despair and poverty, then you are writing your own obituary."[14]

With Malcolm, King, and two Kennedy brothers now gone, with the already frustrated Johnson out of office, and with a decade of revolution now closed, the Black Church returned to the forefront as an advocate for the rights and privileges of the poor and racially oppressed.

> It was the faith of the Black Church that provided black
> people with the courage to fight against great odds, giving them the hope that the goal of justice would eventually be achieved.[15]

13. Ibid.
14. Cone, *Risks of Faith*, 69.
15. Ibid., 64.

By merging a spiritual legacy of hope and redemption from centuries of oppression with the fight for Black Power on a local level, the Black Church soon came to adopt a doctrine known as Black Liberation Theology. Previously, the Black Church had done little "systematic reflection in the area of theology" and all previous attempts had been "presented in the forms of sermons, songs, prayers, testimonies, and stories of slavery and oppression."[16] With such minimal experience in the field of theology, their beliefs would be thrown out by the orthodox Christian worldview. And as members of the Black Church turned their attention to the streets, orthodox Christians began their own debate over how much a heaven-bound believer should be engaged in the complicated political affairs of the world.

∾ ∾ ∾

In order to more fully engage the subject of Black Liberation Theology in the pages ahead, the following chapter will be a timely detour into this uncomfortable debate between people of an orthodox Christian worldview. My own theological views are likely to emerge.

16. Ibid., 78.

8

Between Heaven and Earth

FOR THE better part of two millennia, Christian theology has been regarded as an intellectual crusade to understand and interpret the Bible. Humans being imperfect as they are, theologies have often resulted from human debate over complex issues found within the pages of Scripture. One recent example is the conversation between *covenant* theologians and *dispensational* theologians. The former believe that all Scripture was written to and for Christian application, while the latter believe that God dealt with the nation of Israel under a system of law far different from the system of grace he later instituted for the body of Christ. On the surface, the argument may seem mindlessly petty, but the consequences of either view can affect how people interpret the biblical instructions of God for their lives.

To continue this illustration, there are few Christians of either persuasion who disparage the other for failing to use the Bible as the basis for doctrinal disagreement. If anything, dispensational believers often accuse covenant believers of *misusing* or poorly applying a biblical text and vice versa. The common denominator has, in fact, always been an attempt to carefully handle the Word of God in good counsel: "Study to show thyself approved unto God, a workman that needeth not to be ashamed, rightly dividing the word of truth."[1]

When theology is without a shared basis in Scripture as its final authority, it can only be rooted in the imperfections of hu-

1. 2 Timothy 2:15.

man experience. This is not to deny the realities of our existence, but to defend the authority of God's written word. Without it, Christians frequently end up creating their own version of God, based on any number of human emotions and possibilities. If Scripture becomes a secondary, or worse, an irrelevant source to one's belief system, then this hardly constitutes a sound theology. In order for a set of doctrines to be understood and appreciated by the greater community of faith, there must be a divine constant that all members acknowledge as their solid foundation.

As the previous chapter described, Black Liberation Theology soon emerged from the localized struggle for Black Power but would receive little or no recognition within the evangelical community as a viable creed. For those who knew it existed, Black Theology was seen as nothing more than a bitter and confrontational cult. Angry or not, the challenges faced by impoverished blacks were immense, and the gradual emigration of whites from urban America during desegregation—commonly known as "white flight"—left a hole of unresolved problems throughout the inner city. And it was here that proponents of Black Liberation would begin establishing a permanent residence in the church.

For the rest of the Christian community, an escalating conflict arose over the level to which people of faith should continue interacting with world affairs like politics and poverty. In many ways, their debate was a convenient way of excusing their political disagreements. Believers could fall back on the promise that they were heaven bound and allow themselves to become disengaged from the problems of a dying and sinful world.

Evangelical Christians have always been torn between the hope of heaven and the stranglehold of earth. With an eye toward heaven, many will testify that faith teaches them to steer clear of anything political that might entangle them in the present world.

> And be not conformed to this world, but be transformed
> by the renewing of your mind, that ye may prove what is
> that good, and acceptable, and perfect, will of God.[2]
> For we brought nothing into this world, and it is cer-
> tain we can carry nothing out.[3]

Others will contend that an absolute detachment only hinders the plan and purpose of the believer who was made to serve
as the light of a dying world.

> That ye may be blameless and harmless, the sons of
> God, without rebuke, in the midst of a crooked and
> perverse nation, among whom ye shine as lights in the
> world.[4]

For those who testify of their biblical responsibility to
evangelize the world unto Christ—hence the familiar term of
evangelical Christians—this conflict becomes even more difficult. During a recent political rally, an elderly gentleman was
overheard speaking to a nearby woman about an awkward experience he had shared with two Christians the previous week.
He explained that on a bright and sunny afternoon, two men
approached his door with a Bible and a question.

"Can we have a few minutes of your time?" they asked.
Almost immediately, he brought them inside and showed them
the things he had left to do in the backyard. The old man offered
them a rake and a shovel and said, "I'll hear whatever you've got
to say if you give me a hand with my work." Rather than sharing
an afternoon of fellowship, the two men perceived this singular
task as a hindrance to their door-to-door endeavor and asked
if they could come back later. He wasn't interested and they
never returned.

2. Romans 12:2.
3. 1 Timothy 6:7.
4. Philippians 2:15.

The gospel, for all that it offers eternally, can seem like a cold and lifeless message to those who view Christians as disengaged from the present world. Evangelism has, in many ways, become an intellectual exercise for much of the Christian community who wish to share their faith but have difficulty merging the doctrines they know with the practical grace they were called to share. This imbalance has left an open door for many believers—even Bible believing Christians—to see the *traditional* gospel as wholly insufficient to the task of evangelism.

Still, the truest gospel is inextricably tied to the word of God and cannot, therefore, be molded and reshaped at the whim of frustrated people. A distinction must be drawn between those who preach the gospel and the gospel that is preached. Where humans are fallible, the gospel is not. Two men who fail to seize an opportunity will never invalidate the soundness of the eternal hope that they could and should have given.

> Moreover, brethren, I declare unto you the gospel which I preached unto you, which also ye have received, and wherein ye stand; by which also ye are saved, if ye keep in memory what I preached unto you, unless ye believed in vain. For I delivered unto you first of all that which I also received, how that Christ died for our sins according to the Scriptures; and that he was buried, and that he rose again the third day according to the Scriptures.[5]
>
> Wherefore, as by one man sin entered into the world, and death by sin; and so death passed upon all men, for that all have sinned . . .[6]
>
> For all have sinned, and come short of the glory of God.[7]

---

5. 1 Corinthians 15:1–4.

6. Romans 5:12.

7. Romans 3:23.

> For by grace are ye saved through faith; and that not
> of yourselves: it is the gift of God: not of works, lest any
> man should boast.[8]

The unequivocal gospel teaches that everyone was born into sin through the fall of Adam but that through faith and trust in Jesus Christ, who suffered and died, everyone has the hope of being redeemed from an otherwise eternal separation from God. This life being just a flicker compared to the next, the gospel has always been about preparing for what is to come. Those who put their faith in Christ are given the promise of a future in heavenly realms, but they know they must first endure this present world with all its problems.

> For we wrestle not against flesh and blood, but against
> principalities, against powers, against the rulers of the
> darkness of this world, against spiritual wickedness in
> high places.[9]

In the midst of hardship, some have come to accept an alternative gospel in which they are, in fact, fighting against flesh and blood. Under this new gospel, human beings work against one another to improve social conditions for themselves and those around them. Not surprisingly, the Apostle Paul once "marveled" at the way believers could "pervert" the message of heavenly redemption in order to fight a war with one another over temporary concerns of a terrestrial world.

> I marvel that ye are so soon removed from him that
> called you into the grace of Christ unto another gospel:
> which is not another; but there be some that trouble you,
> and would pervert the gospel of Christ. But though we,
> or an angel from heaven, preach any other gospel unto
> you than that which we have preached unto you, let him
> be accursed. . . . For do I now persuade men, or God?

8. Ephesians 2:8–9.
9. Ephesians 6:12.

> or do I seek to please men? for if I yet pleased men, I should not be the servant of Christ. But I certify you, brethren, that the gospel which was preached of me is not after man. For I neither received it of man, neither was I taught it, but by the revelation of Jesus Christ.[10]

With regard to social responsibility, few believers can or should argue against doing good for the unfortunate. But doing good in one's community is not in keeping with the tenets of a biblical gospel unless the primary goal is to represent and teach the hope of eternal salvation though the blood of Jesus Christ. This is a crucial and missing piece for many, whether they be extreme in their theology or not.

Over the years, many Bible believing ministries have conjured up a false illusion of Christianity to suggest that faith is a means to human prosperity. The price paid two thousand years ago on the cross of Calvary does not exempt anyone from trouble in this life. Nor should vulnerable onlookers to Christianity be misled by haughty suggestions that faith will make them rich or bring them health. The gospel of salvation gives hope toward the next life and strength to achieve contentment in this one. Hence, when people of faith suffer oppression from their enemies they ought not interpret every negative experience as unjust. To suffer and endure tribulation is a known consequence for every body broken by the sin of Adam.

> For unto you it is given in the behalf of Christ, not only to believe on him, but also to suffer for his sake; having the same conflict which ye saw in me, and now hear to be in me.[11]

10. Galatians 1:6–13.
11. Philippians 1:29–30.

In the world ye shall have tribulation: but be of good cheer; I have overcome the world.[12]

And he said unto me, My grace is sufficient for thee: for my strength is made perfect in weakness. Most gladly therefore will I rather glory in my infirmities, that the power of Christ may rest upon me.[13]

If, then, the gospel espoused in the word of God is a hope based in eternal life and not a hope that releases us from suffering in the present world, the church can and often does play a role in helping to lighten the load of any weaker members until the Lord's return.

But this I say, He which soweth sparingly shall reap also sparingly; and he which soweth bountifully shall reap also bountifully. Every man according as he purposeth in his heart, so let him give; not grudgingly, or of necessity: for God loveth a cheerful giver. And God is able to make all grace abound toward you; that ye, always having all sufficiency in all things, may abound to every good work: (As it is written, He hath dispersed abroad; he hath given to the poor: his righteousness remaineth forever. Now he that ministereth seed to the sower both minister bread for your food, and multiply your seed sown, and increase the fruits of your righteousness;) being enriched in everything to all bountifulness, which causeth through us thanksgiving to God. For the administration of this service not only supplieth the want of the saints, but is abundant also by many thanksgivings unto God; whiles by the experiment of this ministration may glorify God for your professed subjection unto the gospel of Christ, and for your liberal distribution unto them, and unto all men.[14]

12. John 16:33b.
13. 2 Corinthians 12:9.
14. 2 Corinthians 9:6–13.

Believers will endure their own share of weaknesses, but through those infirmities, they realize that God's grace is sufficient for their need.[15] Having recognized the personal sufficiency of grace, believers should "abound to every good work" on behalf of those who lack. In other words, those who have much have much to offer. Those who have little know not what it is to have enough.

Bearing in mind all the history and politics that were covered in the preceding chapters, it is curious to note the praise of Scripture for those who provide a "liberal distribution" to all. The use of "liberal" is most intriguing in the classical text because political liberalism today is often understood as unrestricted generosity. Conservative Christians tend to oppose reactionary giving in favor of conditional gifts and the discretionary use of abundant finances. To give exceedingly without limit is to risk being foolish with one's own charity. Yet, to restrict one's giving is to risk being anything but gracious.

Finding the balance between unconditional grace and discretionary spending is, perhaps, one of the most overlooked problems in the *active* Christian church today. If a church is compassionate enough to serve in the local community, the most liberal assembly will tend to give graciously above and beyond the call of duty, sometimes at the expense of caring for their own needs. On the other hand, the most conservative assembly will tend to give cautiously and earn praise for their budgetary wisdom, at the expense of ignoring the most troubled areas where grace was needed more abundantly.

Biblical grace is an unmerited favor given to those who are not deserving. Christians often speak of grace in abstract and spiritual terms without acknowledging the need for its practical application. Nonetheless, it is difficult to deny the fact that applicative grace is needed most in the poor and impoverished areas of our local communities. Sadly, however, there are some who would contend that grace is greater when given to those

15. 2 Corinthians 12:9.

who have plenty. This type of rationale can be found in the voice of a classic conservative who spoke on issues of poverty during the stalemate years of World War I.

> The poor will always be with us. They always have been; why change? They have always been uncomfortable; why experiment? Time has sanctified poverty, made it sacred. It has always been. Let it always be.[16]

These are obviously harsh words from a man who might have second guessed his own opinions if he had survived to live through the challenges of the Great Depression. But speaking when he did on the matter, his views are summarized this way:

> Without slums there would be no charity organizations and spirit of social service and benevolence. . . . While the poor themselves may not receive much of what is donated for charity, if there were no poor, nothing would be donated. Hence the poor are indispensable.[17]

However cold and hopeless his words may seem, they express an honest point nonetheless. If we were capable of creating a world where all had plenty, benevolence would quickly disappear. What reason would people have to give anything if their neighbors already had everything? The ongoing existence of poverty in the world teaches people of faith to graciously give of themselves in the way that Christ gave of himself on the cross.

> The poor shall never cease out of the land: therefore I command thee, saying, thou shalt open thine hand wide unto thy brother, to thy poor, and to thy needy, in thy land.[18]

---

16. Weeks, "Conservative's View," 780.

17. Ibid., 781.

18. Deuteronomy 15:11.

> For ye have the poor with you always, and whenso-
> ever ye will ye may do them good: but me ye have not
> always.[19]

While these verses indicate a responsibility to do good for
the needy, one of the great challenges for many Christians is a
biblical belief that the poor are penniless because of their own
idle foolishness. Unlike the rebel wanderings of a rich man who
wants to experience a poor man's life, Scripture often speaks of
those who make foolish choices and thus end up in a form of
poverty that could have otherwise been avoided.

> Poverty and shame shall be to him that refuseth instruc-
> tion: but he that regardeth reproof shall be honored.[20]
> He that loveth pleasure shall be a poor man: he that
> loveth wine and oil shall not be rich.[21]
> For the drunkard and the glutton shall come to pov-
> erty; and drowsiness shall clothe a man with rags.[22]

Clear as it is that pleasure, drunkenness, gluttony, and the
refusal to heed instruction are among the pathways to poverty,
the fool's behavior does not free the wise from their duties of
compassion. The prodigal child who falls to his father's feet with
no excuse will not be left to die on the ground. A gracious father
will take him in, clean him up, offer the same instructions of wisdom, and send him on his way again. This is the nature of grace
when given in its simplest form.

Regardless of its causes, the condition of poverty has never
been one in which its members are simply free to escape at will.
Whether they put themselves in the poorhouse or happened to
be born there, there is no biblical warning to avoid helping the
poor. On the contrary, Christians were urged to give aid where

19. Mark 14:7.
20. Proverbs 13:18.
21. Proverbs 21:17.
22. Proverbs 23:21.

and when it could be given. The Apostle Paul, writing to the body of Christ, gave extensive instructions to believers about how they should treat the poor, both inside and outside the church. Lengthy as it is, the list below is hardly exhaustive of the biblical command to love thy neighbor.

> Be of the same mind one toward another. Mind not high things, but condescend to men of low estate. Be not wise in your own conceits.[23]
>
> Therefore if thine enemy hunger, feed him; if he thirst, give him drink: for in so doing thou shalt heap coals of fire on his head.[24]
>
> We then that are strong ought to bear the infirmities of the weak, and not to please ourselves. Let every one of us please his neighbor for his good to edification. For even Christ pleased not himself: but as it is written, The reproaches of them that reproached thee fell on me.[25]
>
> For though I be free from all men, yet have I made myself a servant to all, that I might gain the more.... To the weak became I as weak, that I might gain the weak: I am made all things to all men, that I might by all means save some.[26]
>
> Even as I please all men in all things, not seeking mine own profit, but the profit of many, that they might be saved.[27]
>
> Moreover, brethren, we do you to wit of the grace of God bestowed on the churches of Macedonia; How that in a great trial of affliction the abundance of their joy and their deep poverty abounded unto the riches of their liberality.[28]

23. Romans 12:16.

24. Romans 12:20.

25. Romans 15:1–3.

26. 1 Corinthians 9:19, 22.

27. 1 Corinthians 10:33.

28. 2 Corinthians 8:1–2.

For ye know the grace of our Lord Jesus Christ, that, though he was rich, yet for your sakes he became poor, that ye through his poverty might be rich.[29]

For if there be first a willing mind, it is accepted according to that a man hath, and not according to that he hath not. For I mean not that other men be eased, and ye burdened: but by an equality, that now at this time your abundance may be a supply for their want, that their abundance also may be a supply for your want: that there may be equality: As it is written, He that had gathered much had nothing over; and he that had gathered little had no lack.[30]

Every man according as he purposeth in his heart, so let him give; not grudgingly, or of necessity: for God loveth a cheerful giver. And God is able to make all grace abound toward you; that ye, always having all sufficiency in all things, may abound to every good work.[31]

And when James, Cephas, and John, who seemed to be pillars, perceived the grace that was given unto me, they gave to me and Barnabas the right hands of fellowship; that we should go unto the heathen, and they unto the circumcision. Only they would that we should remember the poor; the same which I also was forward to do.[32]

Bear ye one another's burdens, and so fulfill the law of Christ. For if a man think himself to be something, when he is nothing, he deceiveth himself.[33]

As we have therefore opportunity, let us do good unto all men, especially unto them who are of the household of the faith.[34]

29. 2 Corinthians 8:9.

30. 2 Corinthians 8:12–15.

31. 2 Corinthians 9:7–8.

32. Galatians 2:9–10.

33. Galatians 6:2–3.

34. Galatians 6:10.

Let him that stole steal no more: but rather let him labor working with his hands the thing which is good, that he may have to give to him that needeth.[35]

Let nothing be done through strife or vainglory; but in lowliness of mind let each esteem other better than themselves. Look not every man on his own things, but every man also on the things of others.[36]

Now we exhort you, brethren, warn them that are unruly, comfort the feebleminded, support the weak, be patient toward all men. See that none render evil for evil unto any man; but ever follow that which is good, both among yourselves, and to all men.[37]

We are bound to thank God always for you, brethren . . . because that your faith groweth exceedingly, and the charity of every one of you all toward each other aboundeth.[38]

For we brought nothing into this world, and it is certain we can carry nothing out. And having food and raiment let us be therewith content.[39]

Charge them that are rich in this world that they be not high-minded: nor trust in uncertain riches, but in the living God who giveth us richly all things to enjoy: that they do good, that they be rich in good works, ready to distribute, willing to communicate: laying up in store for themselves a good foundation against the time to come, that they may lay hold on eternal life.[40]

Frustrating as poverty may be for members of the church who work hard for the things they have, progress depends on their finding a way to merge liberal generosity with conservative wis-

35. Ephesians 4:28.

36. Philippians 2:3–4.

37. 1 Thessalonians 5:14–15.

38. 2 Thessalonians 1:3.

39. 1 Timothy 6:7–8.

40. 1 Timothy 6:17–19.

dom. No testimony can be worse than that of a man who shares of a grace he did not deserve but in the same breath condemns the poor for a life of oppression that they themselves did not always deserve. When the church wholly fails to practice grace for the poor and undeserving, it should come as no surprise that new doctrines will arise in our collective absence. Such was the case in the controversial rise of Black Liberation Theology.

∽ ∽ ∽

With respect to the freedom of religion espoused in the Bill of Rights, one of the great miracles of our democracy has been the ability for people of faith to graciously discuss the most sacred matters upon which they disagree. But grace often loses its momentum at the juncture between faith and politics. In a recent musing over the need for *patriotic grace*, Peggy Noonan of the *Washington Post* shared similar observations.

> For more and more Americans, politics has become a religion. It has become a faith. People find their meaning in it. They define themselves by their stands. . . . When politics becomes a religion, then simple disagreements become apostasies, heresies.[41]

The underpinnings of Black Liberation Theology can easily be seen as far more political than religious, but the merger between liberation and theology introduced an entirely new racial perspective of God and the purpose of the church for the local community. Traditional Bible believers saw the movement as a departure from sound doctrine, while those within the movement were finding the greater Christian community to be an enemy composed of graceless hypocrites. If the rest of the church was going to ignore the plight of the nation's less fortunate and oppressed citizens, then Black Power would become its own religion, and the Black Church would be the catalytic vessel for its theology.

41. Noonan, *Patriotic Grace*, 50–51.

9

The Most Segregated Hour

ON MARCH 18, 2008, as Barack Obama rose to the stage in Philadelphia, political commentators were on pins and needles over how he was going to address the angry racism of his friend and mentor, Reverend Jeremiah Wright. With an eye toward a more perfect union, the soon-to-be elected president offered his initial thoughts on the current state of race relations in America. "The fact that so many people are surprised to hear that anger in some of Reverend Wright's sermons simply reminds us of the old truism that the most segregated hour in American life occurs on Sunday morning."[1] This "old truism" of which he spoke was, quite literally, ripped from the pages of Black Liberation Theology's most prominent spokesperson, James H. Cone.

> In Bearden, like the rest of America, *Sunday was the most segregated day of the week*. Black and white Christians had virtually no social or religious dealing with each other, even though both were Baptists and Methodists—reading the same Bible, worshipping the same God, and reciting the same confessions of faith in their congregations.[2]

Cone was making a simple yet overlooked point. The Civil Rights Act had forced the integration of public life during the week, but on the weekend, church was the second most obvious

1. Obama, "More Perfect Union," par. 33.
2. Cone, *Risks of Faith*, xi (italics added).

place of segregation (inner city being the first). On a Tuesday morning, white prejudice might have to stomach working in an office with black prejudice, but when it came to the Sunday service, each man went his own way. By law, the government was never going to intrude on matters of the church or force white men to worship in the pews with black women, so the fires of segregation continued in the most sacred place of all.

When the nation lost Malcolm in 1965 and Martin in 1968, it seemed as though the tables had begun to flip in American race relations. Prior to the civil rights era, whites were all too often the face of violence against black equality. But by the end of the 1960s, whites had become far less violent and far more subtle in their discrimination. Instead of burning crosses and lynching citizens, the message of white supremacy turned much more quiet. Fathers would explain to their children that an inner city thug life was no way to live, and the kids would invariably learn that the face of the American ghetto was black. Quite simply, the successful black man was gradually seen as an exception to the rule in the white community. He would be, to the average white citizen, what others in the black community could be if they weren't quite so black.

As a result, *blackness* came to embody for most Americans a symbol of crime, poverty, and gang violence. And the black community heard the message loud and clear. Long after the days of slavery and public segregation, blackness was being portrayed as a lesser part of society. One of the few remaining institutions willing to combat this downgrading ideology was the Black Church. Through the writing and teaching of Cone, they found "a new way of doing theology that would empower the suffering black poor to fight for a more liberated existence."[3]

To a mainstream Christian, the concept of "doing theology" in light of human experience was like saying that truth could be entirely relative. And as the Black *Church* attempted to represent

3. Ibid., xxii.

the black *community*, fighting for "a more liberated existence" meant doing theology in ways that were strangely unorthodox. Cone was without any peer accountability for his theology. And as it turned out, if accountability meant hearing the voice of a theologically-minded white majority, he would have no part of it. Nor would Scripture have any authority if it contradicted his own experience.

> I still regard the Bible as an important source of my theological reflections, but not the starting point. The black experience and the Bible together in dialectical tension serve as my point of departure today and yesterday. The order is significant. I am black first—and everything else comes after that. This means that I read the Bible through the lens of a black tradition of struggle and not as the objective Word of God.[4]

In the mind of Cone, the white community of faith were not welcome to assess Black Theology and certainly not if they were intending to hold his feet to the fire of Scripture. In the twenty-first century, it may seem absurd that anyone's theology could be untouchable by the criticisms of those who wear a different color of skin. After all, no one would have questioned the right of a black man, then or now, to argue against the teachings of Billy Graham or Joel Osteen simply because these were white men. Still, whites were being written out of the equation, and it was deemed taboo for anyone in the white community to engage the subject.

> The term black theology was created in this social and religious context. It was initially understood as the theological arm of Black Power, and it enabled us to express our theological imagination in the struggle of freedom independently of white theologians.[5]

4. Quoted in Mansfield, *Barack Obama*, 41–42.
5. Cone, *Risks of Faith*, 42.

As the objects of great oppression for many years, it seemed understandable that Cone might want to argue for a new and more humanizing independence from the white community for blacks. But in doing so, he was countering the very efforts of integration that had given him a voice in the first place. And it got worse.

> There is no use for a God who loves whites the same as blacks. What we need is the divine love as expressed in Black Power which is the power of black people to destroy their oppressors, here and now, by any means at their disposal. . . . The black theologian must reject any conception of God which stifles black self-determination by picturing God as a God of all peoples.[6]
>
> Black theology must realize that the white Jesus has no place in the black community, and it is our task to destroy him. . . . For too long Christ has been pictured as a blue-eyed honky. Black theologians are right; we need to dehonkify him and thus make him relevant to the black condition.[7]

Black Liberation Theology was now serving as a theological justification for Black Power, designed to "politicize Christianity" as a wing of violent self defense in the black community. Cone was going after the most sacred images of the church.[8] Sunday school material that painted every biblical character with white skin was now at the forefront of controversy. If these were residents of a Middle Eastern society, Black Theology argued, a blond-haired, blue-eyed image was entirely misleading. Inner city churches even took stock of God's physical image and contemplated a more difficult problem among those oppressed by poverty and racial discrimination.

6. Williams, "Black Theology," 564.

7. Mansfield, *Barack Obama*, 42.

8. Calhoun-Brown, "Image of God," 206.

> The radical idea that God or Jesus, the ultimate value
> of religion, shares the race of the oppressed was to be
> a source of strength for liberation. . . . It was not and
> is not a question of whether God is physically black,
> but it is a question of whether a man who is black can
> identify with a white God and depend on his love and
> protection.[9]

If white skin was the image of past oppression and
Christianity had long been painting the savior of the world with
a white face, it was argued that members of the Black Church
would never be willing to fully embrace the faith of Christ.
Rational as it may have been to someone like Cone, what it pro-
duced was a theological reason to see whiteness as the enemy of
blackness. And for the darker brothers of poverty who were easily influenced, this was an easy sell. Cone managed to convince
the most vulnerable black citizens that their very plight was the
continued and endless fault of the white man. In the scattered
pulpits where Black Liberation Theology was preached, Cone
was on par with, if not greater than, the most valuable theologians of world history.

Due to the complex nature of poverty and the challenges of
war, most Americans were content to remove their hands from
the inner city and allow the Black Church to practice its social
theology. Johnson's War on Poverty had been a five-year government solution for the "other America." It didn't work. Cone's Black
Liberation Theology was now a long-term spiritual solution for
empowering the darker brothers of poverty. But instead of cur-
ing the ailments of a weaker society, he instilled within the poor
a self-defeating anger that blamed the white world and justified
its own actions as the never ending curse of white oppression.

However good their intentions may have been, both
Johnson and Cone were up against an institution of poverty that
has plagued social progress in nation after nation throughout

9. Ibid., 199.

history. Both men had tried to formulate a proper remedy to solve past and present wrongs, but the end result was the same as that of all who came before them. For Johnson, the War on Poverty dissolved in the evolution of Washington politics. For Cone, Black Liberation Theology took root in the pulpits of inner city black communities but managed to solve few of the historic problems it had set out to fix.

∾ ∾ ∾

During a recent early morning classroom session at a predominantly white Christian university, several students were roused to a debate over a group of state legislators who had apologized for the historic sanction of slavery and segregation. The most vocal class members shared concern that these apologies (at least five states had made similar confessions) might lead to reparations—federal compensation to the descendants of slavery. It wasn't long before the conversation turned to white frustrations about the black community.

One girl in particular mentioned that she had recently tried to get involved in a childhood social services program downtown but found that several of the black children were quick to say, "I don't want no white girl tryin' to tell me how to live my life." Alas, from an early age, inner city kids had learned that white skin was the equivalent of an oppressive and patronizing group who had no purpose or value in the black community. Cone's approach to theology could now be heard from the lips of the innocent.

Over the years, Black Liberation Theology has proved itself incapable of producing any kind of measurable change for the weaker members of society. The poor of the inner city are not in a better condition today than they were decades ago. The rhetoric and *audacity* of Black Theology may be preached every Sunday, but the people for whom that hope was intended still remain desperate and angry. The current guards of the inner city will either need to alter their message or accept that the time for theological accountability between black and white Christians has come.

10

Faith, Work, and Politics as Usual

IN THE sandwich line of a local Burger King was where I learned my earliest lesson on racial profiling. As I quietly worked on my side of the Whopper table, one of the supervisors began speaking in Spanish with an employee on the other side of my line. And with casual immaturity, I asked, "What part of Mexico are you from?"

Almost immediately, our eyes locked. Had he been any younger I might have been thrown to the floor. But he held his composure and answered, "Listen, kid. Just because someone speaks Spanish doesn't mean they're from Mexico. Do you know how many people speak Spanish in this country? For that matter, do you know how many Spanish-speaking countries there are in the world? Let me give you a word of advice. Don't ever ask that question to an American unless you're looking for a fight."

Prior to our conversation, I had taken two trips to Mexico with two different church youth groups. I had two years of high school Spanish under my belt and no reason to think myself ignorant of geography. Still, I had managed to profile a man based on unfair assumptions. We were both Americans. Yet I was looking at him as though he were an illegal alien in my country, as though he didn't belong because his language and features were not like mine.

Ignorance is not a cause for shame if we learn from our mistakes. But not all profiling is ignorant or accidental. Much of it, as I've witnessed, is perpetual and slanderous. Forty years after the civil rights movement, at a time when the vast majority of racism is exercised by those who declare themselves "not racist," these personal stories may come as a shock to many who thought the lingering effects of white supremacy were over.

∽ ∽ ∽

Below is a letter I wrote to the regional director of a local restaurant after several years of tolerating some of the most disturbing scenes and conversations of my entire career in hospitality.

> As an original member of [your] opening waitstaff, I wanted to thank you for always taking time to visit and encourage our store to be the best in the business. However, as an original member of this restaurant, I must confess that the following information is not going to sit well.
>
> Over the past two and a half years, I've become a silent witness to endless counts of racial discrimination toward guests and fellow employees, personal threats of violence (no joke), sexual harassment with no thought for who is watching, and an ever-present supply of unprofessional language within earshot of children and families who simply want a peaceful dining experience. During my tenure, I have brought every one of my concerns up to management at different times, but have generally been passed over with statements like, "We're taking care of it." Without fail, I witness these things every week, every day, and every shift.
>
> One white employee has threatened to "slit" a black employee's throat and yet, when management was made aware of the threat, the white employee was retained. Employees have joked about having a "noose" for fellow black employees and yet they are laughed at even by the managers. Employees who have slandered their own guests and the guests of others as "f---ing n---ers" are patronized and told to relax. These staff members seem to enjoy the laughter of the majority who accept

this as "the way it is around here." And my list could go on and on.

Just yesterday, a server approached me and asked, "Would you mind taking Table 213?" At which point, I leaned around to notice who they were and asked why. Her reply was quite simple. "Because I don't feel like dealing with black people today." This, of course, falls on the heels of hearing another server stand at a computer saying, "Well, you definitely know a person's color of skin by the way that they tip." How is this a business that any adult can or should be proud to serve and cheer?

As a man of faith, a man of principle, and a man of business, my toleration level for these things has reached its boiling point and I'm beyond angry. Early on, our first General Manager made it clear that ours was a "zero tolerance" policy for discrimination and racism. But within about a year, my respect for his words went out the window. For every intolerable act that I witnessed and testified in private, both he and other managers continually let such actions pass with hardly a reprimand or a concern. And the problem continues to be ignored.

Speeches in staff meeting never have resolved the practical disregard that happens on the floor of this restaurant. We can preach, shout, or declare from the rooftops that these things need to end, but words have yet to bring about a change. No one would ever publically admit to misconduct, nor have I chosen to use names in this letter. More than likely, you could read this in the middle of a staff meeting and the notable perpetrators of these accusations would look around baffled as though it couldn't possibly have any reference to them. So honestly, I'm not sure how you heal the wounds of such a vastly unprofessional restaurant without starting over with a complete personnel overhaul. But that's again why I'm appealing to you and your drive to make us the "best" in the business.

When this store came to town, I was incredibly honored to have a spot serving the guests who walked in our front doors. I've been in hospitality for more than twelve years and always enjoy the chance to make a grumpy person smile or a hungry man satisfied. That's the business. That's what we do. That's what we're here for. And somewhere in the past two years, our staff and our management have used that sense of hospitality as a mask. In theory, we say we believe in it, but the racism, the threats, the private (and public) disregard of every guest . . . these things remind me that we have a long way to go.

My hope is that through these words and any action you may take, we might begin to set in motion the steps that once again make this a proud place to work. Thank you in advance for your time and your listening ear.

On the day that I had planned to give this to our regional director, it occurred to me that such a scathing assault on my place of employment would do little good if the chain of command were to be ignored. The intended recipient was three pay scales above any supervisor or manager to whom I was directly responsible. So, in the interest of keeping peace where possible, I sat down with two managers and three staff members and had them read through my words. Of the five who read through it, both managers were ready and willing to admit their own negligence. They expressed a firm desire to make this their number one priority over the next several weeks. Needless to say, the letter landed in the glove box of my truck, and no one else has read it until now.

At the time I wrote those words, the subject of race had become a dominant issue in several areas of my life. When I wasn't working at the restaurant or teaching school, most of my spare time was spent building and moderating a Web site for dispensational believers around the world. The purpose of the ministry was and is to coordinate a list of churches and interactive forums for isolated men and women looking for a place to fellowship with those of like mind.

Late in the previous year, I had been asked by several members of our ministry to review the video of an affiliated preacher who was allegedly teaching his Bible students the basics of racial prophecy. If it was true, I knew that something would have to be said or ties would need to be broken. By no means would I allow myself to continue sending believers in the direction of a church where such things were openly declared from the pulpit. Others who were much closer to the man expressed a similar sentiment. No one would want to be associated with such blatantly false teaching. Or so I thought.

Racial prophecy, as referred to in chapter 1, is based on the dispersion of families that began after the flood in the house of Noah.

> And the sons of Noah, that went forth of the ark, were Shem, and Ham, and Japheth: and Ham is the father of Canaan. These are the three sons of Noah: and of them was the whole earth overspread. And Noah began to be an husbandman, and he planted a vineyard: And he drank of the wine, and was drunken; and he was uncovered in his tent. And Ham, the father of Canaan, saw the nakedness of his father, and told his two brethren without. And Shem and Japheth took a garment, and laid it upon both their shoulders, and went backward, and covered the nakedness of their father; and their faces were backward, and they saw not their father's nakedness. And Noah awoke from his wine, and knew what his younger son had done unto him. And he said, Cursed be Canaan; a servant of servants shall he be unto his brethren. And he said, Blessed be the Lord God of Shem; and Canaan shall be his servant. God shall enlarge Japheth, and he shall dwell in the tents of Shem; and Canaan shall be his servant.[1]

1. Genesis 9:18–27.

According to those who teach racial prophecy, the "black man" is a resultant child of Noah's curse on Ham. In other words, the "curse" of Ham is that he and his descendants became slaves to the other families of the earth—more specifically, that they became *black* slaves. During and before the Civil War, this was called the *Noahic curse,* as taught by Southern preachers (known as "divines") seeking to maintain their sacred right to slavery.

> Most divines turned to the Noahic curse to provide a racial justification for the specific enslavement of blacks ...[2]
>
> Many divines did invoke the Noahic curse and the supposed black descent from Ham in an ideology that took deep root among the people, but [over time] other prominent divines regarded it with suspicion since neither the Bible nor science demonstrated that the blacks descended from Ham.[3]

After watching the content I had been asked to evaluate, it was clear that the charge of teaching racial prophecy was indeed more than an empty accusation. Here, in late 2007, I was sadly watching the video of a contemporary preacher who saw "the black man" as the object of a biblical curse. I documented all my concerns and conveyed them to the men who had asked for my input. As I waited for decisions to be made, another issue in American race relations soon caught my attention.

Politics had given rise to an eloquent black orator named Barack Obama. But his Achilles heel, at least initially, was his close affiliation with a fire-breathing reverend from Chicago. With Obama under pressure to speak on the current problems of racism, most of the country eagerly awaited the Philadelphia speech that would quickly be dubbed "A More Perfect Union." As a student of politics, I was already familiar with "Obama Fever" before it reached the presidential stage. Only two months after

2. Genovese, *Consuming Fire,* 4.
3. Ibid., 81.

his towering win from Iowa and the early chants of "Yes, we can," a growing number of Americans were beginning to question his controversial church affiliation. And he was responsible to give an answer.

My spiritual concerns were two-fold at the time. I wanted to know what his plain-spoken views were on the controversial message of Black Liberation Theology. And secondly, if he disowned such a racially-oriented teaching, why had he remained so long affiliated with those who preached it from the pulpit?

At the time, the Illinois senator had practically catapulted into the spotlight, and many of the people in my social circle were already demonizing him with accusations that every credible source had consistently proven false. The slightest defense of Obama on my part, as an independent voter, was met with rolled eyes and ridiculous nonsense. As far as I could see, no one cared to discuss the problems with Obama's theology because there was greater joy to be found in passing along false rumor and innuendo. Granted, a few were willing to think outside the box of propaganda, but as the weeks went on, I heard more and more Christians talking as though they were political experts with a background in exorcism. By some estimations, Obama was inhabited by the devil (or "many devils" depending on the source), and those who believed this to be the case were eager to testify of their remarkable insight.

Political news junkies like myself were eating up the coverage, but I was gradually getting more and more discouraged by the number of friendly believers who had fallen in love with campaign gossip. Such conversations made it incredibly difficult to break through the heart of necessary concerns like Black Liberation Theology. If, for instance, this theology was as dangerous as many were making it out to be, then it needed to be a subject of discussion apart from Senator Obama. Between the "Perfect Union" speech and the latter half of the primary, most of the news and argumentative posturing grew quiet on the subject of race relations in America. But for me, three racial problems were still nagging at my conscience.

The first, of course, was whether I could continue to ignore the teaching of racial prophecy by a familiar preacher. Secondly, when it came to white Christians talking politics, I found few who could see Obama for anything more than a black man from a racist church. Any attempt to discuss the root problems that might have led to that racism was a futile effort. For most, it didn't matter, so long as he didn't get elected to the White House. I, on the other hand, felt that if it was problematic enough to keep a man from winning an election, then it was problematic enough to be assessed as a spiritual and biblical concern within the church.

It was my third issue of conscience, however, that sent me over the top. On one particularly hot summer day at our restaurant, several of our staff members were lounging outside between shifts. Occasionally, those who were still taking tables inside would wander out to enjoy a little conversation or a quick meal. Exhausted from the sun, I was sitting with my eyes closed when someone whispered quietly to another server, "Listen, do you want my Mondays from table 53?" The question didn't make sense as it was worded, so I opened my eyes in bewilderment.

"Do you really want to know, Jeremy?" He asked.

"Sure, I guess."

"Well, see, Mondays are a term that we use to describe black people who sit in our sections. They take a lot of work, but they don't pay any extra in the end. Just like a typical Monday."

"You're right, brother. I didn't want to know."

Later that month, my ears caught the edge of another, far more disheartening conversation. Three fellow staff members were huddled around the coffee machine as one said to the other. "I think he has AIDS. Look at him. Table 13. What do you think?" When I turned in the direction of their voices, all three were staring out into the dining room to catch a glimpse of a black man in African dress. Gradually, the discussion turned to ridiculous methods by which someone could or could not acquire the AIDS virus, but no one thought to chastise the originator of such foolish accusations. Later that hour, I brought lunch to the guests at table 13, then returned to the server who had begun the racial slander.

"You make me sick," I said.

Upon hearing me get so serious, he replied, "Listen, man, it was just a joke. We were just foolin' around."

"Then explain to me the punch line because as far as I can tell, it isn't funny. And my guess is, the people at table 13 wouldn't find it funny either." As I walked away, he began offering up a series of excuses. Only later did he approach me with a worthless apology, as though I were the offended party.

The problem wasn't an isolated joke in poor taste but racism itself. Only, in the twenty-first century, perpetrators of racial denigration typically count themselves innocent for fear of being labeled a racist. When it appears they've caused an offense, they justify their actions by declaring a momentary lapse in judgment. Or worse, when no one speaks out, racism just bubbles in the pot of our allegedly civil society.

By the middle of the summer, none of my concerns had been addressed. When it came to an affiliated teaching of racial prophecy, I was eventually rejected as someone who had made an issue out of nothing. When it came to standing up against racism at work, my letter was forgotten by those who had been eager to help. And when it came to dealing with the flawed theology of Black Liberation, most of my evangelical peers were enraptured with the goal of slandering a presidential candidate.

Perhaps I had become too ideological. Perhaps I had become just another face in the crowded terrain of white guilt. But whatever it was I had become was irrelevant. I was looking for an open and gracious audience with whom I could process these truths of segregation still hindering our advancement as Christians, as Americans, and as a people.

Conclusion

THE PRESENT state of race relations in America is an interesting one to say the least. For the first time in our history, an African American has been elected to serve in the highest office of our land. And aside from any liberal views or controversial associations he may have, the fellowship between Barack Obama and his primarily black church in Chicago is one that many still find themselves unable to comprehend. After all, his cool talk is the polar opposite of an angry walk.

But mine is not a case against Barack Obama. For that, I leave you to read the credible and often challenging works of David Freddoso (*The Case Against Barack Obama: The Unlikely Rise and Unexamined Agenda of the Media's Favorite Candidate*), Shelby Steele (*A Bound Man: Why We Are Excited about Obama and Why He Can't Win*), David Mendell (*From Promise to Power*), and Stephen Mansfield (*The Faith of Barack Obama*). Or, if you're determined to live among the limitless stories of political fantasy, I leave you to enjoy the frequently absurd writings of Jerome Corsi (*The Obama Nation: Leftist Politics and the Cult of Personality*), Webster Tarpley (*Obama: The Postmodern Coup*), and Andy Martin (*Obama: The Man behind the Mask*). Plenty has been and will be written to deal with the pros and cons of our forty-fourth president, but those matters belong to another controversy. Mine is a case against the understandable but flawed teaching of Black Liberation Theology.

Deep within the controversy of Black Liberation is one notable strength. Whether it be the impoverished, the veteran, or the child with no future, all Americans should have an equal opportunity for a better future, regardless of the conditions that have made their path more difficult. Followers of Black Theology have long represented this power and strength for the weak and weary. They are, for the inner cities of this nation, a social alternative to government intervention. Indeed, when more churches are willing to serve the people of their local communities with comparable vigor, the rhetorical visions of hope and change won't have to come from Washington.

Unfortunately, Black Liberation has more weaknesses than it has strengths. At least three immediately come to mind. First, in an effort to empower the oppressed, its proponents have segregated their message and brought about a new generation of racial misunderstanding. Preaching of this kind fosters an image that whites are, in all cases, part of the problem. And where whites are made eternally guilty for the color of their skin, blacks—both congregants and preachers—receive a natural upper hand.

Some might argue that in the middle of the last century, the time had come for blacks to be empowered by their *blackness* after so many years of being oppressed by whites who flattered themselves with their *whiteness*. That may be true, but *white* power was never an acceptable part of our nation's history. Although it seems justifiable that at some point there would have been a need for such a radical push against the grain of an oppressive white power, that time has come and gone.

The second, more theological problem with Black Liberation is that it lacks the moderating influence of accountability to a credible and sound Christian community. Those who preach an exclusionary message of God are often cited as cultish, and Black Theology cannot be immune to this criticism. Being an exclusive assembly of believers does not automatically make a group wrong, but where conflicting counsel is not considered, there can be no sound judgment.

Third and most disturbing is the humanized makeover that Black Liberation gives to God. Instead of acknowledging scriptures where the Lord presides over the rich and the poor without racial preference, adherents insist on presenting an image of God that fits the mold of their social necessity. He becomes a part of their creation, rather than they being a part of his. Wiser counsel would insist that the God we serve in this present age is neither black nor white but eternally impartial. Whatever the color of his flesh in time past, he is a risen Lord today, for whom racial definitions are no longer relevant. Believers with sound judgment do not worship a picture or a symbol but a timeless and immortal king.

> Wherefore henceforth know we no man after the flesh: yea, though we have known Christ after the flesh, yet now henceforth know we him no more.[1]

> Now unto the King eternal, immortal, invisible, the only wise God, be honor and glory forever and ever. Amen.[2]

Orthodox Christians have often enjoyed paintings and relics that display their beliefs, but faith is not based on visible images. If, indeed, we have put our trust in Christ as the ultimate sacrifice, we have trusted in something we did not witness but now proclaim as true. This is a faith based not on what is seen, but on what is unseen: "For we walk by faith, not by sight."[3]

Advocates of Black Liberation may have once felt that the painted face of Christ from the white community was a troubling image of oppression, but I would contend that any image then or now was and is irrelevant. Whether Da Vinci was more accurate in his portraits than a modern forensic expert, Christ is now a risen savior whose form is without color, size, or age. Artists are certainly free to exercise a liberal imagination, but to *preach* Christ as the God of racial preference is to sidetrack the gospel of impartial grace from the pulpit. And all too often,

1. 2 Corinthians 5:16.
2. 1 Timothy 1:17.
3. 2 Corinthians 5:7.

listeners simply do not challenge what they hear, no matter how outlandish or contrary it might be to the word of God.

Much of our present dilemma in the Christian church is a lazy congregation. Pastors and teachers have been let loose to dictate whatever doctrines they believe will best accommodate their audience, and the people just nod their heads with enthusiasm. Fewer and fewer congregants are willing to consider that what they are hearing may not always be right, no matter how good it sounds from the lips of an eloquent preacher. Such ignorance and blind obedience can be found in all modern churches, regardless of race. Sadly, people who question the things being taught are frequently railroaded as divisive members of their assembly. So naturally, the people learn to keep quiet.

From the moment that Barack Obama came under scrutiny for his affiliation with Black Liberation, members of the evangelical community have pondered his capacity to sit under misguided theology. "If he disagreed with such extreme views," they say, "he should have left long before it became politically inconvenient." But for that matter, how can anyone hear bad teaching and not acknowledge it? The truth is, the more we embed ourselves in a particular fellowship, the more difficult it is to recognize the errors that may surround us. It happens all the time. And in that respect, Obama is no different from the rest of us.

Black Liberation Theology is just one of many imperfect teachings in the Christian church today. I have not attempted to make this guide a comprehensive history of the subject but a catalyst for further study. May you find it profitable to that end.

Bibliography

AfricanAmericans.com. "Significant African American Firsts." Online: http://www.africanamericans.com/FirstsMore.htm

Armstrong, Karen. *Islam: A Short History.* London: Weidenfeld & Nicolson, 2000.

Bennett, William J. *America: The Last Best Hope.* Vol. 1, "From the Age of Discovery to a World at War, 1492–1914." Nashville: Nelson Current, 2006.

Benson, J. Kenneth. "Militant Ideologies and Organizational Contexts: The War on Poverty and the Ideology of Black Power." *Sociology Quarterly* 12 (1971) 328–39.

Boyd, Herb, ed. *Autobiography of a People: Three Centuries of African American History Told by Those Who Lived It.* New York: Anchor Books, 2000.

Calhoun-Brown, Allison. "The Image of God: Black Theology and Racial Empowerment in the African American Community." *Review of Religious Research* 40 (1999) 197–212.

Cone, James H. *Risks of Faith: The Emergence of a Black Theology of Liberation, 1968–1998.* Boston: Beacon Press, 1999.

Davidson, Roger H. "The War on Poverty: Experiment in Federalism." *Annals of the American Academy of Political and Social Science* 385 (Sept 1969) 1–13.

Divine, Robert A., et al. *America: Past & Present,* 8th ed. Vol. 2. New York: Pearson Education, 2007.

Fogel, Robert William, and Stanley L. Engerman. *Time on the Cross: The Economics of American Negro Slavery.* New York: W.W. Norton & Company, 1974.

Foner, Eric. *A Short History of Reconstruction.* New York: Harper & Row, 1990.

Genovese, Eugene D. *A Consuming Fire: The Fall of the Confederacy in the Mind of the White Christian South.* Athens: University of Georgia Press, 1998.

Goldwater, Barry. *The Conscience of a Conservative.* New York: MJF Books, 1960.

Haley, Alex, and Malcolm X. *The Autobiography of Malcolm X.* New York: Random House Publishing Group, 1965.

Harrington, Michael. *The Other America.* New York: Simon & Schuster, 1962.

Harris, Jessica C. "Revolutionary Black Nationalism: The Black Panther Party." *The Journal of Negro History* 86 (2001) 409–21.

Hughes, Langston. "I, Too." In *The Collected Poems of Langston Hughes,* edited by Arnold Rampersad and David Roessel, 46. New York: Vintage Books, 1996.

Humphrey, Hubert. "The War on Poverty." *Law and Contemporary Problems* 31 (1966) 6–17.

Johnson, Michael P., et al. *Reading the American Past,* 3rd ed. Vol. 2. Boston: St. Martin's Press, 2005.

Jones, LeAlan, and Lloyd Newman. *Our America: Life and Death on the South Side of Chicago.* New York: Simon & Schuster, 1997.

King, Martin Luther, Jr. "Letter from a Birmingham Jail." In *I Have a Dream: Writings & Speeches That Changed the World,* edited by James M. Washington, 83–100. San Francisco: Harper Collins, 1986.

———. "The Power of Nonviolence." In *I Have a Dream: Writings & Speeches That Changed the World,* edited by James M. Washington, 29–33. San Francisco: Harper Collins, 1986.

Locke, John. *The Second Treatise of Civil Government.* n.p., 1690. Online: http://www.constitution.org/jl/2ndtr02.htm.

Mansfield, Stephen. *The Faith of Barack Obama.* Dallas: Thomas Nelson, 2008.

Noonan, Peggy. *Patriotic Grace: What It Is and Why We Need It Now.* New York: Harper Collins, 2008.

Oates, Stephen B. *With Malice toward None: A Life of Abraham Lincoln.* New York: Harper Collins, 1977.

Obama, Barack. *The Audacity of Hope: Thoughts on Reclaiming the American Dream.* New York: Three Rivers Press, 2006.

————. "A More Perfect Union." Speech, Constitution Center, Philadelphia, March 18, 2008. No pages. Online: http://www.npr.org/templates /story/story.php?storyId=38478467.

Penn, Sean. *Into the Wild.* DVD. Directed by Sean Penn. Hollywood: Paramount Pictures, 2007.

Perman, Michael, ed. *Major Problems in the Civil War and Reconstruction.* Boston: Houghton Mifflin Co., 1998.

Powell, Adam Clayton Jr. *Adam by Adam: The Autobiography of Adam Clayton Powell, Jr.* New York: Kensington, 1971.

Schulman, Bruce J. *Lyndon B. Johnson and American Liberalism: A Brief Biography with Documents.* New York: St. Martin's Press, 2007.

Senate Historical Office. "Hubert H. Humphrey, 38th Vice President (1965–1968)." U.S. Senate: Art & History. Online: http://www. senate.gov/artandhistory/history/common/generic/VP_Hubert _Humphrey.htm.

Silverman, David S. *You Can't Air That: Four Cases of Controversy and Censorship in American Television Programming.* Television and Popular Culture. Syracuse, NY: Syracuse University Press, 2007.

Steele, Shelby. *The Content of Our Character: A New Vision of Race in America.* New York: Harper Collins Publishers, 1990.

Sundquist, James L. "Co-ordinating the War on Poverty." *Annals of the American Academy of Political and Social Science* 385 (1969) 41–49.

U.S. Census Bureau. "Race and Hispanic Origin: 1790 to 1990." Online: http://www.census.gov/population/www/documentation /twps0056/tab01.pdf.

U.S. Congress. *Report of the Joint Select Committee to Inquire into the Condition of Affairs in the Late Insurrectionary States.* Vol. 1, "Ku Klux Klan." Washington, D.C., 1872. Online: http://www.archive. org/details/reportofjointsel01unit.

————. *Report of the Joint Select Committee to Inquire into the Condition of Affairs in the Late Insurrectionary States.* Vol. 5, "South Carolina." Washington, D.C., 1872. Online: http://www.archive.org/details /reportofjointsel05unit.

U.S. Constitution. Thirteenth Amendment. Library of Congress, Primary Documents. Online: http://www.loc.gov/rr/program/bib/ourdocs /13thamendment.html.

U.S. Reports. *Dred Scott v. John F. A. Sanford.* 60 (Dec Term 1856) 393. Online: http://openjurist.org/60/us/393.

———. *Plessy v. Ferguson.* 163 (May 1896) 537. Online: http://openjurist .org/163/us/537.

Wagner, Richard. *American Conservatism: An Encyclopedia.* Wilmington, DE: ISI Books, 2006.

Watkins, T. H. *The Great Depression: America in the 1930s.* Lebanon, IN: Little, Brown & Co., 1993.

Weeks, Arland D. "A Conservative's View of Poverty." *The American Journal of Sociology* 22 (1917) 779–800.

Wheeler, John W. "Civil Rights Groups: Their Impact upon the War on Poverty." *Law and Contemporary Problems* 31 (1966) 152–58.

Williams, A. Roger. "A Black Pastor Looks at Black Theology." *The Harvard Theological Review* 64 (1971) 559–67.

Wilson, William Julius. *The Truly Disadvantaged: The Inner City, the Underclass, and Public Policy.* Chicago: University of Chicago Press, 1987.

Yarema, Allan. *The American Colonization Society: An Avenue to Freedom?* Lanham, MD: University Press of America, 2006.

YOUR TRAUMA HEALING JOURNEY

Lifeprint Reiki's Guide to Reconnecting to Self-Love

STEVE FOGELMAN

To all those who've struggled for years trying to find the happiness they deserve and to make sense of the world. Your inner strength and perseverance to move forward despite all the obstacle you've faced is inspirational. I hope you find the insights in this book like the cavalry arriving to help vanquish your seen and unseen opponents and facilitating the life of your dreams.

CONTENTS

PART III: THE SELF-LOVE JOURNEY

PART IV: LIVING LIFEPRINT REIKI

PART 1:

IN THE BEGINNING

CHAPTER 1:

Inciting Events

The hero's journey is about the courage to seek the depths;
the eternal cycle of change within us;
the uncanny discovery that the seeker is the
mystery which the seeker seeks to know.

—JOSEPH CAMPBELL

WELCOME TO *Your Trauma Healing Journey!* In this chapter, I share my own journey from trauma to healing, to show you how I learned the insights I share in this book, as well as to show that it is indeed possible to move from trauma to healing. Though your life and journey may be different, I found comfort and healing in gaining understanding of universal truths of life on earth before—and after—traditional religion.

I felt compelled to share the success I experienced from my trauma healing journey and the spiritual clarity that came with it. Before, I was living in deep pain from toxic situations, yet I knew the answers lay within, and that this journey was the only path to survival.

I was drowning in a lifetime of traumas until the 2020 pandemic, when I finally had the solitude needed to heal and reconnect to my authentic self and purpose. But the critical point in my spiritual development happened in 2018.

I moved to New York City in 2012, to pursue theater and playwriting, believing the darkest moments of my life had passed. But in 2014, I moved into a studio apartment with my seven-year-old dog, Mossi. I didn't know then, but my building was owned by New York's most prolific, unindicted crime family, the Goldmans.[1] Though patriarch Sol Goldman, a well-documented racketeer and sex trafficking slumlord, died in 1987, his youngest daughter, Jane Goldman, runs the business, Solil Management, to this day, exactly as her father did.

Daily, I was subjected to the unbearable jackhammering noise of constant illegal apartment renovations and filed several complaints with the city, only to find each case was closed after two denials of entry, not escalated.

I reached out to then Public Advocate Leticia James and every member of city council but no one replied. Knowing there was no one in the city government willing to help me deal with a criminal landlord who ignored her contractual obligations dropped me into a deep depression where I lost all interest in everything I used to love, like cooking, writing, and art.

But I finally had the wherewithal to seek professional help. At the age of fifty-five, I was diagnosed as being on the autism spectrum, at which point my whole tumultuous life made sense. I needed medication to help with the depression and was also diagnosed with General Anxiety Disorder. It became clear I had been suffering with undiagnosed anxiety my entire life and would later learn the cause. Through all this, my inner drive for civil justice wasn't dampened, and at the apartment, I was finally able to have illegal construction shut down. Unfortunately, that only lasted a day, so further action was needed. I was so naïve and felt brokers needed to know

---

1   A compilation of published and recorded evidence of the Goldman family's eighty-year crime spree in New York City can be found at tinyurl.com / 228tjvry.

about the illegal apartments and started emailing the larger real estate brokers letting them know Jane Goldman's apartments were illegal, as it's also illegal in NYC for licensed brokers to show illegal apartments.

Jane found out about my activism and, one afternoon in February 2018, called to threaten a lawsuit against me and my mother as guarantor, if I didn't stop notifying brokers, on some business interference grounds. The lawsuit never happened as it was only meant as a RICO violation type of intimidation.

Because the doormen were so hostile towards me, I moved before the end of my lease. Once I found a new, safe place to live, I could really appreciate how traumatizing the experience had been and realized I needed to find a way to heal. I absolutely hated Jane Goldman, but knew my journey was to find a way to love all the horrible experiences she brought to my life.

I thought I had hit rock bottom, but just a year later, in May of 2019, the love of my life for thirteen years, my dog Mossi, experienced degradation of his hip dysplasia to where he could no longer walk, and had to be put down. I was absolutely devastated, realizing I was actually living my life for him; I was always thinking about getting home to feed or walk him and constantly checking the weather to be dressed appropriately for those walks. But now he was gone, and the grief was unbearable.

I was already familiar with the many meditations available on YouTube. But now I focused on self-love videos and affirmations, listening several times a day, and furiously journaled my feelings. I also scoured the internet for ways to properly grieve, and found an article about post-traumatic growth, making that my mantra. With the help of a therapist, I began the transformation to Steve 2.0, which I discuss more in chapter 8.

A shaman I met through a mutual friend came over to perform a Tibetan Healing Bowl ceremony on me, which propelled me to investigate the healing powers of sound, where I learned that the bowls are tuned to Solfeggio Frequencies.

I discovered Reiki at this time, too. After one in-person session, the pandemic hit, making it necessary to continue remotely. My practitioner felt I had negative entities attached to me, and after ten remote sessions I was finally healing and gaining back my inner strength.

Many traumatic events lead up to that moment. Ever since I was a young boy, I felt there was something different about me, and looked to astrology and other spiritual practices in search for answers about the otherness I felt. I was born into a Jewish family and raised in Allentown, Pennsylvania (made famous by the Billy Joel song). I'm the third of four children, and developed Middle Child Syndrome, which is now simply called trauma.

I was born two weeks late and jaundiced and had to be put under a bright light, unswaddled, for hours a day. A week later was the ceremony of my circumcision. Psychology Today's January 2015 article *Circumcision's Psychological Damage,* confirms circumcision can create sex abuse trauma and even autism when done without anesthesia. At age one, I had to have surgery for an undescended testicle, and my mother said I absolutely howled with distress when she had to leave. Off to a great start, setting the stage for a lifetime of anxiety and abandonment issues!

As a toddler, I was a rocker. At night to fall asleep, or if I woke in the night, I'd rock myself to sleep, banging my head against the plaster wall while hugging a pillow. Today we recognize that as a stimming behavior to soothe deep feelings of a lack of safety. But back then, I was judged as a weird child, never getting any help to deal with my overwhelming emotions. Instead of my family being sympathetic or even compassionate to the situation, I was further teased about the bald spot the head banging left on my scalp.

There were psychologists in the 1960s, so I always wondered why, as a parent, one wouldn't want to figure out why their kid banged his head every night. What I experienced is what psychologists call "Benign Neglect," which is when physical needs like food, clothing and shelter are met, but emotional needs are ignored, creating feelings of not being worthy of love.

What I remember most about growing up is always being nauseous. Every day, it seemed. The unhelpful response from my exasperated parents was always: "Take a shower, you'll feel better," "Go for a walk, you'll feel better," or "Have something to eat, you'll feel better." Today, my digestive problems would be considered a symptom of something much more complicated, along with my other behavioral issues.

I also suffered severe motion sickness, which is a psychological sign of lack of control. Simply getting into a car, I would throw up. Motion sickness manifested the trauma of humiliation, because it's impossible to control and everybody knew about it. Even close friends of my parents, if they took a flight somewhere, would collect air sickness bags from the plane to bring back for me, which didn't make me feel good about myself. They were kept in the backseat pocket of our station wagon, just like on a plane.

I endured an Orthodox Jewish day school education from kindergarten through sixth grade. Since we were Reform at home, all the rituals I was taught at school as important parts of my religion weren't practiced at home, adding religious trauma to an ever-growing list of unresolved traumas.

Although I was fortunate to have friends, I suffered from such emotionally arrested development that intimate relationships eluded me, since I never felt safe talking about my feelings or asking for what I needed. Not to mention, when puberty hit, I was alone dealing with all the changes in my body, and turned to food for comfort. I was considered an overweight tween, and when my mother took me to the doctor to help me lose weight, it sent the subliminal message that I wasn't loveable as I was. My sixth-grade class photo exists as a record of all the pain I was feeling.

On top of all that, I was a closeted gay teen in the 1970s, creating shame for who I was. I could never be myself, even around friends, and even after I came out around thirty, intimate gay relationships eluded me. I was scarred with self-hatred and being with another gay man meant the world would know and judge me.

Another pivotal traumatic event was set in motion when I was twenty. Sadly, my uncle Arnold, my mother's brother-in-law, dropped dead from a heart attack at the age of forty-four.. He was the only one in the family that tolerated me, and we spent a lot of time together since I was interested in his crafting hobbies and DIY projects. He was part of the inspiration behind my pursuing a degree in architecture.

Arnold, along with my father, ran the family garment business after my maternal grandfather retired. My father was in the process of leaving the business, but since he was still legally involved, he had to return, and my uncle's share in the business were sold to my father. It was at this time that the factory became phenomenally successful, leaving my aunt and her family out of the ensuing windfall, instigating a building resentment between my aunt's family and ours.

When I was thirty-six and launching a private chef business, I sent my parents a copy of my marketing brochure to keep them in the loop. I received a voice message from my father congratulating me and wishing me luck in the business. I had always considered him a dream killer, because every time I had an idea for something, all he could offer was reasons why it wouldn't work. That validating voicemail was a message I had waited all my life to hear. The next day he was dead.

Though the business was now owned by my mother, my brother took over running it. My aunt had remarried, and her new husband came to work for us as head of Human Resources. This was the late 1990s, and much work was going overseas. The business found itself in such tough times that my brother asked all office executives to take a temporary 20 percent pay cut to help. This prompted my aunt's husband to quit and sue us two weeks before my brother's second wedding. I was understandably furious and sent my aunt a scathing letter expressing how I felt. Because I apologized for it the next day,

I was shocked to find out I had been villainized over it by not only my cousins, but also friends of my aunt who now looked down on me—but not on the guy who filed the lawsuit. I was confused and deeply saddened that writing a letter expressing feelings could be viewed as worse than suing your own family. This experience plummeted me into the beginning of my midnight of the soul.

The situation tore the family apart. Although, several months later, all the executives were reimbursed for their temporary sacrifice, it would be another twenty years before I realize I was the subject of what psychologists call a narcissistic smear campaign with transfer of blame, and that narcissism was an ancestral trauma.

My mother was especially upset, as the relationship with her sister was in turmoil. I was searching for comfort and answers when I discovered the Kabbalah Center. I enrolled in classes and attended regular shabbat services because I felt welcomed, and stayed an active member for over four years despite it being a cult of Judaism.

The true Kabbalah is an esoteric practice with hidden meanings in multiple layers of consciousness, instilling the need to look at all things for deeper, hidden personal meaning and insight. I learned Kabbalah's ten interdimensional aspects of life through which the divine manifests in the world, and that the divine energy flows and interacts with creation. That everything in the universe is interconnected, forming a single tapestry of existence, fostering a sense of unity and belonging. Kabbalah also emphasizes the importance of personal growth and transformation to refine character, overcome negative tendencies, and cultivate positive qualities.

At the end of my tenure at the Kabbalah Center, the 2008 mortgage crisis hit and I lost my house and most of my savings. My midnight of the soul became a deeper depression that only went away when I went off to improv classes. Otherwise, there were days I didn't even have the energy to walk the dog past the front lawn. I didn't have the wherewithal to seek the needed professional help, as it's common for traumatized people to have difficulty asking for help, since they never had helpful people in their life as a child.

Though many suffered through the 2020 pandemic, it was the best time of my life. While I was able to empathize with the loss and grieving everyone experienced due to my own past loss, I was also overjoyed I no longer had social obligations to my toxic family.

The pandemic also awakened my inner need to help. I was a professional actor, and all my theater friends were out of work for who knew how long. Would theater ever return? Everyone might need help finding new passions in life, so I enrolled in an online life coaching certificate program through Life Purpose Institute. LPI has been around for thirty years, and is the forerunner of the style of life coaching we have today. Within four months, I was a certified life coach with clients in NYC, Los Angeles, Canada, England and Cyprus.

I realized that most actors suffer trauma. Wanting to be seen is an unconscious search for love, and acting helps process trauma, and why play acting is used in trauma therapy. "Self-care" has become a popular buzzword, but true self-love, is more than massages and walks in the woods. It's a spiritual lifestyle and mindset rooted in one's humanity.

I never in a million years thought my destiny included becoming a spiritual coach, but realizing my own spiritual growth, I soon felt adding a spiritual component to my coaching would help me succeed. I returned to LPI to add certified spiritual coach to my resumé.

In learning effective techniques to help others, I found myself healing even more deeply from my own past, and connecting to more of my own self-love. I found myself able to stop dwelling on my painful past with self-pity and to view it merely as an opportunity that led me to be the authentic person I was now becoming. My life couldn't possibly be as fantastic as it is now if I hadn't gone through those difficulties, because working through them is what brought me to now.

After a series of non-coincidental coincidences, Reiki healing became an obvious path to explore. My level 1 Reiki master mentioned he attuned autistic children to Reiki to help heal themselves. Before then, it never occurred to me that an individual could be attuned to Reiki merely to heal themselves. How empowering it is to unlock one's inherent healing powers! Think about when something hurts in your body; your hands automatically go to the point of pain to start sending healing energy. We're wired to heal ourselves, mostly, but society teaches us we need someone outside ourselves to complete the healing. When you perform Reiki on yourself, in addition to calming your mind, you can also clear your chakras, heal joint pain, body aches, and pains, and grow confidence in your proactive strength.

As I continued healing myself and offered to help friends and family, I had another empowering epiphany. Reiki was also a way to heal my ancestral trauma of a lifetime of narcissistic abuse. It became clear: **gaining the ability to heal ourselves and our families is part of many a soul's purpose.** The ubiquitous phrase "To heal the world, you have to first heal yourself," became my driving force

Although there's still plenty to clear, I became empowered with a new emotional intelligence, gaining agency to feel safe speaking up for what I wanted and needed.

Lifeprint Reiki was born as a new, non-religious, spiritual lifestyle and societal blueprint based on the empowerment of first and foremost healing your trauma to create happiness, with the understanding that everyone's spiritual needs are as unique as a fingerprint.

CHAPTER 2:

You're Not Broken, Only Disconnected

If you want to awaken all of humanity,
then awaken all of yourself.

If you want to eliminate the suffering in the world,
then eliminate all that is negative in yourself.

Truly, the greatest gift you have to give is
that of your own self-transformation.

—LAO-TZU

THE PHILOSOPHY OF LIFEPRINT REIKI is predicated on the notion that all challenging human behavior and desires, as well as physical ailments, are a product of unresolved trauma stored in the body. This unresolved trauma disconnects us from self-love and feeling the happiness we desire. The purpose of this book is to help awakening the individual to their own hidden traumas and offer healing methods, assisted by Reiki, to reconnect to their inherent humanity and divinity. Think of Lifeprint Reiki as my attempt at compiling a human user's manual.

You're not broken, only disconnected from self-love. Which means developing self-love isn't selfish, but rather the cornerstone of a fulfilling, happy, and successful life. By cultivating the lost deep appreciation for themselves, individuals unlock a world of possibilities, becoming more resilient, confident, and empowered to pursue passions without fear of judgment. Those who embrace self-love experience greater emotional well-being, stronger relationships, and a heightened sense of purpose. In contrast, those lacking self-love may struggle with low self-esteem, social anxiety, unhealthy relationships, and difficulty reaching their full potential.

Self-love is our inherent human spirituality. Why, then, do we get disconnected from it? If you haven't already realized, you're not a human with a soul, but a soul having a human learning experience. We're here on earth to experience some of the most complex and challenging soul lessons in the entire universe. But without knowing how to best navigate this lifetime of learning, it's like we're brought into the world spiritually blindfolded and handcuffed, and the trauma created by all those struggles not only disconnects us from self-love, but also leaves us without emotional intelligence to navigate through life.

Everyone has their own definition of happiness. For some it's an ego vision of having millions of dollars, an expensive car, and a four-bedroom house with a pool. That's not the happiness goal of this book, but certainly could be a by-product. While material possessions, social status, or external validation might bring a sense of accomplishment, these are often superficial and temporary fixes.

The happiness this book helps with is that which comes from embracing the simple joy of being by healing all that's disconnected us from self-love.

This understanding enables us to align with our soul's desires, and fulfill that deep yearning for purpose, growth, and divine connection that transcends a wounded ego's fruitless fight for control. To accomplish that end, there's a lot of work ahead to gain awareness of our thoughts and behaviors, why we have them, and to understand that none of them are our fault. We're all destined for abundant, happy lives but limiting beliefs are the unconscious blocks holding us back.

There are many reasons why we may not have yet achieved our desired happiness in life. Most disconnections from self-love can be traced back to childhood. Not having our feelings acknowledged, feeling shame, being bullied, feeling abandoned, or enduring any number of experiences, whether horrific or seemingly benign, traumatized us, leaving us without the ability to understand our emotions nor express them in a healthy manner. In other words, these left us with a lack of emotional intelligence. Disconnected from self-love, our survival personality developed unhealthy coping behaviors and limiting beliefs to fill the love void.

These challenges are our Earth soul lessons. But we can only learn from them if we stop to reflect on what happened and how we can grow from those experiences. Otherwise, we'll likely keep finding ourselves in the same or similarly unpleasant situations until the lesson is learned.

It's also important to be aware that every single soul is here for different reasons, with different skill sets, for different experiences. That makes life a challenge, and why one spiritual path or faith can't possibly be a good fit for everyone. That's why it's called Lifeprint Reiki, because everyone's spiritual needs are as unique as a fingerprint, and its practice is intended as a philosophical foundation from which to explore auxiliary physical spiritual practices that enhance your soul's specific needs.

Lifeprint Reiki offers the Shamanic point of view: life has no inherent meaning. Instead, we bring meaning to life by clearing past karma and traumas that we don't even realize we have.

This non-religious path to more peace in life can begin a spiritual rewiring toward self-love, or work through a religious deconstruction. Gaining only a bit of awareness can free your soul from arcane or fearful religious beliefs that disconnect you from your inner power. Independent divine connection is the future of humanity in the Age of Aquarius.

This book can also help answer the question of why you can't seem to find a life partner. Those who are chronically single are likely in need of a stronger inner divine connection. You might have heard the ridiculous phrase, "You can't love somebody else until you love yourself." Every toxic relationship is rooted in self-hate, so there's more at play.

Perhaps you're the black sheep of the family, which means your 'problematic behavior" is the response to narcissistic abuse, and have no clue how to find the strength to create a healthier emotional environment. Family gatherings are a nightmare and breaking free of this cycle seems impossible.

Perhaps you unknowingly find yourself unhappy in life, feeling like you were born and bred into the social matrix of society merely to serve it, never learning how to find your own purpose and life meaning. Individual talents aren't appreciated by the matrix, and anyone above or below average in any of a million ways, is made to feel they don't fit in.

Lifeprint Reiki is the key to breaking free from the societal matrix, by gaining self-awareness and self-acceptance. This is the core of your self-love journey—a process that may challenge your ego's resistance. But, as we embark on this journey of creating your personal spiritual path together, you'll find the rewards far outweigh the emotional challenges.

Lifeprint Reiki helps us undo the limiting beliefs and negative programming we've endured by showing how to reframe challenging past experiences to uncover the positive aspects and shed the victim mindset. You can't change the past, but you can change the way you feel about it. It's also important to understand you're perfect at every stage of growth. **You can be a masterpiece and a work-in-progress simultaneously.**

Bringing together the effective modalities and understandings I've explored over my years of healing from trauma may save you years of spiritual growth. Rooted in Usui Reiki, Lifeprint Reiki offers a few key universal spiritual and psychological teachings to change the energy of this modern age. These are the 11 Insights. The goal is to develop a deeper, unique independent divine connection with a unity consciousness.

The process starts with learning to connect to the sanctity of every moment. Our homes are as sacred as any religious structure; it's just that we currently don't believe that to be the case. We don't need to be part of a congregation to connect to a higher power. Sitting alone on a dock by a lake enjoying a spectacular sunset is equally, if not more, spiritual.

There's a lot of information out there on self-love, but Lifeprint Reiki differs in the scope of determining what affects self-love. We can't create a vaccine for an unknown virus because we need to know its DNA. You'll learn more about what Carl Jung calls your shadow and may even discover that there are more than eleven insights into what's holding you back from the life you prefer.

Lifeprint Reiki also includes a powerful new symbol I discovered, the *Shin Zo Ho Go*, that can be used with or without attunement.

Shin Zo Ho Go literally means "heart protection," in Japanese, facilitating a heart center release while creating protection for it. Meditating on this symbol helps release the energies that no longer serve you, while protecting the heart center while it heals.

Not everything in this book is for everyone, yet there's something to gain for everyone. It's okay if the 11 Insights to Happiness is the only portion you connect with, or the aspect of gaining self-awareness. A goal of Lifeprint Reiki is to inspire you to find the collection of spiritual practices that work to not only help you heal your trauma while on Earth, but also motivate you to continue searching through other modalities that may resonate even more strongly with you. The sooner you clear your traumas, the more opportunities for happiness you'll have.

This book includes three more parts. Part 2 details the principles of Lifeprint Reiki, and the attunement process. Part 3 is The Self-Love Journey, offering a spiritual and psychological foundation necessary for this journey, steps to gaining self-awareness, and the 11 Insights. Part 4 details what living Lifeprint Reiki could be like in your life, and what a compassionate society could look like in the future. You'll also find an appendix of helpful spiritual resources at the end of the book.

Such a tremendous amount of information is included here that it can't all be absorbed in only one reading. The best way to use this book is to first read it entirely, and simply allow any thoughts and emotions to surface. Next, identify the topics that caused the greatest discomfort or resistance. These are the areas most in need of attention; however, it's okay to return to the chapters that feel easier to get started. Don't rush into anything, and revisit only one of the 11 Insights per day. You may take it at any pace that feels right for you, which could be weekly revisits, or even a monthly revisit, to give yourself a healthy year to grow into the new you, though your desired growth may take longer.

Depending on where you are on this spiritual growth journey, some concepts might not make sense right now. I remember, as a young actor, reading Uta Hagen's famed book *Respect for Acting*, and not understanding a single thing. Reading it again thirty years later proved I had learned everything she wrote about! Patience is required in this process. As you move along your journey, you can revisit this book many times to monitor your growth. You might even repeat the process annually for the rest of your life.

I invite you to share this book with people you feel are open to the benefits of a self-love journey, so that you can talk about the feelings and findings that come up as you move through the 11 Insights.

YOU ARE WORTHY.

PART II:

THE CORE PRINCIPLES OF LIFEPRINT REIKI

CHAPTER 3:

Why Lifeprint Reiki Now?

The Age of Aquarius is an opportunity for humanity to evolve into a more conscious and compassionate species.

—RAM DASS

IN RECENT YEARS, RELIGION has lost much control over a large portion of Earth's population. According to the 2019 Pew Research poll, *US Decline of Christianity Continues at Rapid Pace,* those identifying as Christian have dropped from 78 percent in 2007 to 65 percent in 2019, while those identifying as religiously unaffiliated have grown from 16 percent to 26 percent in the same period. This dramatic decline is illustrated by seven thousand congregations leaving the United Methodist Church, in 2023 alone, finding the church's intolerant stance toward LGBTQ+ people offensive. Since 2018, over 300 Catholic schools across America have shuttered due to dwindling enrollment.

No religion lasts forever. The Egyptians no longer pray to Ra as they did 6,000 years ago. No one prays to Zeus or Poseidon as they once did. What was practiced as a religion by the Greeks has been downgraded to mythology. In fact, the oldest current widely practiced religion, Hinduism, dates back only about 3,500 years. Judaism dates back less than 3,000, and Christianity 2,000 years. Islam has only been around 1,250 years. Buddhism, Jainism, and Taoism also came about within 900 to 200 BCE, during a period Swiss German philosopher Karl Jaspers coined the Axial Age, in his 1953 book, *The Origin and Goal of History*. In this era of history "the spiritual foundations of humanity were laid simultaneously and independently. And these are the foundations upon which humanity still subsists today." But for how much longer?

It's interesting to note that this Axial Age also corresponds to the Zodiac Ages of Aries and Pisces, but since 2012 we've moved into the Age of Aquarius. Just as the Zodiac energies change for the individual based on the planetary positions, so does that of the collective. For the past tens of thousands of years, humanity has repeatedly moved through each of the twelve ages approximately every two thousand years, responding with evolving spiritual understandings to complement the changes.

The Zodiac ages move in reverse through the signs of the common horoscope, as the spinning of Earth wobbling on its axis appears to move backwards in relation to the constellations. No doubt, then, being in the Age of Aquarius holds a new spiritual understanding to support the next two thousand years that you're already experiencing.

Four thousand years ago, during the Age of Aries, the most significant spiritual legacy was the proclamation of codes of laws by several civilizations. The eighteenth-century BCE king, Hammurabi of Babylonia, is known for one of the first written codes of law in recorded history, the Code of Hammurabi. This set of laws to control the masses also brought us the toxic "eye for an eye" belief of justice. The story of the Ten

Commandments, as revealed by Moses, came four hundred years later. Aries also brought the polarity of "good" and "bad" which, connected to religious beliefs, was the birth of the concept of sin. In India at that time, the four Sanskrit Vedas, which laid the ground for the Hindu way of life, appeared.

Then came the Age of Pisces, a water sign symbolized by the fish. Its significant influence was the growth and spread of monotheism, particularly Christianity and Islam. Not surprisingly, the rise of global religions centered primarily on symbols of water: baptism, walking on water, changing water into wine. Not to mention that the fish is used as a symbol for Jesus, who was actually born during the March equinox, not in December—coinciding with the beginning of the Piscine month of the year.

But the actual teachings of Christ, of loving all and the power of divine connection within us all, was pirated and altered by modern Christianity to become the complete opposite. Society became firmly entrenched in religious dogma and monarchical hierarchies, with strict frameworks and a focus on material wealth and power as the ultimate goal, instead of the all-loving message of the man called Jesus.

This led to zealotry, self-righteousness, and the urge to establish fundamentalist guidelines. The Spanish Inquisition, lasting three hundred and fifty years (1478–1834), stands as a perfect example of an era of religious intolerance. Large populations were expected to show unquestioning allegiance to the monolithic belief system of Christianity, or be murdered. In America today, this intolerance is represented by the Evangelical and Dominion Christian nationalist movements, copying Islamic Sharia Law by attempting to mandate that those of differing faiths must also adhere to their singular oppressive dogma.

Thankfully we're now in The Age of Aquarius, an air sign, associated with collaboration, freedom, creativity, and taking action — almost the opposite of Pisces. You feel it already as New Age spirituality, mindfulness, and the buzzwords of "self-love" and "self-care" fill popular consciousness. All are

Aquarian ideas. Although old religions won't suddenly die, Christianity is continually losing a following.

Though Christianity dissipates, what has been known as Christ Consciousness expands in the Age of Aquarius. The man called Jesus Christ was a pre-Talmudic Jew who didn't create Christianity. What he brought to earth is the idea that each one of us possesses the ability to gain awareness of the higher self as part of a universal system. A person can find self-realization and unity with their inner divine power and their humanity; the name is not intended to relate to the personality of Jesus Christ. To eliminate any unintended sense of religious connection, I refer to it as Unity Consciousness.

In the Age of Aquarius, the harsh concept of "sins" being punished by a vengeful God with eternity in a non-existent Hell is replaced with the compassionate understanding that these actions are mostly trauma responses that create karma, which can be transmuted. The idea of worship, recognized for its arcane root in fear and hierarchy, is replaced with the simple notion of connection to a higher power, with whom we are on equal footing.

The Age of Aquarius also supports less focus on material wealth, and in turn, the energy on Earth shifts from consumerism, material values, and hierarchies, to intellect, information, and collaboration. We already see that happening as people are more focused on spending money on experiences rather than objects.

The Black Lives Matter movement and the popular notion of "woke" as finding reasons to express empathy for those less fortunate and marginalized, are supported by this Aquarius energy. Those who attack this empathetic revelation of compassionately repairing past injustices are actually expressing trauma responses from their own unconscious self-hate. They can't accept any wrongdoing of the past, because they support the same horrendous acts in the present. They need to feel they're better than others to exist which makes the idea of equality an existential crisis for them. If they're not better than someone, then who are they? Theirs is a futile last stand against the steamroller of change that is the Age of Aquarius.

Lifeprint Reiki purposefully address these evolving spiritual needs, desires, and concerns as a lifestyle that's not a religion.

One purpose is to help the vibrational changes currently happening around the globe. If you're not familiar with the concept, the energy of the planet is shifting from a 3D (three-dimensional) reality towards a higher 5D vibration. The world we see, with the heaviness of polarity and reaction, of betrayal and revenge, war and control, is 3D; 5D is the unseen world of unity and response, of support and gratitude, peace and freedom. Know we don't have to "get there," to this desired space and time. We already exist in this dimension, though unresolved trauma and the toxic people we keep in our lives can prevent us from connecting to it effectively. Lifeprint Reiki is designed to help you transmute the negative effects of unresolved trauma with a new spiritual practice without a savior.

The savior archetype often dictates a specific path or set of doctrines. Rigid adherence to these external frameworks can stifle the exploration of diverse spiritual avenues and the development of our unique spiritual identity. This can ultimately lead to a sense of inauthenticity and conformity. Investing undue trust in a single savior creates vulnerability to manipulation and exploitation, causing significant societal and individual harm.

The concept of a savior outside us is also detrimental to individual and collective growth. Placing faith in a savior fosters codependency, hindering our ability to connect with our inner guidance and engage in proactive spiritual practices. **The only one who can truly "save" you, is you.**

Lifeprint Reiki emphasizes the potential for inner transformation within everyone. By cultivating self-awareness, self-compassion, and critical thinking, you can become responsible for navigating the spiritual needs of your unique trauma healing journey. As a result, you'll feel personally empowered, with a renewed emotional intelligence, leading to a more authentic and fulfilling spiritual experience and, by default, a happier life.

Additionally, there's no worshiping in Lifeprint Reiki. As mentioned earlier, the idea of worship is rooted in caveman fears of a higher power with a need to appease the Gods. With Unity Consciousness, there's no hierarchy with the divine, because we reflect it. All that's required is connection and gratitude. Religion is obsolete. We're no longer followers but our own self-empowered leaders, full of self-love.

Reconnecting to self-love isn't a new concept in spirituality; it has just been lost. Multiple religions promote cultivating a loving, independent connection with the source of being, similar to unity consciousness that because we are part of Source, we are Source.

That simple understanding will help you live a life free of anxiety, chaos, toxic influences, and uncontrollable trauma responses to find inner peace and happiness. You'll learn to strip away the existing unconscious barriers to that happiness to freely express your soul's desires and authentic self.

CHAPTER 4:

The Lifeprint Reiki Difference

Reiki power is like an aura or glow you radiate
out, where no darkness can penetrate you.

—MRS. HAWAYO TAKATA

THERE ARE AT LEAST A DOZEN different types of Reiki, such as Violet Flame, Kundalini, and Karuna Ki, to name but three. Each contains different symbols and healing intentions. I encourage you to explore these as well to see what resonates with you. However, Lifeprint Reiki builds upon the classic Usui Reiki, founded in 1922.

Just like yoga is an entire spiritual path beyond the familiar poses and stretches, and Zen Buddhism is far more complex than simply meditating, Lifeprint Reiki, too, is an entire way of life.

While there's no magic bullet for a journey toward happiness, attunement to any of the many forms of Reiki offers a powerful spiritual jumpstart.

Imagine hiking a dusty path leading to a mountaintop view. Step by step, you build strength and resilience. A Reiki attunement is like finding a hidden cable car, whisking you up to the breathtaking vista where the vastness of the spiritual landscape unfolds before you.

This attunement awakens and enhances our ability to sense and channel universal healing energy using various symbols. These symbols can be used to not only heal the physical body, but transcend space and time to heal past pains and send positive energy to the future. It's not about gaining a magical power, but rather a heightened sensitivity to the subtle energies around us.

Reiki is Japanese for "spiritual life force energy." This healing technique was thought to have been discovered in Japan in 1922, by a Buddhist monk named Mikao Usui. Learning the legendary story of Usui's life, that he's some kind of savior who came to rediscover the lost art of Reiki, is often part of the Usui Reiki attunement process. However, he didn't actually discover Reiki, nor was he a savior or Buddhist monk.

Born October 9, 1865, into a practicing Buddhist family, and dying on March 9, 1926, Usui lived during a time of great conflict, upheaval, and social change in Japan. The end of feudalism and its ancient ways removed generations' worth of traditions that had held Japan together. Though he was a practicing Buddhist, he was also a working man who faced business failures and personal hardships, leading him to seek a deeper understanding of his purpose. We'll never know Usui's history for sure, as he wrote nothing down, and his teachings were all orally conveyed.

Reiki had been previously practiced by other groups in Japan and Tibet, but Usui contributed deeper empowerment to the attunement process, possibly as a result of his legendary three-week meditation on Mount Kurama. Because of this new understanding of Reiki, Usui Reiki became the most popular method in Japan and is why he's so revered to this day. He then spent the rest of his life working to find ways to improve the practice, help people heal themselves, and spread the teachings of Reiki.

Another noted master, Mrs. Hawayo Takata, was a Japanese woman from Hawaii, credited with introducing Reiki to the United States. In the 1930s, Takata traveled to Japan to learn Reiki from Chujiro Hayashi, one of Mikao Usui's first students. After returning to the United States, Takata opened a Reiki clinic in Hawaii and began teaching Reiki to others. It's Mrs. Takata who fabricated Usui's mythical savior story to connect Reiki to Christian faith, since nothing sells better to Christians than the familiar savior.

Takata died in 1980, after teaching Reiki to hundreds of students, and is remembered as a pioneer of Reiki in the USA. Her legacy lives on through the many Reiki practitioners who continue to teach and practice.

HOW DOES REIKI WORK?

Reiki works with the body's intrinsic ability to heal itself. If the body's energy flow is disrupted by illness or injury, Reiki assists our own ability to restore balance. Since Reiki can also span space and time, there are distance Reiki techniques to send energy to far away people or situations in need of healing. There are Reiki healing videos on the internet that do, in fact, work.

In 2019, Natalie L. Dyer, Ann L. Baldwin, and William L. Rand published a scientific study of Reiki in *The Journal of Alternative and Complementary Medicine* that examined 1,411 reiki sessions by 99 different practitioners, concluding that a single session of Reiki improves multiple variables related to physical and psychological health. Other published studies have looked at the effect of Reiki on measures of stress hormones, blood pressure, heart rate, and immune responsivity, and on subjective reports of anxiety, pain, and depression.

The study groups to date are typically small; however, overlapping data from various studies support the ability of Reiki to reduce anxiety and pain, and suggest its usefulness to induce relaxation, improve fatigue and depressive symptoms, and strengthen overall well-being. While the healing technique of Reiki is a fantastic self-care tool, it's not a substitute for Western medical treatment. If you have any serious health concerns, always consult a medical practitioner.

By channeling Reiki energy, practitioners facilitate a connection to universal life energy, believed to be intelligent and inherently healing, to promote balance and well-being on physical, emotional, mental, and spiritual levels. The practitioner acts as a conduit for this energy, allowing it to flow into the recipient to support their own healing abilities. Reiki practitioners don't actually possess any power to heal, but merely to stimulate our own intrinsic healing abilities.

THE SPIRITUAL PRACTICE

Beyond physical healing, Lifeprint Reiki can be experienced as a transformative journey, fostering personal growth, spiritual awareness, and a deeper connection to one's inner self and the universe.

The four parts to Lifeprint Reiki, based on Usui Shiki Ryoho method, are: healing, personal development, spiritual discipline, and mystic order.

Healing

The premise of all Reiki is that pains and illness are caused by negative energy trapped in the distressed body part. These trapped negative energies are unresolved trauma, which I explain in detail in chapter 5. Because of that revelation, I developed my own style of practice to focus on treating trauma that starts with aura cleansing. Not all Reiki practitioners are even aware of this healing modality, but my level 3 training used the *Usui/Tibetan Advanced Reiki Training Manual* by William Lee Rand, which describes the practice.

Aura cleansing removes the root of the traumatic energy. I equate this practice to treating a gunshot wound. A doctor must first remove the bullet for anything else they do to be effective. I had one client come in needing crutches to walk, and after a twenty-minute aura cleansing, they stood without them. Another client suffering with neuropathy left the session free of foot pain. Because all these illnesses are caused by the energy of trauma, guiding a client through my simple modified aura cleansing meditation allows them to effectively heal themselves and learn the practice.

In my spiritual coach training, I also learned a practice called Body Tracking, which is similar. I had tremendous success with using it on my coaching clients. Rand's method includes the practitioner utilizing symbols (explained below) while the client is in a meditative state. But my intention is to eliminate the co-dependent nature of the practitioner/client relationship and empower the client to learn to heal themselves. I have adapted the technique so that it can be performed alone.

Because trauma dysregulates brain and nervous system functions, I focus on healing the head. The brain is the root of the entire nervous system, and Reiki energy has the intelligence to travel through the nerves to the area most in need of healing.

Personal Development

Reiki isn't just about feeling good physically. It's a catalyst for personal development. As you practice Reiki, you become more in tune with your body's needs. You might find yourself drawn to healthier foods or discover a need for better sleep habits. Reiki itself can also bring hidden emotions to the surface, allowing healing from those past experiences. Imagine Reiki as a mirror reflecting our inner world, helping us understand ourselves better and grow as people. Through practice, we learn to look at our life choices and address underlying unhealthy principles and limiting beliefs we acquired over our lifetime, and to clear them for our path towards authenticity. Lifeprint Reiki adds the 11 Insights to further your personal growth towards a happier life experience.

Spiritual Discipline

Reiki is a spiritual discipline, meaning it requires dedication and a willingness to learn. There are specific practices and principles associated with Usui Reiki, like the Five Reiki Precepts for living a compassionate and mindful life.

Just for today…

Don't be angry.
Don't worry.
Be graceful.
Work diligently.
Be kind to people.

When recited morning and evening, with palms together, while meditating on the heart, this chant is so powerful that it keeps the focus in the present moment. When we learn to live in that singular moment, we create more happiness and peace.

These precepts have become a popular part of recovery programs. The sitcom *Mike & Molly*, about two overweight people falling in love, often set scenes at an Overeaters Anonymous meeting. I was pleasantly surprised to see, written in large letters on the blackboard in the background, the five precepts!

But what if some days you're angry, lazy, or mean? It means there will forever be challenges. Even someone at a highly enlightened status has moments or days where the shadow peeks through.

Reiki also encourages any type of daily meditation, a powerful tool for quieting the mind and connecting with our inner selves. By incorporating these practices, we deepen our connection to the universal life force and gain a greater understanding of our place in the world.

Mystic Order

The practice of Lifeprint Reiki isn't meant to be a solitary journey. The concept of a "mystic order" emphasizes the importance of community and shared experiences as a spiritual practice. Reiki practitioners often gather for Reiki Circles to learn more, practice, or simply to connect with others on a similar path. This creates a supportive network where we can learn from each other. Imagine a group of friends who not only understand our passion for Reiki, but also actively support our growth. Support groups and Reiki Circles are an important part of Lifeprint Reiki.

These four aspects of Lifeprint Reiki are not separate but interconnected. As we practice self-healing, we'll likely experience personal growth. Spiritual discipline strengthens our connection to the universal life force, which can enhance our healing abilities. The supportive community becomes a source of strength and inspiration for personal development. By weaving these aspects together, Lifeprint Reiki becomes a holistic spiritual foundation to living a more fulfilling and balanced, happy life.

THE ATTUNEMENT PROCESS

A Reiki attunement is a meditative and physical ritual performed by a Reiki master teacher. It's what strengthens the existing connection in you with the universal light force energy in a moment of enlightenment. During the Reiki attunement, you learn how to impart this energy to yourself and another person by meditating on a variety of Reiki symbols.

The Symbols

One of the most important elements of Reiki attunement is learning its symbols, which allow people to use the energy for a specific purpose. Until rather recently, Reiki symbols were kept secret, which some say was to protect their sacred nature. But that doesn't resonate as true with me, as it was always Usui's intention for people to learn to heal themselves.

Symbols, in their essence, are bridges between the seen and unseen realms. They're potent vessels that carry the weight of collective and individual consciousness. Their power lies in their ability to bypass the rational mind and directly engage with our subconscious, tapping into deep-seated archetypes and emotions. When we encounter a symbol, it resonates with our inner world, activating a profound connection to something greater than ourselves. Through this resonance, symbols can inspire, heal, and transform. Whether it's the cross, the mandala, or any of the dozens of Reiki characters, each carries a unique vibration that interacts with our energy field.

To work with a symbol, one can either draw them with a finger in the air, visualize the symbols, or say their names out loud or in one's head. It's all about intention in the activation process, so anyone can make it happen.

Four different symbols are commonly used in Usui Reiki, but there are dozens more in the other types of Reiki practiced around the globe. Lifeprint Reiki introduces a new symbol, the Shin Zo Ho Go. The four symbols used in Level 1 Usui Reiki are the Cho Ku Rei, Sei He Ki, Hon Sha Ze Sho Nen, and Dai Ko Myo.

Cho Ku Rei: The Power Symbol

Cho Ku Rei is most used at the start of a Reiki session to help boost Reiki power. It's excellent for healing all kinds of injuries, from light aches and pains to more serious damage.

Outside of the body, Cho Ku Rei can be used to clear negative energy. It can be used in our daily life by drawing the symbol on walls of rooms where we want the energy to be light and positive. Cho Ku Rei can also act as a protection against misfortunes and give our meals a nutritional boost.

Sei He Ki: The Emotional/Mental Symbol

When we're in need of mental and emotional balance, turn to Sei He Ki. The general meaning is "God and man become one," and the drawing of this symbol resembles either a wave cresting and getting ready to crash over a beach or a bird's wing.

This symbol can aid in balancing the right and left sides of the brain, and therefore can be helpful in many brain activities like memorization, kicking bad habits, and cultivating a better self-image. It can even be helpful in eliminating headaches. Sei He Ki is not only effective in self-Reiki treatments for alleviating stress and emotional pain, but also protects us from negativity, and can actually remove negativity from the body.

Hon Sha Ze Sho Nen: The Distance Symbol

The Hon Sha Ze Sho Nen is a bit more difficult to grasp than some of the other Reiki symbols, as it's used to send Reiki energy across time and space. For example, although Hon Sha Ze Sho Nen can't change the past, it can help heal old wounds by reframing and turning it into a learning experience, rather than simply a random, devastating event.

Hon Sha Ze Sho Nen can also send Reiki into the future, ahead of challenging events, such as travel, exams, and doctors' appointments.

While this symbol is considered one of the most powerful, it works best when used on the energy of the body rather than the physical body. Calling upon on it daily effectively encourages past and future healing in the body.

Dai Ko Myo: The Master Symbol

This symbol is nourishing and enlightening, and it is the most universal Reiki symbol, healing the upper chakras, the aura, and the soul, helping bring users closer to Source energy.

This symbol also helps in strengthening our relationship with ourselves, our self-awareness, or a stronger spiritual practice. Using it in combination with other Reiki symbols makes it even more effective. Dai Ko Myo is also an excellent way to improve our immune system, by improving the flow of energy throughout the entire body.

Shin Zo Ho Go: The Lifeprint Reiki Symbol for Heart Center Release and Protection

This symbol is about healing and protection of the heart, and literally means "heart protection." Meditating on this symbol helps release the energies that no longer serve you, while protecting the heart center as it heals.

The discovery of this symbol began in 2010, when I wanted to get my first tattoo. After some thought, I chose a simple triquetra, what you might know as a Celtic knot, on my left shoulder. To me it symbolized the Infinite, with no beginning nor end, like a Möbius strip. You may be familiar with the triquetra associated with Irish Catholicism, but its use predates Christianity, to the Norse, or early Scandinavian culture, which led to it becoming part of the early Celtic faith.

Just like the cross was a symbol for the sun millennia before it was used in Christianity, the three points of the Celtic triquetra came to symbolize the father, son, and holy ghost in Christianity. The Celts held the number three in high regard, believing that many important aspects of life came in threes. The triquetra's three interlocking loops came to represent various triads, like the balance between land, sea, and sky; birth, life, and death; or the body, mind, and spirit—anything with a beginning, middle, and end. Past, present, and future are also intertwined within the triquetra's design, signifying the interconnectedness of time and the ever-flowing nature of existence.

It wasn't until the 2020 pandemic, when I began my journey with Reiki, that I learned the triquetra is also a symbol of infinite protection. The very form of the triquetra, with its interwoven loops, suggests that these interconnected forces—life stages, realms, or moments in time—offer a form of security. By acknowledging and respecting these interconnected aspects, one can be shielded from harm.

The symbol of Reiki is a circle, so when I saw a more elaborate triquetra that included an inner circle, it seemed like kismet: an ancient symbol representing exactly what I was trying to achieve in reviving ancient wisdom would be the perfect icon for my logo.

But as I was working on my logo, I had the idea to have a large triquetra above and below my business name, and turned the triquetra upside down. At that moment I felt a surge of energy, with a release in my chest area. I began meditating on it for a few days to see how it further affected me, to finally realize its power of heart-centered release, transformation, and protection. I moved the circle to the outside to enforce the concept of protection.

The Shin Zo Ho Go became not only a symbol of the three stages of everything in life and a symbol of protection, but also one of healing and empowerment. I liken it to the Old Testament story where Jews in Egypt marked their doorposts with blood to ward off the angel of death from taking their firstborn.

Effects of Attunement

After a Reiki attunement, it's common to experience physical changes and emotional shifts. Since the purpose of the Reiki attunement is to raise our vibrational level, this shift creates changes in our body and chakra system. (The chakra system is an ancient concept originating in Hinduism and Buddhism that describes energy centers in the body said to influence physical and emotional well-being.)

Most people experience positive Reiki attunement side effects and are left with a feeling of unconditional love and harmony with the universal life force energy. In fact, many students who are attuned to the first level of Reiki end up getting all the attunements up to level 3, with only the intention of healing themselves.

The following possible changes, although positive, can seem daunting and uncomfortable in the newness of their experience.

1. Energy Rush Around Your Body

This might be the most beautiful side effect of an attunement. You feel a huge energy rush of love, making you laugh and cry in pure happiness, grateful for the fact that you are alive in this wonderful world.

2. A Shift in Consciousness

This is a big one, as we start thinking differently, with more gratitude and consideration for all living beings. We'll feel like we're a whole new, happier person.

3. Crying

Crying is the ultimate release of stuck emotions, whether pleasant or unpleasant. It's the best emotional detox you can experience, and it will make you feel a whole lot better afterward.

4. An Increase in Psychic Abilities

Due to the increase in vibration, attunement may heighten our sensitivity to positive and negative energies with increased connection to intuition, allowing us to see and feel what others can't.

5. A Stronger Connection to Nature and the Divine

With a higher personal vibration, we feel in complete harmony with nature and crave to spend time outside, because spending time in nature is spiritual.

6. Affinity for Certain People

The increase in vibration heightens the need to be and speak with other people at the same level or higher, because we attract the same positive energy. The inverse happens with people who are at a lower vibration; we feel the need to distance ourselves from them.

7. The Need to Reduce or Stop Drinking Alcohol

Alcohol reduces personal vibration, and the body processes it as a toxin. That's why you won't crave it as much as you used to and you'll feel the desire to limit its intake into your body. I found myself not wanting alcohol after my master attunement, only partaking in toasts that create a positive intention for imbibing.

8. A Reduced Pleasure in Smoking

Just like alcohol, your body recognizes tobacco as a toxin. Due to nicotine addiction, you might still have a craving for tobacco, but your pleasure of smoking is greatly reduced. The attunement can facilitate stopping.

9. See Colors and Patterns

The colors and patterns you often see with your eyes closed, known as phosphenes, will change. They can become more dramatic, as you see a representation of high vibrational energy in a visual way, or the phosphenes disappear altogether.

10. A Change of Perception

Once you increase your connection with the universal life force energy, you will feel the need to do something more meaningful with your life. Instead of seeking more material possessions, you will seek more meaningful experiences. The same goes for your job. If it doesn't fulfill you, you'll want to do something else, even if it means earning less money.

Challenging Reiki Attunement Side Effects

Any major changes we go through can be uncomfortable. Puberty is uncomfortable. Menopause causes symptoms. Spiritual awakening causes symptoms in a similar fashion. These challenging attunement effects can appear two to five days following the attunement session.

Challenging side effects of Reiki level 1 attunement, though rare, are mostly physical. I experienced no negative side effects at any level of attunement; however, when I began working with the Shin Zo Ho Go, I experienced a few days of minor physical ailments and a few nights of difficult sleep.

Some of the possible temporary side effects during the detox period are: dizziness, diarrhea, body aches, fatigue, insomnia, abdominal pains, cold symptoms, constipation, fever, weight gain, limb heaviness, headaches, tingling, chest pain, loss of appetite, mood swings, and emotional releases.

Fortunately, easy steps can alleviate most Reiki attunement side effects. Doing them all together can produce the best results and improve your mood.

- Drink a lot of water, especially during the initial detox phase, because proper hydration can speed up the detoxification process in your body.

- Welcome any emotional release with an affirmation to tell the body it has permission to detoxify. For example: "I ask for this energy to flush out anything that no longer serves me."
- Stay grounded by walking barefoot on grass to ground to the earth's magnetic field, to help reduce physical symptoms.
- Spending time in nature is the best medicine after getting an attunement, as the body will crave that time and it'll make the emotional detoxification much easier.
- Perform Reiki on yourself with the Sei He Ki symbol to bring back harmony and balance.

HOW TO FIND A REIKI MASTER

You'll greatly benefit from any form of Reiki attunement, not just Usui. The two questions to ask a prospective Reiki master are:

1. Do you think Usui was some kind of saint and do you spend a whole day telling that story?
2. Do you believe there's a wrong way to perform Reiki?

If they answer "yes," to either, I suggest you keep looking.

Healers are all deeply wounded people who've found some healing and want to relieve others of their suffering. But what type of trauma they've healed from can leave scars of their shadow that affect their abilities as a healer and teacher. Case in point was my level 1 Reiki master. The program was two days long, and for the first day all he did for hours was tell this most incredulous over-the-top story of Usui, canonizing him as a saint, along with manipulating the tale of Takata's journeys across the seas from Hawaii to Japan as harrowing, to selflessly study these healing arts. Not only was it boring, but it was also demeaning, like telling adults to believe in Santa Claus.

Then came the big red flag the next day when we were practicing the hand placements. The teacher said that if we didn't do Reiki exactly as he showed us, we could connect to negative energy. The truth is, it's impossible to connect to negative energy while performing Reiki, if that's not your intention.

While there's no rule precluding a Reiki practitioner from practicing a religion, I would surmise this person suffers from religious trauma, perhaps from being brought up in a fundamental Christian household, or they were taught by Catholic nuns. It appears they still see everything through that fundamentalist lens, with a lasting need for a savior and rules that, if broken, create evil. His unsuspecting students now hold toxic fear in what they do, unwilling to try new things to personalize their treatments. Usui himself wanted practitioners to experiment, as that's what he spent his life doing. We'll go more into how religious dogma can stifle our inherent curiosity in other areas of our lives in the 11 Insights.

I found all my Reiki teachers through a simple Google search. Often level 1 and 2 are taught together, which is a great way to jumpstart your Reiki connection.

THE LIFEPRINT REIKI HEALING PROCESS

Aura Cleansing

My version of aura cleansing starts with sitting quietly and focusing on where there's pain or discomfort in the body. The next step is to begin to visualize the exact size, shape, color, and texture of the sensation. This begins the separation of the pain from the self.

After identification, continue sitting quietly and begin taking deep breaths, holding for a few seconds, then exhaling with a sigh. Perform this three times, each time trying to take an even bigger breath, and hold it a bit longer.

Then we call upon the Reiki energy, by visualizing a beautiful white light descending from above that envelopes the body like the most comforting cocoon. Visualize breathing this white light into the body and feel it moving from the lungs and traveling throughout the body from head to toe, releasing all that no longer serves you.

Next, begin breathing the white light into the area of pain or discomfort, with the intention of clearing it. Continue this process and observe changes to the sensation. Has the shape, color, or size changed? As it reduces in size, continue the process, observing changes until the pain or discomfort has disappeared. This may take five to ten minutes, possibly longer.

Once the sensation is gone, breathe the white light into the area that once held the pain and hold the breath for a few seconds. This will not only help prevent the discomfort from returning, but also helps prevent any feelings of lack that can arise from moving forward without that energetic attachment.

This process can work on more than just strong physical pain: it's also effective on energies left from past toxic people and situations. As you gain more awareness, it'll be clear that thoughts of these people are the cause of various discomforts in your body. For example, I personally would feel an energetic crust on my shoulders at the thought of past abuse that was relieved by the aura cleansing process.

Once you gain a mastery of the process, the deep meditation won't be necessary, and simply breathing into the discomfort will clear it. I eventually found myself able to clear these unwanted energies as they arise with just breathing, even while walking down the street.

Hands-On Healing

STEP 1: Create a calm environment, a quiet space free from distractions. Put your phone on silent, light some calming candles, and/or play some soothing music. Get comfortable and lie down on a sofa or yoga mat, or sit on a chair with your feet flat on the ground. Do whatever feels best.

STEP 2: Breathing is important in calming the body, so take a few minutes to focus on your breath. Close your eyes and inhale deeply through your nose, feeling your belly expand. Hold for a few seconds, then slowly exhale through your mouth. Repeat this several times, letting go of any tension with each exhale.

STEP 3: Reiki works best when you have a clear goal. Is there physical or emotional pain that needs to be addressed? Are you feeling stressed about something or sore from that intense workout? Maybe you just want some overall trauma healing. Silently set your intention for what you want to achieve with your self-treatment.

STEP 4: Connect to the symbols by writing them in the air, visualizing them, or saying their names. Place your hands palms together, first against your chest and then on your forehead, and say, "Reiki energy flows into me from above, through my heart and out my hands."

STEP 5: Now comes the "hands-on" part. When healing trauma, we start with the brain.

- Head: Place your flat hands, fingers together, lightly on top of your head, palms facing down. The brain is the organ most affected by trauma and connects to the entire nervous system. Treating the head treats the entire body. You can also move the hands to the sides, back, or base of the skull, and to your forehead.

Trauma can also be stored in other areas of the body. You might additionally try placing your hands on these areas:

- Stomach: Place one hand above your navel and the other below. The abdomen is the location of the solar plexus chakra, which you may want to cleanse.
- Chest: Rest your hands on the chest. It's called a broken heart for all the stored negative energy in the heart chakra. This position also treats the lungs, which in traditional Chinese medicine are known to store grief.
- Throat: Position both hands overlapping, with the throat in the curve between the fingers and thumb. Because trauma makes it hard to verbally express needs and emotions, this area is often heavily blocked.

There's no right or wrong way to place your hands. Trust your intuition and go where your body feels drawn.

STEP 6: Once your hands are in position, simply focus on your breath, the symbol(s), and intention. Don't worry about "feeling" the energy; the goal is to be present and allow the healing to occur naturally. If your mind wanders, gently guide it back to your breath and intention.

STEP 7: Stay in each hand position for several minutes (three to five minutes is a good starting point). As you hold your hands there, visualize a warm, healing light flowing through your body. Imagine all the tension or discomfort releasing with each exhale.

STEP 8: When you're finished and have addressed all the areas for your intention, slowly remove your hands. Take a few more deep breaths, feeling refreshed and revitalized. Then, slowly move your hands up and down a few inches away from your body, with the intention to seal in the healing. Finally, take a moment to express gratitude for the healing and the new life you're creating.

It's important to remember that, like building muscle, regular practice is crucial for optimal results. Aim for fifteen to thirty minutes of self-treatment a few times a week to start. But don't push yourself. If you feel any discomfort during self-treatment, gently adjust your hand placement or shorten the session.

Healing Others

On an airplane, we're instructed to put the oxygen mask on ourselves before assisting others. The same holds true with healing. It's important to first heal ourselves to the point where we're not drowning in our traumas before we try to help another person.

Offering healing to adult family members can be precarious compared to healing friends. Although no one can change who doesn't want to, the person who rejects healing comes from a fearful ego perspective. A damaged ego is content in the known commodity of misery and pain. It fears the unknown of happiness and is unwilling to accept its flaws.

In-Person Healing

Preparing ourselves for healing someone else is the same as when we heal ourselves, but we'll now be placing hands on or near someone else. Ask them if they are open to this healing.

They can lie down on a sofa or bed, or be seated in a chair, while you stand or sit behind them. Be sure your hands and arms will be comfortable for fifteen to twenty minutes in your chosen position. After connecting to the four symbols, simply place your hands on or near the person's head. Every five minutes or so, you can reposition the hands to cover all areas from the forehead to the back of the skull.

This can even work on our pets. I recently adopted a three-year-old rescue dog from Georgia. She came with all sorts of trauma, and was also recovering from heartworm. She was afraid to go in the elevator and even to explore other rooms in my house. I performed Reiki on her every day for fifteen minutes after my morning meditation, with one hand on her head and the other on her heart, and in less than a week she began to blossom.

Remote Healing

It may be a difficult concept to grasp, but Reiki healing energy spans all space and time. We don't need to be in the same room as the person we offer healing to, nor even in the same dimension. This makes it possible for you to send this healing energy to your childhood self, to begin to release your current attachment to the past.

The only difference with remote Reiki is that we can't specify where in the body the healing energy goes. The other person's higher self makes that determination. And while verbal consent is required for all in-person healing, distance healing practices vary.

When the person rejects healing, we must respect their autonomy. However, we can ask their Higher Self for permission when we're in a meditative state. Or we can offer Reiki with the intention that the recipient receives only what their Higher Self is willing to accept. The Higher Self is much more open to this process.

Others, like myself, view Reiki as a form of channeling universal energy that flows regardless of permission. Love, a core aspect of Reiki, knows no boundaries and the energy flows based on the recipient's need, not consent. From a scientific perspective, proponents of this viewpoint of the interconnectedness of all things argue that separate entities are an illusion. Reiki simply acts as a conduit for the already-present universal energy.

Regardless of approach, the toxic or abusive people in our lives won't suddenly become compassionate, and holding onto that expectation can cause us more suffering. **If toxic people are not out of our lives, it's impossible to become the healed, authentic person we desire to be.**

Whether performing a session over Zoom or using a photo, or simply through meditation in our mind's eye, we prepare ourselves the same way: connecting to the four symbols, with a special focus on Hon Sha Ze

Sho Nen, which facilitates the remote healing. Direct your hands at the computer, photo, or up to the heavens and allow the healing energy to flow. This is tremendously useful in healing our ancestors, whether or not photos of them exist.

CHAPTER 5:
All About Trauma

Trauma in a person, decontextualized
over time, looks like personality.

Trauma in a family, decontextualized over
time, looks like family traits.

Trauma in a people, decontextualized
over time, looks like culture.

—RESMAA MENAKEM

THROUGH ALL MY SEEKING, I concluded that life's traumas are at the root of disconnection from self-love. Validation came when I discovered my belief is supported by psychologist and *NY Times* best-selling author Bessel van der Kolk. When we understand how life's unresolved traumas disconnect us from self-love, we can become more empathetic and compassionate people. The entire world is victim to thousands of years of unresolved human trauma, and a path to world peace starts with mental health.

Because people treat others the way they feel about themselves, it's crucial to learn to see that all the unpleasant people in our life—and the world—are struggling with their own self-hate. The need to control, from a sociopathic dictator, down to the individual struggling with perfectionism, can be seen as rooted in unresolved childhood trauma. Each bigot, homophobe, and antisemite are projecting their unconscious self-hate on others.

When people love themselves, they lose all judgment of others. Feeling compassion for the homeless and addicts on the street is to understand they're not weak, but merely overwhelmed by past traumatic life events.

Since we treat others the way we feel about ourselves, the Golden Rule, "Do unto others as you would have done to you," becomes so important. Originating with Confucius 2,500 years ago, it's noted in all major world cultures. The Golden Rule underlies acts of kindness, caring, and altruism that go above and beyond the minimum. (Unless you're a People Pleaser. Then there's a toxic root to treating people well.)

Nobody wants to be bullied, embarrassed, or abused, yet there are those who will perpetrate such offensive acts, not just on strangers, but also on friends and family. This is an expression of unresolved trauma.

Unresolved trauma shows up in many ways you may not expect as part of your survival personality and not part of your authentic self.

The need for attention and to be seen

Procrastination

Long screen times

Promiscuity

Workaholism

Feeling we're not good enough

Immediately saying "no" to everything

Constant complaining

Trouble focusing

Fear of failure or success

Trouble asking for help

Not picking up after the dog

Always needing to plan for everything

Hoarding

Messy house or room

Poor hygiene

Low self-esteem

Being longingly single

Continually needing external validation

Practicing "shop therapy"

Afraid to be alone

Easily triggered

Sarcasm

Always finding the negative

Always filled with anxiety and worry

Adrenaline junkie behavior

Traumas are created by feeling unsafe for any period of time and keep us in survival mode, unable to fully enjoy many of life's intimate moments and connections. The accumulation of trauma response behaviors becomes our survival personality.

Cortisol, often referred to as the "stress hormone," plays a crucial role in regulating various bodily functions, including blood sugar levels, blood pressure, and the immune system. In short bursts, cortisol is essential for survival. When faced with a stressful event, the body initiates a "fight or flight, freeze or fawn," response and the adrenal glands release cortisol, which in turn increases heart rate, blood pressure, and blood sugar levels to prepare the body for action. This is a normal and adaptive response. However, prolonged or excessive stress can lead to chronically elevated cortisol levels. When the body is in a constant state of fight or flight, it dysregulates the entire nervous system.

High cortisol levels can manifest in a variety of detrimental physical symptoms. Because cortisol increases one's desire for sweet and salty foods, weight gain results, particularly around the abdomen. Other effects include a weakened immune system, high blood pressure, digestive problems, muscle weakness and chronic fatigue.

Being in this constant fight or flight response affects long- and short-term memory, which hinders learning and sociability, and increases poor decision-making. I would even argue, from a spiritual perspective, that ADHD symptoms can be seen as trauma responses, because of how they're all maladaptive behavior related.

The more difficult it is to admit unresolved trauma, the more serious its hold is on us. The driving force behind most addictions (alcohol, cigarettes, drugs, gambling, sex, or even food) is to fill an energetic void left by trauma. When we're motivated through guilt or shame, that's trauma. Victims of racism, discrimination, sexism, or those part of a marginalized community, have all experienced trauma.

Trauma affects the soul by shattering our sense of safety and security to participate in life events. Detachment can be a coping mechanism, but it can also lead to feelings of isolation and numbness, making it hard to find meaning in life or motivation to pursue goals.

THE FOUR TYPES OF TRAUMAS

The four types of traumas we deal with every second of the day are:

Current life trauma
Past life / soul trauma

Religious trauma

Ancestral trauma

Unless we have specific memories of events, it's difficult to pinpoint which type of trauma triggers our challenging behavior, because they can overlap.

Current life trauma typically suggests severe events like physical abuse or war, because of the more obvious effects on a person's behavior. However, as I mentioned, trauma occurs from feeling unsafe for any length of time, making seemingly innocuous past events the source of many of our present personal difficulties. The terms "wounded inner child" or "middle child syndrome," are phenomena rooted in trauma.

Most of us believe we've resolved whatever happened to us as kids. The teasing. The rejection. The toxic family environment. However, unless we've had professional help, it's not likely we've properly processed the past trauma. We've merely unconsciously accepted it into our lives, and no longer recognize why we may have an addiction, lack trust, or find ourselves isolated.

Past life trauma is the belief that negative experiences from other incarnations can carry over and influence our current emotions, behaviors, and phobias. A sudden and intense fear of heights, water, or public speaking might not have a clear root cause in our current life. Unexplained physical ailments like chronic pain or recurring illnesses that defy medical explanation could be echoes of past life injuries or illnesses. Schizophrenia may have links to past life trauma, as those suffering appear to live in more than one reality.

Repetitive toxic patterns in relationships, or constantly attracting the same kind of unavailable partner, could be a sign of unresolved past life trauma related to betrayal, abandonment, or attachment issues.

Vivid déjà vu experiences or recurring dreams with specific themes (e.g., war, betrayal) could be fragments of past life memories trying to surface. An unexplained affinity for a certain historical period or culture, even if we have no prior exposure to it, could be a clue.

About thirty years ago, I was living in Los Angeles, and participated in past life regression therapy. I discovered that in a previous life I was a Catholic teenage girl in France, near Lyon, in the 1930s or '40s. There was a boy I was crazy about, a real hot bad boy, who got me pregnant. But he didn't love me. I'm not sure he even liked me. And the depths of shame from being an unwed pregnant Catholic girl all alone in a devout French family made taking my life the only viable solution. I must've seen carbon monoxide poisoning from a car exhaust in a movie and I sat in the backseat of the family Citroën 2CV, windows open, parked in the barn. As part of the regression, you move through the death, and I was there in the French car, vomiting all over the red interior. The reason for my childhood motion sickness connected for me.

Religious trauma disconnects us from self-love by unconsciously paralyzing us with fear. Fear of repercussions from not being a good follower, fear of a higher power who blackmails us with spending eternity in hell, or fear that we're unworthy of our higher power's love just being us.

From this perspective, one can see the Old Testament stories as deeply traumatizing, from Adam and Eve being expelled from the Garden of Eden to God asking Abraham to kill his own son. And that's just Chapter 1!

Many religions tell followers they're born sinners. *Sin*, translated from its original pre-biblical Greek origins, of *hamartia,* merely means "to miss." The term has been mistranslated from the original biblical text by religions to imply a deliberate offense against a moral or religious law. But these laws are man-made and don't exist in the eyes of the divine.

Religion also argues that it provides the only framework for a moral or ethical life, yet the fact remains that a July 2021 Department of Justice investigation into chaplain services in prisons, found 75 percent of prison inmates identify as following some type of Christian faith. A June 23, 2024, article in *USA TODAY,* by Nicole Russel titled, *Evangelicals Need to Focus on the Church's Sexual Abuse Epidemic,* says it all about its pastors and church employees' disturbing behaviors.

Some people believe they thrive on the limitations of religion, but others silently suffer with the dilemma of being part of a religion that simply doesn't fit their soul. There was a young Southern woman in my spiritual coaching class distraught with anxiety and depression because she didn't know how to come out to her parents and grandparents with the fact that their Christian faith didn't serve her.

Atheism is a type of religious trauma, too. The notion that when we die that's the end is a purely ego perspective. Our body does in fact die, but our souls are eternal. Atheists are spiritual, despite rejecting the notion of a higher power. They might appreciate beauty or feel part of something grand, but that doesn't make it any less spiritual. Like everyone else, atheists seek meaning and purpose in life. They might find it in personal growth, helping others, contributing to a cause they believe in, or simply creating a fulfilling life for themselves and loved ones. That's living spiritually.

Remember, every soul is here for different lessons. Because our souls learn from suffering, the suffering brought on by following a religion is thought to be spiritual. Even though we have free will to end our religious suffering, it's not every soul's destiny to move away from religion into a healing, independent spiritual practice in this lifetime.

Ancestral trauma can be difficult to define, since we likely grew up exposed to toxic behaviors deemed normal in our family. Yet science has discovered that trauma is passed down through our DNA and affects our behavior. This is the focus of the field of epigenetics, which explores how our environment and experiences can modify gene expression without changing the underlying DNA sequence. Studies suggest that trauma can leave epigenetic marks on parents' genes, potentially affecting how those genes are expressed in their offspring. For example, a 2013 study published in Nature

Neuroscience (Epigenetic Transmission of the Response to Battlefield Stress by Sperm in Mice) demonstrated that exposure to stress in mice could be transmitted to offspring through epigenetic changes in sperm.

This theory's premise is that the psychological effects of trauma in parents can indirectly impact their children. Trauma can affect parenting behaviors, creating a stressful environment for the child and recreating the trauma. A November 2014 study lead by Lynne Murray and published in *Development and Psychopathology*, found that mothers with high levels of negativity were more likely to have children with heightened physiological responses to stress. Different proteins are created in our genes by trauma, allowing a propensity for unpreferred behaviors to be expressed.

As the woman I consider the founder of the modern self-love movement, Louise Hay, says in her 1984 book, *You Can Heal Your Life,* "If you want to find the root of your ailment, look in your family tree."

Imagine that your great-grandmother lived through a terrible famine. Her body, under extreme stress, might have switched off genes related to hunger. This change could be passed down to you, making you more prone to over-eating, even if you've never experienced hunger.

Maybe an ancestor fled a war-torn country. Their experience of constant fear could have changed genes related to the startle response. We might be extra sensitive to loud noises or sudden movements, even if we don't know the family history.

This unresolved trauma is stored in the cells and various parts of the body, so hereditary diseases can be hereditary traumas. Some irrational fears or compulsive behaviors can be inherited, and not of our own volition.

Other mental health issues that can be based in inherited traumas are:

Narcissism
Bi-polar disorder
General anxiety disorder

Compulsive eating
Criminal instinct
Poverty
Autism

In 2014, Carol Torgan, Ph.D. published findings in the National Institutes of Health reporting that scientists have identified hundreds of genes that seem to be involved in autism risk. These genes might influence brain development in subtle ways. Unlike diseases with clear inheritance patterns, causes of neurodiversity are trickier. Having a family member with ASD increases your risk, but it doesn't guarantee you'll develop it yourself. Environmental factors might also play a part.

Though trauma is not our fault, the onus is on us to heal and reconnect to self-love and our authentic selves. Lifeprint Reiki encourages learning to be gentle on ourselves while we heal, and not wallow in the pain and blame in the process.

HOW THE BODY RELEASES TRAUMA

In the animal kingdom, a traumatized gazelle surviving a chase by lions will shake to dissipate the energy. You may have experienced hands and legs shaking after a traumatic event. That's the body automatically trying to release the trauma. But the emotion of that trauma still gets stored in the body if not fully processed As we participate in more releasing exercises, our body, too, will find more ways to release. Some of the ways our bodies release emotions are:

Crying: Releases the gambit of emotions from sadness to joy, from fear to inspiration.

Laughing: It's the best medicine!

Yawning: One of the more pleasant ways; learn to generate a yawn as you focus on releasing something.

Screaming: Excellent way to release suppressed anger.

Vomiting: Emotions stored in the abdomen become overwhelming and need to be purged.

Coughing: The lungs carry much grief, so coughing can release it.

Sneezing: Like coughing, relieves tension in the chest and dispels pathogens.

Bowel movement: Again, emotions held in the abdomen are being released.

Shaking: A natural way to release, and can be enhanced with Trauma Release Exercises (TRE).

Vigorous physical activity: Exercise as simple as walking, when done to muscle exhaustion, has a releasing effect on the body.

Sex: When given a healing intention, it creates a whole new level of experience.

Let's explore three of the most pleasurable approaches.

Yawning

I found yawning to be the most prominent way my body naturally releases trauma, and one of the more innocuous releases. Often associated with tiredness or boredom, yawning is a somatic response, meaning related to the body, not mind. Most people likely haven't heard of somatic therapy, but unlike other mind-body approaches, such as mindfulness meditation, somatic therapy is gaining popularity.

What's the fundamental concept? Somatic therapy is a treatment focusing on the body and how emotions appear within it, that posits that our body holds and expresses experiences and emotions. Beyond fulfilling its primary function of oxygenating the brain, according to the Cleveland Clinic's website, yawning triggers a cascade of physiological and neurological responses:

Increased vagal tone: Yawning activates the parasympathetic nervous system, responsible for relaxation and calming, counteracting the heightened fight-or-flight response often associated with trauma.

Muscle stretching and release: The deep inhalation and exhalation stretch and relax diaphragm and intercostal muscles, potentially releasing physical tension held in response to trauma.

Brainwave entrainment: Studies suggest yawning synchronizes brain waves across individuals, creating a shared state of emotional resonance and catharsis.

Neurochemical regulation: Yawning reduces stress hormones like cortisol and increases the neuropeptide oxytocin, promoting feelings of calm and connection.

Here are steps to take to explore yawning as a tool for emotional and trauma release.

Cultivate awareness. Start by observing your yawns. Notice the triggers (fatigue, social interaction, stressful situations) and the accompanying sensations in your body and mind. This mindful awareness paves the way for deliberate yawning practices.

Initiate the yawn. When you feel emotionally charged or triggered, try to gently initiate a yawn. This can be done by watching someone yawn, visualizing a yawn, or gently stretching your mouth and taking a deep inhale.

Deepen the response. Once a yawn starts, encourage it to fully extend. Open your mouth wide, stretch your throat and lungs, and let out a slow, deep exhalation. Repeat this several times.

Embody and release. Focus on the bodily sensations during and after the yawn. Notice any tension releasing, emotional shifts, or changes in breathing. Allow yourself to fully experience the sensation of release.

Journal and reflect. After practicing yawning exercises, take some time to journal about your experience. Did you notice any emotional or physical shifts? How did your body feel before and after? This reflection deepens your understanding of your personal response to yawning.

Trauma Release Exercises

Another innocuous way to release trauma is Trauma Release Exercises, or TRE. The process was developed by David Berceli, a former Israeli special forces medic, who noticed a common thread amongst his patients who had experienced trauma: involuntary shaking. He realized that this shaking was the body's natural mechanism for releasing deep-held tension and trauma.

A simple shortcut is to bypass much of the exercises and lie flat on your back with legs straight in front. Bend the knees up, then drop them twisting at the hips. Bring both legs up an inch off the floor and hold for a minute. Raise another inch and hold a minute. Continue raising until you reach a point where the legs begin shaking.

There's no need to force or control the shaking; the body does the work. The tremors can vary in intensity and duration, and may even feel pleasurable or cathartic.

Sexual Healing

Sex is often used unconsciously as a coping mechanism when our traumas leave us feeling lack; it's an easy form of validation. This shows up as promiscuity, anonymous sex, and various kink behaviors. None of this is to be judged in a negative way, as these behaviors are deemed necessary to the survival personality. But because sex also has a strong spiritual component, it can be healing if given that intention between two consenting, compassionate adults. (This is not advised for survivors of sexual abuse trauma without a therapist's recommendation.)

When both partners enter into sex with the intention of healing the other, a truly magical, heightened experience is possible. Our bodies are complex organisms of chemicals, emotions, and desires that intimacy can utilize for our spiritual benefit. Tantric practices, originating in Hinduism and Buddhism, view sexual energy as a powerful life force that can be used for spiritual growth.

During consensual sex, the body releases oxytocin, often referred to as the love hormone, which promotes feelings of trust, bonding, and safety. This hormonal response can counteract the feelings of isolation and fear often associated with trauma. However, this release of feel-good hormones can create sex addiction, if one has no other means in their life of feeling loved.

While trauma disrupts the nervous system, leading to hypervigilance and difficulty relaxing, sexual intimacy can activate the parasympathetic nervous system, promoting relaxation and feelings of safety through increased vagal tone.

Open communication is crucial for a healing experience. Sharing feelings and boundaries with your partner creates a space for emotional processing. Aftercare rituals like cuddling or conversation deepen the connection and emotional safety.

Conscious connection and present-moment awareness during sex are important, because this is what creates a safe space for emotional and energetic release.

OTHER PATHS TO HEALING TRAUMA

Trauma can't be released by simply talking about it. As trauma is stored in the body, moving the body around to the point of fatigue greatly helps. All forms of sports, dance, aerobics, or any vigorous physical activity where you're moving until you can't, works. Practicing yoga has proven especially helpful as it helps integrate the healing.

Deep tissue massage was a godsend of healing for me. My journey led me to Thai massage and eventually abdominal massage. Most negative emotions are held in that area, and abdominal massage gently manipulates and stimulates the organs. It was one of the most releasing massages I ever experienced.

Art or drawing is used in trauma therapy with children, and is also effective with adults. It's why art and music are so important in public education. Play acting is also used in trauma therapy, and why some get "the acting bug" after appearing in school plays.

Another great starter practice is spending time in nature, be it gardening, hiking, camping, or even bird watching. Repeatedly immersing yourself in the ocean, forest, or mountains has a spiritual cleansing effect like meditation. Wading in the salty waters of the ocean can especially draw the negativity out. Frequent Epsom salt baths, with at least a cup of salts, are an option for those who are not near the sea.

The EFT Tapping Solution, a powerful holistic healing technique, is based on the combined principles of ancient Chinese acupressure and modern psychology. The basic technique requires you to focus on a negative emotion, and tap at certain points on your face and body while speaking about letting the emotion go.

Another powerful course of action is breath work. There are dozens of practices for different goals, including:

- Prana breathing as a core part of yoga
- Mantak Chia, an Eastern breathing practice that intends to release traumatic energies from the organs
- Concentrative breathing, which creates high levels of DMT (dimethyltryptamine) in the blood (a practice not to be performed alone)

The most advanced methods are shamanic medicine ceremonies like Ayahuasca that create altered states of consciousness. You need to first be at a place where you can relinquish control, as the medicines create intense imagery with a challenging physical purging reaction. Other psychedelics, like psilocybin and ketamine, have also been clinically proven to provide relief from trauma symptoms, like depression, for a great percentage of test subjects. https://www.medicalnewstoday.com/articles/psychedelic-therapy

A search on the internet will turn up many more options. It's up to you to find what works best for you. It's possible one modality may create great change—I would never say it can't—or you may have to try several to peel away the proverbial onion layers of pain.

BUT NOT ALL TRAUMA IS BAD

After all I've said about the horrors of trauma, it can actually be a motivational force in our lives if properly resolved, propelling us to do great things. It's when fear and self-doubt get in the way of our path to greatness that the unresolved issues become toxic.

Here are five ways trauma can lead to positive outcomes:

1. **Increased resilience and strength:** Trauma can push us to our limits, forcing us to develop new coping mechanisms and discover a well of inner strength we never knew we had. Overcoming adversity can build confidence and make us feel that we can handle anything.

2. **Deeper relationships:** Trauma can bring people closer together. Sharing a difficult experience can foster empathy and understanding in our relationships. We might discover a newfound appreciation for supportive loved ones, or forge strong bonds with others who have been through similar struggles.

3. **Positive reevaluation:** Trauma can cause us to re-evaluate our priorities and what truly matters. We might develop a greater appreciation for the good things we have or find the courage to pursue a passion we had previously neglected.

4. **Spiritual growth:** Facing existential questions and challenges can lead to a deeper exploration of our spirituality or purpose. Trauma can prompt us to seek meaning and understanding, fostering needed growth

5. **Increased empathy and character:** Trauma can make us more sensitive to the suffering of others. Having gone through a difficult experience ourselves, we might be more attuned to the struggles of others and feel compelled to help those in need.

Only someone willing to change can change, and we can only change ourselves if we're brave enough to gain objective awareness of not only our behaviors that negatively impact our life, but also *why*. Why do we need to be brave? Because the happier "you" you desire to be lies outside your comfort zone, so this spiritual growth process is inherently uncomfortable.

The degree to which a person can grow is directly proportional to the amount of truth they can accept about themselves without running away. The speed of our transformation is determined by us. The ego resists change, fear arises as part of the process, and the ability to recognize the resistance and to push through it is crucial to moving forward.

PART III:
THE SELF-LOVE JOURNEY

CHAPTER 6:

Spiritual Foundation for the Journey

Just as a candle cannot burn without fire,
men cannot live without a spiritual life.

—BUDDHA

WHETHER YOU'RE SPENDING A WEEK at the beach, cruising through Europe, or climbing Mount Everest, you prepare mentally and physically by educating yourself on all that location has to offer, and by packing everything you'll need while away. Taking a journey to reconnect to your inherent spirituality is no different, though it can last a lot longer. That's why it's helpful to know why you're taking the journey.

Most of us either take for granted the spiritual aspects of our lives, or don't even recognize them as such. Have you ever been awestruck by a sunset, felt a deep connection with nature, or questioned your place in the universe? These experiences tap into something fundamental to being human; our spirituality is a deep sense of wonder and connection to something bigger than us.

Humans are intrinsically curious creatures. Asking big questions like, "Why are we here?" "What happens after we die?" "Is there a force guiding the universe?" While there are no simple answers, spirituality allows us to objectively explore these questions to find comfort, hope, and direction.

This search for meaning plays out in countless ways across cultures. In some Native American traditions, spending time in nature is seen as a way to connect with the spirits that inhabit the world. Buddhist monks meditate to find inner peace and enlightenment. Even attending a concert or feeling part of a team can be a spiritual experience.

Most human beings live rather mindlessly. Yet the more mindful we become, the more we're aware of these higher truths and insights. The less we suffer (more on this under the 11 Insights), the more we grow, and the more meaning and happiness we can find in life.

As I've mentioned before, Lifeprint Reiki asserts that our spiritual needs are as unique as a fingerprint. Every point of view is valid for that soul's growth. I came to this epiphany one day that I call "Everybody's right." I was engaged in my own spiritual studies at the time and experienced a vision during a meditation where I saw the Tree of Life as a three-dimensional apple tree, with all souls as the apples. Some hang low, while others are elevated. Some are in the dark behind the leaves, while others bask in the sun. Some in the dark believe they're in the light and some in the light believe they're in the dark. As each apple looks out, what they see is their reality, so every single apple has a different point of view. If each is asked, "What do you see?" each answer would be correct.

All eight billion of us currently on Earth have a slightly different response to the question "What do you see?" Some are interested to know what life is like from different branches of the tree, and some prefer not to know what they can't see. Understanding that everyone has a different point of view that's completely valid to them helps increase tolerance and dispel the need to forcibly unify thought, which in turn creates a peaceful, compassionate Earth.

This hypothesis has been proven by science, as in quantum mechanics the act of observing a particle can influence its state. Our viewpoint shapes how we experience the world. Two people looking at the same situation might see different things based on their past experiences, biases, and expectations. When we gain the ability to consider different perspectives as valid for those with them, we begin to build empathy.

This concept is like the ancient parable "The Blind Men and the Elephant," which originated in the Indian subcontinent millennia ago, and has been widely interpreted in various cultures. It's a story of six blind men who've never come across an elephant before, and who learn and conceptualize what the elephant is like by touching it. Each has just one piece of the elephant—the ear, tail, tusk, skin, and foot—and each comes to their own fundamental, and very different, definition of what the entire elephant is.

WHY WE ARE SPIRITUAL

Spirituality is intrinsic to the human condition. But unresolved trauma disconnects us from easily connecting to, and even the understanding of, our gift. Therefore, you may not be aware of all that spirituality fulfills in our lives:

Happiness / Peace / Overcoming Suffering
Suffering is the initial door to spirituality, as the soul needs these painful lessons to grow. Many people no longer desire to experience the accompanying anxiety, grief, or fear. Learning how to let go is a radical spiritual practice that leads towards happiness.

Purpose / Direction

Spirituality is the search for meaning, purpose, and direction. Whether or not you're succeeding materially, you may feel an underlying sense of dissatisfaction, limitation, and emptiness, creating anxiety about existence. Some people are sensitive to it, and will compensate by pursuing externally validating activities. Spirituality is about the genetic need to be aligned with something bigger than our egos and individual lives.

Unity / Love / Connection

Being alone can be painful, as it's a natural human need to seek connection and love with the community, the universe, or the divine. To feel complete, we crave to receive and give unconditional love, which brings a sense of total acceptance and of happiness. This search can also manifest as the feeling of a new sense of sacredness to life.

Growth

Many of us have a desire to grow, improve, and push through our limiting beliefs. This motivation enables continuous growth: to learn, to live real lives with our truth, to develop our minds, and to expand our consciousness beyond what we can see or hear.

Answers / Truth

Questions like "Who am I?" "Why are we here?" and "What else is there?" together with a passionate questioning to understand how life works as well as ourselves, all need answers. This manifests in the form of understanding, absorbing, and becoming one with Source.

Transcendence / Enlightenment

Different traditions describe enlightenment differently, but the common thread characterizes it as a state of rising above the physical human condition, beyond all possibility of further suffering. There's a radical expansion of consciousness and a permanent shift in our perception and experience of the world, with a sensation beyond the sense of being an individual.

Exploration / Mystery

Diving into one's own consciousness and exploring other aspects of reality speaks to our thirst for knowledge, experience, and adventure. The worlds of physics and spirituality are merging as one, as quantum mechanics finds mathematical ways to explain phenomena previously beyond our comprehension.

Serving

The urge to serve people on a deeper level, making a big difference in their lives, and helping uplift and awaken humanity, is a form of spirituality.

HOW SPIRITUALITY DIFFERS FROM RELIGION

I've already mentioned the detrimental effects of following a savior. Essentially, **spirituality is not about what you believe, but about your experience**. Spirituality isn't about faith, but of feeling. Religion offers a detailed map that must be followed, complete with marked routes and specific destinations. This map is not optional. Spirituality, on the other hand, is more like a compass—it helps us find our own direction and meaning to connect, not to a savior, but to our inner divine power. This is the key difference between these two concepts.

Religion motivates by instilling a fear of eternity in hell for sins or noncompliance, while spirituality is motivated by gaining the ability to connect more strongly to love and enlightenment. The most powerful spiritual tools are labeled "work of the devil" by religion to instill a fear of any empowering practices. If some aspect of a spiritual practice is deemed too "woo woo" for someone, they carry a religious fear of their spirituality.

Spirituality is a more personal experience. The path can look completely different for everyone. Some people find spiritual fulfillment through rituals, meditation, spending time in nature, or helping others.

Think of it this way: religion provides a pre-built, one-size-*must*-fit-all house of faith, while spirituality is about laying the foundation and doing the work building your own unique belief system. Both can offer a sense of belonging and purpose, but often religion is forced upon someone from childhood, and its practice can cause great unconscious distress if that system isn't congruent with their authentic self.

TYPES OF SPIRITUALITY

Now that we understand how spirituality serves humanity, let's look at the different ways spirituality can manifest. there are five common types of spirituality, and within those are many paths. We have free will to work with as many or few of them as desired and change our minds at any moment.

Authoritarian Spirituality

This type of spirituality is the basis of all religions, which we have already discussed intensively. Authoritarian spirituality follows precise rules in the praise of a single savior, prophet or sage. People following an authoritarian spirituality can develop fundamentalist attitudes, meaning they believe their religion is the only truth. Meeting as a congregation or being part of an auxiliary group is what's actually spiritual, not the practice of the religion.

Intellectual Spirituality

This type of spirituality emphasizes the importance of knowledge. Intellectually spiritual people tend to learn about spiritual theories and analyze the information they gain. One form of this spiritual journey, for example, is theological studies. But this type of spirituality is not only related to the study of religion. Any knowledge that helps people lift their spirits and expand their consciousness is a form of intellectual spirituality. Scientists often fall into this category.

Service Spirituality

Human DNA contains genes programmed to serve our tribe. There are many ways to achieve this spirituality, that, at its core, is about giving without receiving, as a way to get in touch with our spiritual selves.

Social Spirituality

Many people desire to be with others in search of a greater spiritual purpose in life. Belonging to a religious group is one way of living this spirituality. However, this can also be achieved with other groups, like team sports, exercise, nature activities, and meditation. Even wanting to go out with friends or go dancing on a Saturday night has its roots in social spirituality. That's why a concert at an arena or a night at the theater can feel like a 'religious' experience.

Mystical Spirituality

This type of spirituality focuses on connection to something larger than oneself, without hierarchy. The human is on an equal footing with the divine. People with mystical spirituality believe there's a greater unity in all life experiences, and that reality goes beyond what we can see. All experiences transcend the physical or material world. People with this type of spirituality may support the idea that everything happens for a reason. Since there are no rules to follow, there's never a "good" mystic or "bad" one.

Most of us believe the world consists of only what we see and hear when awake. Mystic spiritual traditions explore the concept that awakened 3D perception is only a small percentage of reality, and that human reality is multifaceted, with deeper, unseen dimensions influencing our waking consciousness. These other dimensions could be spatial or non-spatial, encompassing different realms of consciousness or energy.

Mystics believe in the "collective unconscious." Carl Jung explained this as not being about our personal experiences, but rather a mutual connection to shared ideas and patterns that have been passed down through generations, like a mental library of humanity's common experiences, fears, and desires. The idea of the collective unconscious suggests that there's a deeper level to human experience that connects us all. It helps explain why certain themes resonate across cultures and why we tend to be drawn to the same characters and stories throughout the ages.

CORE TRIALS OF SPIRITUAL GROWTH

I wish I could tell you that going on a self-love journey to meet your authentic self and inner connection to spirituality is like a walk in the park. But the truth is, healing the traumas experienced in childhood create many emotional pitfalls to navigate as an adult. A damaged ego will desperately fight the changes our soul desires, even if they are for its own good. Because healing is grieving, the process of spiritual growth can be emotionally painful. Creating a new discipline to practice our spirituality presents challenges, as does finding gratitude for not only what we have, but for all the horrible things that made us the great person we are today.

Revealing the Ego

I've mentioned the term *ego* several times so far, and wanted to delve a bit deeper. Imagine yourself as a superhero. Not just any superhero, but one with two very different sidekicks. One sidekick is wild and impulsive, always wanting fun and excitement. The other sidekick is cautious and rule-following, reminding us of what's ethical and safe. These sidekicks are like parts of our mind that Sigmund Freud, the early twentieth century father of modern psychology, first defined.

The wild sidekick is like the **id**. It's all about our needs and desires, like eating pizza for breakfast or staying up all night partying. The cautious sidekick is like the **superego**. It represents our conscience, the voice that tells us what's "good" and "bad" based on what we've learned from parents, teachers, and society.

Who decides between these two sidekicks? That's the **ego**. It's like the manager of the superhero team, trying to balance the wild id's wishes with the superego's rules. A healthy ego figures out how to get what we need in a way that works in the real world.

The ego is basically our sense of self. Everyone has one, kind of like a mental fingerprint, and it's essential to our personal constitution and survival. Carl Jung was the first to believe the ego is also shaped by our experiences, especially in childhood. If we go through something frightening or upsetting, like a fight with a friend or a scary accident, or abuse, our ego might get bruised or worse, shattered. This can make it harder for the ego to manage the desperate id and superego, and why we may end up doing something dangerous, unethical, or illegal to satisfy a desire.

Humans are the only animal on the planet with an ego. The ego triggers us with anger when an appointment is canceled, the store is out of the one thing we went there for, or someone expresses differing points of view online. When that Amazon delivery is a day late, do you react like a crime has been committed, or know that the package will eventually arrive? Your ego reaction is not because of what happened, but the fact you had no control over it. **When we can relinquish control of everything we can't control to a higher power, that's letting go of the ego**.

The ego is the source of much personal suffering. Many mystic practices include the goal of "breaking the ego" or "killing the ego," but I believe "revealing the ego" may be a more helpful goal. The only part of the ego that we need to release is the one that prevents us from forgiving others and ourselves. (Refer to the section on forgiveness in chapter 8.)

A wounded ego has no concept of patience: the calm acceptance that things can happen in a different timeframe than expected. Developing patience is at the root of inner peace. With a healthy ego, a person is confident, kind, resilient, handles challenges, celebrates the successes of others, and builds strong relationships.

If there's one thing the ego hates, it's change. The ego would rather wallow in known misery than venture into the unknown world of growth and healing. This makes spiritual growth challenging. Yet just like a broken arm can heal, a bruised ego can too.

Navigating Growing Pains

As a past trauma is released, one might relive the emotional pain as part of the healing process. The healing could take a moment, an hour, or several sleep or lunar cycles to process.

During what's known as the "midnight of the soul," you may experience heightened anxiety, depression, insomnia, feel crazy, and a whole list of other ailments while a new reality emerges. These unpleasant symptoms can last for days, weeks, months or even years, depending on your level of active healing practices.

Another pain comes from making progress, when the new you mourns the loss of the old you. We may feel grief for no reason, especially right after something great happens to change our lives. These are the true growing pains, but any physical distress qualifies.

The best thing you can do is be kind to yourself. Accept what's happening and know it'll pass. Know also that these symptoms will likely reoccur as we continue to grow. The good news is we'll be able to acknowledge this occasional irritated state more quickly, and become experts at moving through it.

With my background in architecture, I enjoy watching home renovation programs. A spiritual growth journey is analogous to the discomfort of living through a renovation. Imagine yourself as the fixer, needing to address a leaky roof, install larger windows to let in more light, and rearrange walls to create a better flow. The process starts when the place is gutted, and walls are stripped back to the studs. There's irritating noise and choking dust to deal with daily. You're sleeping in a sleeping bag on the floor. The heart of the house, the kitchen, is gone and you're cooking outside off a camp stove, rain or shine. It may be too cold or hot with no insulation.

Then the rebuilding begins. New walls are framed in to make the rooms flow better, with larger windows flooding the interior with sunshine. Safe and new electric wiring and plumbing complete the inner workings. The insulation is restored, followed by new drywall. You begin to see how much more livable your house will be! The kitchen and bathrooms are finished with your favorite tile and fixtures and your house is finally livable again. It's the same house, but with a brand-new sense of home.

You'll have to get used to a host of other challenging situations as you evolve into the new you. As therapist Dr. Vasillia Binensztok so aptly states on her counseling website, "When you're not used to being confident, confidence feels like arrogance. When you're used to being passive, assertiveness feels like aggression. When you're not used to getting your needs met, prioritizing yourself feels selfish." It's a struggle to not allow your survival personality to hinder your growth.

Having Discipline

Discipline, in the context of spirituality, is the practice of self-control that allows us to focus our energy and actions towards achieving our spiritual goals. It's about developing the mental fortitude to resist distractions and temptations that pull us away from our spiritual path.

Someone might lack discipline for various reasons. Without a clear vision of spiritual aspirations, it's easy to feel lost and unmotivated. Procrastination is rooted in trauma, and simply not knowing where to start can hinder progress. Distractions like social media, unhealthy habits, or negative influences can derail our focus.

You can develop discipline by first setting clear intentions and goals. Define what spirituality means to you and what you hope to achieve through your practice. Don't overwhelm yourself with drastic changes. Begin with small, achievable goals and gradually increase the challenge. Create consistent practices like meditation, or spending time in nature. Repetition strengthens resolve. Find an accountability partner who can offer support and encouragement. Learn to forgive yourself. Everyone slips up. Acknowledge setbacks, learn from them, and recommit to your path.

By following these simple steps, you'll begin to develop the discipline that becomes the foundation for not only your spiritual growth, but anything you wish to accomplish.

Finding Gratitude

Gratitude is a conscious awareness of the good things we receive, big or small, and a recognition that these things enrich our lives. It seems like such a small act, but the truth is, gratitude is one of the most powerful states we can be in. It involves acknowledging that these blessings come from something outside us, whether it be a higher power, other people, or just fortunate circumstances. Even if life is challenging, one can always be grateful for being alive, having a roof over one's head, and having food to eat.

Gratitude might be a struggle for those focused on negativity because of trauma, as our brains are wired to prioritize threats. This negativity bias can make it easy to dwell on problems and overlook the good. A sense of entitlement can make us take for granted things that come easily and fail to appreciate the effort behind them. And of course, seeing what others have on social media, and societal pressures to be what we're not, can cultivate a sense of lack, making it hard to appreciate what we already have.

The good news is that gratitude can be cultivated. Gratitude journaling is a great way to start. Take a few minutes each day to write down things you're grateful for (I'll talk a lot more about journaling in chapter 8). This simple act can shift our focus towards the positive. Savor the little things, like a warm cup of coffee, a beautiful sunset, or a kind word from a stranger. We also create gratitude by expressing it, like thanking the people in our lives who make a difference, big or small. Also, doing good for others fosters a sense of connection and cultivates a grateful perspective.

Even if you can only find one thing in life to be grateful for, focus on that one aspect throughout the day to open the doors to finding other things for gratitude.

The most difficult moments are finding gratitude for all the painful challenges we've faced: the sources of trauma we're working on processing. We're here on Earth for soul lessons, and that's what all those challenges have been. But our broken egos are in so much pain and don't care why the soul has incarnated. Gaining the ability to find gratitude for those challenges that have made us the stronger people we are today is a clear sign of spiritual growth. (The 11 Insights are meant to help process the pain by reframing challenging situations.)

Choosing Silence

Silence, often misunderstood as weakness, is a potent force for personal and spiritual growth. There are two kinds of silence: "being in" silence, and "choosing" silence as a response. Both practices require patience to acquire.

Being in silence is revered as a sacred space where the soul can connect with the divine. By purposefully spending time abstaining from speech, we quiet the mind's chatter and create room for intuition and guidance.

By choosing silence as a response, especially to toxic stimuli, we cultivate a profound respect for ourselves and the situation, allowing for introspection, discernment, and a deeper connection to inner wisdom. How we respond to something is truly the only thing we can control. The ability to withhold words is a testament to gaining self-control and emotional maturity. Remaining silent in situations where your comments could raise the toxicity level will always be the right choice.

Silence and non-response empower us to reclaim our personal authority and live with greater intention.

Being in Solitude

Solitude, often viewed as mere isolation, plays a profound role in spiritual growth across various traditions. Spending time alone allows us to not only quiet the noise of external influences, social pressures, and expectations, but gives us the opportunity to freely delve into our internal landscape and be reborn as our authentic selves. We can examine our thoughts, beliefs, and motivations, paving the way for a more authentic connection with the spiritual aspects of our being, without outside judgment.

Many people aren't comfortable being alone. When alone, they feel lonely. In the quiet, we may face hidden fears, anxieties, and unresolved issues. And since we often seek validation from others, solitude forces us to find our own sense of worth and purpose, which can be unsettling. Also, many of us have difficulty enjoying being alone because it triggers feelings of abandonment. For those of us who don't enjoy being alone, the self-love journey can be trying.

As we gain self-love, our reality changes, and that means people currently in our lives may not be part of that future. We may turn down invitations to protect our energy. We may turn down invitations because being alone feels better than being around toxic people. We may turn down invitations because we don't need to prove we're lovable by the number of friends we have or how social we are. Enjoying solitude needs to become our superpower.

How do we know if what we're experiencing is solitude or loneliness? Loneliness is a feeling of isolation and disconnection, while solitude is a state of being comfortably alone with an inner divine connection.

Many of us find it boring to be alone, which is a clear marker for disconnection to a higher power and a lack of self-love. How can someone be bored being in a room with someone they love? How can someone be bored having time alone to express themselves however they choose?

To cultivate a love for solitude, start small, such as being alone for fifteen minutes a day, gradually increasing the duration as it becomes more comfortable. Immersion in nature is a powerful way to connect with something larger than ourselves and find peace in solitude. Those of us who are gardening enthusiasts understand this concept.

Purposefully dedicate time alone to fulfilling activities, whether it's reading, writing, or making art. Practicing meditation and other mindfulness exercises can help create more comfort with our own thoughts and cultivate a sense of inner peace in solitude.

You may have realized you do a lot of routine activities that could be considered spiritual. And now that you're aware of all the new choices and reasons for making them, take time to consider what changes could make your routines more spiritual.

CHAPTER 7:

Gaining Self-Awareness

Self-awareness is the foundation upon which
we can consciously create our reality.

—BASHAR

PEOPLE WHO HAVE MORE SELF-LOVE tend to know what they think, feel, and want. This self-awareness creates a greater likelihood they'll achieve goals, cultivate nurturing and meaningful relationships, and feel authentically connected and engaged with all aspects of life.

When we have a better understanding of ourselves, we're able to experience ourselves as the unique and separate individuals we are, empowered to make changes and to build on our strengths. Being clearer about our strengths helps boost confidence by focusing more energy on doing what we're good at. We are conscious of our own impulses, desires, and limitations, and can adapt and accommodate to different social and cultural situations.

However, it's possible to be self-aware to some degree and still be unhappy and unfulfilled, if we don't know how to take further action. And clarity about our weaknesses is also essential, as it can help us to surround ourselves with people who balance us.

How do we know if we lack self-awareness? A good indicator is how well we understand our emotions, actions, and behavior. People who lack self-awareness often feel constantly off-kilter, anxious, or angry. They're passive-aggressive. They don't understand why they act or feel the way they do and have a need to control everything. They're prone to emotional outbursts. They micromanage, nothing is ever their fault, they get defensive and say things they don't mean, and have a hard time laughing at themselves.

On the flip side, being overly self-aware can lead to negative feelings about oneself as there's a fine line between having self-awareness and being self-conscious. Here's a list of things to consider to help with the self-awareness development process. You can find further books and websites on topics below, in the appendix.

Look at Yourself Objectively

Learn your strengths and weaknesses. The ego doesn't like the truth, especially about itself. It won't allow us to believe addictions, habits, or weaknesses that seem uncontrollable are problematic. For example, if someone drinks alcohol or uses marijuana daily but tells themselves, "I have it under control," that's the ego at work. The list may include screen time, smoking, promiscuity, food, toxic friendships or relationships, and so on. But don't forget to also look objectively at your strengths, because they're already there and can be built upon.

Psychotherapy

Psychotherapy or counseling is an invaluable resource. Those with medical insurance can call their provider and ask for referrals for therapists specializing in their area of need. We can also access therapists online or via apps like Alma, Headspace, or Talkspace.

As I mentioned, talk therapy doesn't heal trauma, but it's the perfect solution for gaining self-awareness. And because working with a psychologist, therapist, or counselor in a therapeutic relationship gives us an opportunity to explore our thoughts, feelings, and patterns of behavior, it can help us learn new coping skills and techniques to better manage daily stressors and challenging behaviors. Some of the benefits include:

- Build self-esteem
- Reduce anxiety
- Improve social and community functioning
- Develop better relationship skills
- Understand and achieve personal goals
- Overcome illnesses such as trauma, depression, compulsive behaviors, and eating disorders
- Improve overall mood
- Replace negative thinking with positive thinking

Not every therapist, whatever their specialty, will be helpful to everyone. Many are once-traumatized people, like the rest of us, who moved into psychology to help themselves grow, but never fully transmuted all toxic behavior. If we suffer from low self-esteem, we may not have the courage or feel worthy to move on to another more helpful therapist. I can't tell you how many therapists I had to leave after just a few sessions.

However, there is a type of psychotherapy that has proven successful in treating trauma: EMDR (Eye Movement Desensitization and Reprocessing) removes stagnant energy out of the body through eye movement. It was developed by Francine Shapiro in the late 1980s and is based on the same idea as this book, that unresolved traumatic memories can disrupt a person's emotional and psychological well-being.

The therapy involves guiding the patient to focus on the traumatic memory and its associated feelings, while simultaneously engaging in stimulating both sides of the brain. This can be achieved through eye movements, tapping, or auditory tones. Because it addresses the underlying causes of trauma, therapists who use EMDR overwhelmingly have found clients create a greater sense of control over their thoughts and feelings and alleviate symptoms such as anxiety, depression, nightmares, and flashbacks.

Journaling

Writing down thoughts and feelings every day can be profoundly helpful in releasing the emotional attachment to those emotions, and crucial to those who can't afford talk therapy. It's a powerful healing tool, and I ask you to journal on various topics in the 11 Insights.

Journaling is an incredible stress management tool, a helpful habit that lessens the impact of physical stressors on your health. In fact, the 2005 Cambridge University study, by Karen A. Baikie and Kay Wilhelm, showed expressive writing (like journaling) for only 15 to twenty minutes a day, three to five times over the course of a four-month period, was enough to strengthen immunity and decrease risk of illness. Those who journal boast improved immune system functioning as well as lessened symptoms of asthma and rheumatoid arthritis. Expressive writing has been shown to improve liver and lung function and combat certain diseases; it has even been reported to help the wounded heal faster. Not only does journaling boost memory and comprehension, it also increases working memory capacity. It can improve your mood and give you a greater sense of overall emotional well-being and happiness.

As journaling habits are developed, benefits become long-term, meaning we become more in tune with our health by connecting with inner needs and desires. The practice gives us an opportunity for emotional catharsis and helps the brain regulate emotions. It provides a greater sense of confidence and self-identity. The same Cambridge study also shows that expressive writing can help individuals develop more structured, adaptive, and integrated schemes about themselves, others, and the world. What's more, journaling unlocks and engages right-brained creativity, which gives access to one's full brain power. In the end, journaling fosters growth.

From my coaching point of view, there's no best time for everyone to write, only the best time for you. If you feel inclined to write first thing in the morning, before bed, or during the day where you can write with some regularity, that's your time. Set a goal for how many times a week to write.

What do we write about? To start, I suggest writing about what's bubbling inside. These surface emotions need to be cleared first. Many journals already have writing prompts. Topics to write about include:

- Hopes and dreams: One way to make fantasy a reality is to write it down.
- Goals: Daily, yearly, or five-year goals are best put on paper. Include the steps needed and your progress.
- Achievements: These are the goals reached, what you learned about yourself from the process, and how you feel about yourself.
- Daily activities, and how you felt doing them.
- Epiphanies: That's just a fancy word for your "aha" moments, when you understand things in new ways.
- Gratitude: Focusing on what you have and your overwhelming thankfulness for it being in your life.

- Fears: There's no better way to address worries than writing about them. They always seem much worse in your head. When you start writing down what you're stressed about, you can think about how you're going to meet the challenge that's causing the stress in the first place. Especially for those catastrophic thinkers who always imagine worst-case scenarios, writing about them can help one see that the worries are not even realistic.

Choosing a topic may seem overwhelming to people who have never journaled before. So, to help, you will find journal prompts in chapter 8's Deeper Dives for specific areas of transformation.

Setting Goals

I subscribe to the belief that nothing is real until we write it down. What are your long-term goals? What are your annual goals? What are the steps to achieve them? Who or what do you need to help?

Make them visible. Once you have your goals articulated, take some time to turn them into a creative and artistic visual. One exercise is to sit with markers, crayons, or paint and write them out in a way you might if you were a child. This activates a different part of your brain and will help cement your goals in your mind. The creative process also helps you not get stuck in rational thinking.

Feel them. Rather than simply listing your goals, write at least a paragraph on how it feels to achieve each one. Acting like you've already achieved your goal will start to connect the dots between where you are now and where you want to be. On top of that, it'll also give you the confidence associated with attaining this goal— and this will permeate to those around you.

Share them. Many people are afraid of sharing their goals in case they don't achieve them, but sharing them with truly supportive people helps to keep us motivated. Additionally, once we say them out loud to someone else, we've made an unknowing commitment to make it happen. It has become bigger than us and now it's on us to make it materialize.

Understand them. To set goals that truly motivate us, we must understand why we want to achieve that goal. Without a clear understanding of our motivation, it's hard to find the tenacity or drive needed to succeed.

Take action. Once we have our goals written, we need to take immediate action—even if it's a small step. Momentum begets momentum, and by kick-starting our goal-writing process with a tangible action, we'll immediately create a sense of progress. Change happens as a result of lots of little steps, so don't feel the need to start with a huge, intimidating one. Be sure to celebrate wins and review the goals each month to track progress. Remember, progress is progress!

As a coach I help clients create SMART goals:

Specific: Your goal must be clear and well-defined.

Measurable: Include precise amounts, dates, time, frequency, etc., so you can measure your degree of success.

Attainable: Make sure that it's possible to achieve the goals you set.

Realistic: Is it physically possible to happen.

Time-Bound: Time of day, frequency length of practice.

For example, "I want to start practicing yoga," is a goal, but it's not a SMART goal. What kind of yoga do you want to practice? There are several modalities. Where, at home or a class? How many times a week and for how long? Are you physically capable of this? When do you want to start?

The SMART goal version would be, "Starting Monday, I want to practice Vinyasa yoga at home for thirty minutes, three times a week, streaming from the Exercise channel."

"I want to be happier" is intangible. However, the sole purpose of a self-love journey is to be happier in life, so you're already heading in the right direction. Perhaps in the meantime, contemplate what exactly would make you happy, and create SMART goals to that end.

Daily Meditation

Meditation is the general term for quietly raising the frequency of our brain waves (from Alpha or Beta to Theta or Gamma), for various reasons, from connecting to nothingness to learning to break a habit. Daydreaming is a type of meditation. As is a walk in the woods, or sitting in the park. There are many types of meditation, and each is useful in its own way. Some people enjoy listening to guided meditations, some may breathe or chant or use bells, some may just use the quiet time to check in with themselves and see how they're really doing.

Meditation can give us a sense of calm, peace, and balance that benefits both our emotional well-being and our overall health. And these benefits don't end when the meditation session ends. The healing of the meditation can carry us more calmly through our day and may help us manage symptoms of certain medical conditions and treat insomnia. It also has the power to improve digestion, strengthen the immune system, and maintain normal cholesterol and blood pressure levels.

Meditation helps us focus in the moment, without life's distractions. It helps us tap into our subconscious minds to allow us to consciously effect change we can't effect when asleep. Meditation helps rejuvenate us; it helps us relieve any negativity that may be weighing us down.

We can never meditate wrong. We may learn to do it more effectively, but it can *never* be done wrong. We might choose to start by listening to guided meditations for specific purposes like clearing chakras, reducing fear, or daily affirmations. The speaker uses guided imagery to put our mind at peace. Eventually, the need for guidance will disappear. Hundreds of guided meditations are available for free on YouTube and via terrific apps, like Insight Timer.

For the beginning meditator, I recommend creating a sound bath of Tibetan bells through an online recording. I use Pandora or YouTube. (Be certain they're the metal, not crystal, bells.) A recording with multiple tones works best. This is a sound bath, meaning no earphones. Play the music loud enough to get good bass on the bell tones and feel them vibrate in your body.

Now, sit quietly with eyes closed. Listen to the bells and focus on your breathing, inhaling for a count of four, holding for two, and exhaling for a count of eight. After a few breaths, bring the bells back into your consciousness and allow the vibration to consume you and penetrate to your core. Witness and observe. What are you feeling? Where are you feeling it? What's happening to your thoughts? Continue your observations for ten minutes, or up to an hour.

This simple practice, over time, will not only train the brain to refocus from needless repetitive thoughts, but also tune the body to these higher healing frequencies. Keep in mind that you need four to six consistent weeks to create a new habit. You'll also find meditation prompts in this book.

Occult Readings

Astrology can also hold personality insights. I'm not talking about the daily paragraph in your newspaper, but rather an extensive reading from an experienced astrologer. I found a Sabian reading to be the most insightful. Sabian Astrology embodies all the philosophical, spiritual and practical concepts of the Sabian vision, founded in 1923, and applies it to astrology. They're rare astrologers, but worth the effort to find.

There's also something called Human Design. Created in 1987 by Ra Huru Ulala, it combines astrology, I Ching, and Kabbalah to create a graphic representation of the self and what we're on Earth to achieve. A qualified Human Design reader can be found with a simple Google search.

Uncover Your Social Programming

Social programming is what it sounds like: the process of training people in a society to respond in ways generally approved by the society at large, or smaller groups within it. It's the set of instructions each of us learned in order to fit in. Our family members, schoolteachers, and peer groups were all part of the socialization process. The long-term effect of this socialization is that we don't pursue an authentic inner life, but seek external approval and external goals.

There are several general categories where your social programming may be defeatist:

Money: "I want to be rich."
Falsely believing that we'll be happy when we make more money, so we become workaholics to make more money, yet we never feel we have enough.

Status: "I want to be popular."

Falsely believing that "once I obtain status, people will like and respect me." Trying to "keep up with the Joneses." Becoming popular with lots of people but not building close relationships with individuals.

Approval: "I want to be liked."

Working at a job we hate to pay for our family's high consumption or pursuing a career that Mom or Dad wants us to go after. Not speaking up at work when we have a good idea, for fear of getting shot down.

Power: "I want to dominate."

Using others to achieve our goals. Trying to one-up others, dominate conversations, and pinpoint other people's weaknesses and failures.

None of this is needed to be happy when connected to self-love—though it can still take a lifetime to become better at thinking for ourselves and more independent of others.

Shadow Work

Carl Jung referred to the parts of ourselves that we judge as undesirable and try to conceal as our "shadow." In other words, our survival personality. The shadow is our "dark side" because it consists chiefly of primitive, negative human emotions and impulses like rage, envy, greed, lust, selfishness, desire, and the striving for power. Whatever we perceive as inferior, evil, or unacceptable in ourselves becomes part of the shadow. You might know them as vices.

"Everyone carries a shadow," Jung wrote in his 1938 book *Psychology & Religion,* "and the less it's embodied in the individual's conscious life, the blacker and denser it is." Exploring our shadow can lead to greater authenticity, creativity, energy, and personal awakening. This introspective process is essential for reaching mature adulthood.

Shadow Work is how we integrate the aspects of our unconscious psyche into our conscious experience and allow the positive aspects of the shadow to express themselves. When properly used and channeled, the shadow-self has traits that further our own personal development. The 11 Insights provide a means to reveal the shadow.

Life Mirrors

You don't see the world as it is. You see it as you are. Life is a mirror; its reflection shines our image back to us. Similarly, as I've mentioned, "we judge others for what we don't want to accept about ourselves." Yes, our most annoying qualities that we're blind to show up as intolerable in others. If we're seeking greater self-awareness, examining our life mirrors is an effective place to start.

Who are some of the people you can't stand to be around because of their personality? Who do you and your friends gossip about and criticize? What specific behaviors do you ridicule and seek to avoid? Guess what? Those are all parts of *you*! This is most visible in politics. When a candidate lies about their opponent, they're often projecting their own weaknesses.

Let's remove the blame, shame, and denial that may be coming up right now. It's okay to be who we are. If we don't like it, we have the power to grow. See the section on forgiveness in chapter 6 on how to handle what you may be feeling.

Many of our judgements are never brought to words, let alone delivered in a speech. Most are mere thoughts and may last a split second. Walking down the street, we judge the appearance of people we see: their ethnicity, attractiveness, weight, style, height, hair, and status, to name a few. What's the basis for these judgements? How we feel about our own ethnicity, attractiveness, weight, style, height, hair, and status.

Our home environment is also a life mirror. If someone we most admire—an actor, politician or athlete, for example—is coming to our house, what would we like to change about it? Would we be embarrassed to have them over? Does it need painting? Bathroom a mess? Filthy carpet? If we're not pleased with our surroundings, it's because we're not pleased with ourselves. But guess what? We deserve to live in that place fixed up for our hero, because we are our own heroes.

Many of us immediately focus on economic factors when choosing a city, neighborhood, and dwelling in which to live. And to some extent those conditions govern our choices But what if that's simply a limiting belief? Not that we can suddenly afford to pay $3,000 a month for our home, but rather that our living situation isn't about money; it's how we feel about ourselves. Though we may not have control over how much money we make, we have complete control over taking a self-love journey. As we regain our sense of worth and authenticity, it becomes easier to manifest a better living situation.

Examine your environment. Maybe you can paint an accent wall, lay down a rug, improve the lighting, and really make the home come alive. Or do you need to move? Do you feel safe? Does the place feel bright and cheery? Is the place quiet? The school of thought known as *feng shui* can help create comfortable environments (see chapter 9).

CHAPTER 8

The 11 Insights to Happiness

Find out where joy resides and give it a voice far beyond singing. For to miss the joy is to miss all.

—ROBERT LOUIS STEVENSON

GAINING SELF-AWARENESS of your thoughts and behaviors is paramount to the Lifeprint Reiki process, and grasping and mastering the following 11 Insights is at the core of reconnecting to self-love and the happiness living authentically can offer. We've all likely seen spiritual advice on social media telling us, "Don't do this," or "Stop X, Y, and Z," without telling us *how*. This chapter will help you better understand the thought process behind your uncontrollable triggers, reactions, and behaviors, so that you can make the desired changes.

The eleven concepts in this chapter will help you shed that survival personality and learn to live more authentically, in a new reality, with emotional intelligence. The 11 Insights are: curiosity, suffering and surrender, attachments and expectations, the illusion of polarity, forgiveness, compare & despair, boundaries, power of loss, internal validation, connecting to ancestors, and nothingness.

While there's no hierarchy of importance to the 11 Insights, I discuss them in this order to facilitate their understanding. Their interdependence will become evident as we explore them.

I've already mentioned some of these topics, but now we'll dive deeper into how limiting beliefs affect our authenticity and emotional intelligence. *Authenticity* simply means shedding the survival personality and embracing who we really are at our soul core and then acting in accordance with our own values and beliefs. To succeed in being authentic, we first must reveal our true selves, which requires being emotionally intelligent.

Emotional intelligence is all about understanding and managing our emotions, as well as recognizing and responding to the feelings of others. It's like having an open toolbox for building strong relationships, effectively navigating conflict, and coping with stress. Without this toolbox, people might struggle to connect with others, make poor, impulsive decisions, and even have trouble keeping a job. Unresolved trauma inhibits us from attaining emotional intelligence, since we likely grew up disconnected from our true feelings.

At the end of each insight is a section called Deeper Dives. These are optional opportunities to further explore the topic of discussion. In several instances, you'll be asked to journal using an automatic writing technique, which is the most effective way to journal. Instead of thinking about what to write, simply focus on the body and heart center and let your hand move freely with pen or pencil in hand, writing whatever comes to mind without filtering or judging. This bypasses the conscious mind, allowing deeper thoughts and emotions from the subconscious to surface. Hidden memories, negative emotions, or even forgotten parts of us blocked by trauma, can then be more efficiently processed.

Journaling can only have a healing effect by handwriting, as the physical act of writing engages different parts of the brain, enhancing memory and learning. That's why I don't consider writing on a computer as journaling, although such a practice can be the start of a fascinating memoir. If you don't have a journal, a simple composition book from the dollar store will suffice.

WHAT YOU WILL GAIN FROM THE 11 INSIGHTS

Ability to speak your truth. Asking for what we need is often stifled in childhood, when we had no agency and feared abandonment. Releasing those blockages allows us to speak from a place of truth and positive intention, without censoring or limiting ourselves. The truth sets us free to blossom in our new reality.

Your inner light will be your guide. When we come from a place of trauma, we lose connection to our intuition and the ability to trust our own judgment. Clearing those blockages allows us to connect with the fire inside our hearts. We are open to consult the wisdom of our heart-center when faced with important choices and decisions and rely more on our intuition and less on our mind for decisions.

Easier gratitude. When drowning in trauma and chaos, we become blind to the blessings already in our lives. The 11 Insights help reframe our lives to focus on the goodness, beauty, kindness, light, love, and joy in everything. Gratitude gives love to the universe, and we need to give love to get love.

Recognize synchronicity. When connected to self-love with a personal divine connection, the universe becomes our genie in a bottle, granting more than three wishes. Life has a flow where events line up in our favor, creating a spiritual web of connection between people and events. We understand the way the universe gently nudges and guides us towards our greatest destiny.

Become a freer spirit. Fear of judgment imprisons our souls and prevents them from fully expressing themselves in a myriad of ways. But a freed soul can sing, dance, play, stretch, move, make music, create art, breathe, laugh, and cry freely. A happy soul is a happier life.

Ability to choose love over fear. There are only two emotions: love and fear. All positive emotions come from love, all negative emotions from fear. From love flows happiness, contentment, peace, and joy. From fear comes anger, hate, anxiety and guilt. We cannot feel these two emotions simultaneously.

The love in service. When we're trapped in a lack and neediness mind-set, it's difficult to consider helping others, as we feel we have nothing left to give. The paradox is that, when we give love, we get love back from the universe. The clearing after completing the 11 Insights leaves us overflowing with love and a great desire to share, be it through community service, youth sport coaching, mentoring, or senior care.

Ability to do what you say you'll do. We often say things to meet the expectations of others, but then fear arises in following through. Eliminating the root of those fears allows us to be consistent with the promises we make, which helps others trust that we are who we present ourselves to be. When our speech and deeds match up, we know we're in alignment with the universe.

1: CURIOSITY

We begin with the topic of curiosity because it's at the root of why you're reading this book. Your curiosity began as a childlike wonder that drove you to poke every elevator button, ask a million questions, build forts, play "house," and lose yourself in endless "whys?" Turns out, that's not just a cute phase we outgrow. Curiosity is part of being human.

Have you heard the phrase "knowledge is power?" Curiosity ignites the very potential for that power, and is why education is so important. Curiosity is the fuel that propels us towards self-love, unlocks hidden corners of our humanity, and illuminates the path to spiritual growth. Did you continue your education after high school? Were you curious to learn more about something you're passionate about in hopes it could become a career? Curiosity, gaining knowledge, and self-love are the holy trinity for this day and age.

Curiosity and creativity have a beautifully symbiotic relationship. Curiosity ignites the spark of new ideas, fuels the creative process, and drives us to learn, which in turn, fosters even greater creativity. **This is so important, as creative expression is directly linked to levels of happiness.** As Albert Einstein famously said, "I have no special talent. I am only passionately curious." Perhaps the key to unlocking one's own creative potential lies in cultivating a sense of wonder and embracing the power of curiosity. For example, an artist's curiosity about different color palettes or mediums can lead to creating a unique artistic style.

From the first cave paintings which scratched stories onto rock walls, to the satellite telescopes peering into the vastness of space, our journey as a species is fueled by insatiable curiosity. We question, we challenge, we push the boundaries of what we know, and in doing so, we redefine humanity.

Consider the curiosity of Leonardo da Vinci, whose relentless questioning and exploration from art to anatomy advanced our understanding of the human body and the built and natural world. Or Marie Curie, whose curiosity about radioactivity led to groundbreaking discoveries that reshaped modern science and medicine. How did we get to the moon? How did Gutenberg invent the printing press?

We don't have to change the world with our curiosity. We might create a crowd-pleasing apple pie recipe, a crocheted afghan, a new dance craze, or simply a better way to organize the items on your desk. Our curiosity is why we travel to foreign lands to see how other people live, to experience their cultures, and taste their foods.

The key to unlocking creativity isn't just in asking "why?" but more powerfully, "what if?" Every experiment starts with "what if?" On a personal level, it's what makes us try new things, alter recipes, or buy a telescope.

For example, let's look at how cheese was invented. Thousands of years ago, there was a need to store and carry milk. Someone had the spark of genius to ask: "*What if* I sew the animal's stomach shut to use it as a container?" When they took the milk out, it was different from what went in, separating into curds and whey. The rennet, a digestive enzyme in the animal's stomach, made the milk curdle and cheese was born. That "what if?" brought us hundreds of ways to enjoy cheese, and thousands of years later, rennet is still used in cheese production.

I've seen firsthand how curiosity and creativity can shape a person. As a child, I had art and ceramic lessons and discovered the joy of the relatively instant gratification of baking. I studied architecture in college, spending an exchange year in Switzerland learning a different language and way of life. *Oui, je parle français.* As an actor, I became a standup comedian because I didn't want to fear doing anything. I enjoy photography, singing, and painting. I went to cooking school and became a private chef. I had a resort wear company designing swimsuits. I write plays and movies and even made a few films. Perhaps my curiosity hasn't yet changed the world, but it has certainly changed *my* world.

A 2014 study conducted at the University of California, Davis, headed by neuroscientist Charan Ranganath, found that curious individuals had lower levels of stress hormones and reported higher levels of positive emotions, contributing to their overall well-being. Another study that year from UC Davis by post doctorate researcher, Matthias Gruber, states "Curiosity may put the brain in a state that allows it to learn and retain any kind of information and that when curiosity is stimulated, there's increased reward activity in the brain."

Most importantly, in 2016, psychologists with the University of London's Hungry Mind Lab observed that curiosity leads to a higher sense of satisfaction and can significantly reduce the risk of developing mental health issues like depression and anxiety. A curious mind is a motivated mind, but societal pressures, daily routines, and even fear can dim that spark. We forget to ask, to explore, to truly see ourselves with open eyes.

This lack of curiosity can hinder our self-love journey. "Unused creativity is not benign. It festers, it metastasizes into resentment, grief and heartbreak," said researcher Brené Brown on a 2025 podcast, *Magic Lessons*. Being a little more curious and creative could change your whole life.

How Curiosity Connects to Self-Love

How can you fully appreciate the intricacies of life and your soul without a passionate curiosity to explore their depths? How can we embrace all facets of our being if we never question, never delve beneath the surface? Curiosity is the key that unlocks the treasure chest of self-love—the one holding acceptance, compassion, and ultimately, an unwavering belief in your own magic.

When we meet someone who romantically interests us, passion drives our curiosity to learn everything about them. Faults and all. But people often lack the passion of curiosity to explore themselves. How deep are you willing to go for the thrill of discovering your hidden talents, the awe of understanding your emotions, and the quiet peace of embracing your true self, flaws and all? What if you discover a whole universe right there within you?

As adults, we often encounter a stigma surrounding curiosity. There's a societal misconception that curiosity is a childish trait, that as we grow older, we should have all the answers, or that seeking new knowledge beyond our comfort zones is somehow frivolous or a waste of time. We minimize curiosity, or a toxic family member does it for us. But great minds, like Albert Einstein and Steve Jobs, emphasized that maintaining a childlike wonder throughout life was their key to success.

Reasons for Lacking Curiosity

It's true that education isn't that important in every family. Maybe you were the first to get a college degree. Not everyone has hobbies and interests that keep us wanting to learn more and get better at them. Likely it's something rooted in a childhood or ancestral trauma. The fear of asking questions or venturing into unfamiliar territory for fear of appearing foolish, or shame from not being good at something on the first try, can be a major roadblock to curiosity. Many children are ridiculed for asking questions or making mistakes. This can be especially true for people who have a strong sense of perfectionism as a result of unresolved trauma.

Plus, our egos guide us to seek out predictability and avoid novelty, which can lead to a preference for sticking with what we already know, even if it's not particularly stimulating. This behavior is rewarded by the release of dopamine, a feel-good chemical in the brain. That's why children will often watch the same program or movie twenty-five times. And let's be real: in our fast-paced world, it's easy to feel like there's simply not enough time to indulge in curiosity. Between work, family, and other obligations, there may be little room for exploring new hobbies or interests or delving deeper into existing ones.

Religious faith can also be behind a lack of curiosity. "Why?" questions may be discouraged or outright prohibited. This learned behavior stifles curiosity in other areas of life and disconnects us from self-love. This disconnection can make us feel we're not deserving of indulging in our passions or simply gaining the knowledge needed to thrive in our society.

I've compiled seven ways to get back on course with your curiosity to heighten your creativity.

Reigniting Curiosity

1. Daily Journaling

This cathartic exercise bypasses the inner critic and allows for the exploration of unfiltered thoughts and emotions that can unearth buried curiosities and spark creative ideas.

2. Focus on the Joy

Perfectionism and self-doubt often act as creativity's greatest adversaries, because they make us result-oriented instead of encouraging us to smell the roses along the way. However, by focusing on the joy of exploration rather than the end product, we can bypass perfectionism and embrace the inherent curiosity of the experience.

3. Embrace the Power of Play

Play is important throughout life to foster a state of mind conducive to exploration, experimentation, and risk-taking. Engaging in playful activities, whether it's doodling, playing music, sports, or even board games, can help us loosen up and break free from rigid patterns. Watching silly movies or standup comedy allows us to dissolve the wall that makes us take ourselves too seriously.

4. Ask "Why?" Like a Child

Children constantly ask "why?" relentlessly seeking to understand the world around them. Reconnecting with this childlike inquisitiveness can be a powerful tool. Start asking yourself open-ended questions about everyday experiences. *Why does the sky appear blue? How does Wi-Fi work?* The process of inquiry can spark creativity and a sense of wonder.

5. Step Outside Your Comfort Zone

Challenge yourself to try something new, whether a hobby, visiting a new place, or trying a new food. Novelty can spark curiosity and provide fresh perspectives. For those who've never been outside their hometown, simply exploring the next state over can make a huge impact.

6. Embrace the Power of Nature

There's a reason many creative minds find inspiration in nature. Immersing yourself in nature, whether it's a swim in the ocean, a walk in the park, a hike in the woods, or simply gazing at the stars, can reconnect us with a sense of wonder. One exercise is to simply leave the house on foot or by car with no planned destination, to allow serendipitous discovery and to see the familiar in a new light.

DEEPER DIVES

1: Write Your What Ifs

Take out your journal and start making a list of *what ifs* that pertain not only to your life, but the world as a whole. What if I take a class to learn something new? What if I paint a wall blue? What if I moved to a different city? What if I took a different route to work? What if I tried a new restaurant? What if there weren't cars? What if electricity was free? The possibilities are endless. How do you feel about these new thoughts? Anything surprise you? Anything you could act on making real?

2: Connecting to Past Passions

In your journal, make a list of your passions and the creative things you enjoyed as a child that you no longer pursue. Why did you stop? How did you feel doing those things? What would it take to reconnect to those passions?

3: Keep a Curiosity Journal

Use your journal during this challenge to note down what you did, how it made you feel, and any interesting discoveries about yourself or the world around you. The goal here is not just to learn new facts, but to reignite that sense of wonder and exploration that enriches our lives in profound ways.

4: 30-Day Challenge

I encourage you to do one thing you've never done before each day for thirty days. It could be reading an article on a completely new topic, trying a hobby you've never considered before, taking another route to work, watching a YouTube video about something new, or even asking someone a question about their life that you've been too shy to ask.

Curiosity is a foundational element for spiritual growth, propelling us through the labyrinthine paths of our inner selves. This inward journey might be scary at times, but every step we take on this path, every question we ask, every mystery we unravel, brings us closer to the profound truth of our own being.

2: SUFFERING AND SURRENDER

The word *suffering* often evokes extreme images—war, poverty, natural disasters. It's the cry of a child, the despair of a refugee, the ache of loss that breaks our heart. These are external forms of suffering and addressing them remains an important human challenge.

There's also a subtler, more pervasive, internal form of suffering that affects us deeply, but can be avoided. Our time on this planet has unconsciously woven internal suffering into the fabric of our daily lives, manifesting as emotional triggers, anxiety, worry, anger, and a cacophonous hum of dissatisfaction.

Many of us feel that we don't have options besides a negative emotion when life doesn't meet our expectations, or we feel anxiety over what lies ahead beyond our control. The frustration when things don't go our way, the missed promotion, unrequited love, dissatisfaction with our appearance, the late Amazon delivery, people asking us to do things we don't really want to do, when the fast-food cashier got the order wrong, our favorite TV show was canceled, or our spouse or child needs something from us…and all of a sudden, our patience runs out and we react.

We've all been there. But what's underneath it all?

We're never encouraged to stop and think about why and how we're reacting the way we do. All we know is that we're triggered, and getting upset is the instant response. If that upset feeling only lasted a minute, life wouldn't be so bad. But anger gets stored deep in the body, so the suffering of disappointment can often last days or weeks, dampening any chances of joy and happiness during that time. Getting over a breakup can sometimes take months. The takeaway is that such triggers are a glaring sign of unresolved trauma crying for help, requiring compassionate healing.

All About Control

We learned as children to suffer internally when we couldn't control everything. Our inner child learns to fear abandonment, rejection, or loss of
safety and does anything to prevent the experience from repeating. In Part
I, you read a brief version of my life story. It took me almost fifty years to
figure out that my behavior response to all the trauma I experienced made
me a control freak for the first half of my life. Part of my hope in writing
this book is to save you time in learning these concepts.

The ego forever seeks control as a defense mechanism until healed,
lashing out at disappointment, clinging tightly to the illusion of perma-
nence and certainty, desperately grasping at fantastical outcomes and toxic
relationships to feel a modicum of love. The damaged ego compensates
for childhood pain by needing excessive validations and won't take "no"
for an answer.

In the throes of strong triggers, we might make rash decisions or act
impulsively without considering the consequences. This could involve over-
spending, substance abuse to numb the pain, or reckless behavior. Some
people may shut down emotionally in triggering situations as their fight or
flight, freeze or fawn, response kicks in, as they have no means to handle
the emotions in the moment.

Surrender and Self-Love

The rise of the Karens and Kevins caught in the act of uncontrolled responses
on social media is the perfect example of emotionally wounded people
desperately fighting to make the world fit their unmet childhood needs. "I'd
like to speak to the manager" became their battle cry for the help they never
received as children. And let's face it, this constant wrestling with unattainable
control is exhausting, not to mention, it disconnects us from self-love.

How do we reclaim our inner peace? Surrender.

Surrender is a crucial part of reconnecting to self-love, because we don't realize the unconscious blame we put on ourselves when these uncontrollable things happen.

Surrender is not about giving up, but is a radical spiritual act of self-empowerment. It's about accepting our helplessness in any situation and letting go of the illusion of control, to trust in a higher power, whatever that means to you. It's about releasing the struggle against what we can't control and trusting in our inner divine connection.

Think of life as being on a boat. You let go of the oars and sail with the wind. You navigate, but the universe propels you, guiding you towards your best life. Can you imagine when the flight is canceled or you don't get the job, you'll be able to calmly take the necessary next steps without an emotional response?

Trust issues are the greatest obstacle to surrender. When individuals struggle to surrender due to a lack of trust, they may experience negative outcomes, reinforcing their belief that control is necessary. This can lead to feelings of isolation, anxiety, and a sense of powerlessness, continuing a negative feedback loop of resistance.

This need for control is at the root of most addiction issues. Step three of Alcoholics Anonymous' twelve-step program includes surrender, with their famous quote: "Let go and let God." The idea sounds simple, and can be, now that you're aware of it, but for those with trust issues, this process takes patience.

The whole point to surrendering to a higher power is that it's a spiritual act that allows us to tap into a limitless source of support we may never have experienced. **That act of trust makes us equal partners with the divine**, and the whole universe conspires to help us thrive.

Releasing control isn't always easy. It'll likely take time and practice to develop trust in the universe, like a gradual unclenching of the fist. But with each breath of acceptance, with each moment of letting go, a sense of peace washes over us, leading to more feelings of happiness. Every moment of surrender is a step towards freedom. As we let go, we'll notice our emotional burden lightening.

From there, we can practice self-acceptance. Accept that change is a constant, that outcomes are often beyond our grasp, that even our emotions and thoughts are transient gusts of wind. This doesn't mean passivity; it means facing life with open eyes and an open heart, ready to flow with the current, rather than against it. It's an active pursuit of inner peace. This change won't appear in meditation. We'll only see it in action when, one day, we notice how something that bothered us in the past no longer does.

This understanding of suffering and surrender doesn't negate external hardships. Remember, we're here to learn from experiencing those external challenging events. But we can still strive for justice and alleviate external suffering in the world, without allowing it to affect our inner peace. We may feel heartbreak for atrocities happening around the globe, or the harsh effects of climate change, but by letting go of control, we find a sense of peaceful balance that remains unshaken even amidst life's inevitable challenges.

DEEPER DIVES

1: Make a List of Triggers

Take out your journal, and list all the things that happened in the last week that made you angry, anxious, annoyed, or frustrated, as well as the reasons why. Then list out how you responded to each, and why. If you didn't respond at all, detail what was going on in your mind that kept you silent. How did you feel in your body?

2: Connecting Triggers to Childhood

Dwelling in the past accomplishes nothing, but it's important to look back at childhood to begin to make connections to current behavior. Start making an inventory of the most dramatic events or situations in your childhood. You remember them all. Did a parent have a substance abuse problem? Was it a single parent household? Were your emotional needs met? Did you feel loved? Was there sibling rivalry? Were you bullied? Take those stories and rewrite them with happier endings, where you have agency to say what needs to be said and are heard.

3: Discover What You Can Surrender

The best way to see surrender clearly defined is in black and white. Take a sheet of paper, and at the top left write, "Things I can control"; on the top right: "Things I can release to a higher power." Then, list everything you have control over in all aspects of your life: home, relationships, career, finances, spirituality, leisure, health. When you've completed the list, thoughtfully go over it again and see if anything on the left can be moved to the right.

You might find surrender easier at first with situations outside the home, since family can be so triggering. Just set surrender as a goal with no specific end date. Whether it takes six months, a year, two years, or longer doesn't matter, if growth is your intention.

4: Affirmations to Rewire the Brain for Trust

I've found affirmations to be one of the most effective methods to rewire the brain. Let's try to rewire yours to be more trusting of the universe. Sit back and close your eyes. Take three deep breaths, then repeat each phrase three times:

- "I am surrounded by love and support, seen and unseen."
- "I trust the universe to support me."

- "I let go of control and open myself to peace, with the guidance of a loving higher power. With each breath, I release fear and embrace the flow of life with an open heart."
- "I trust that the universe is unfolding perfectly, even when I cannot see the bigger picture."

Journal about the changes you experience.

3: ATTACHMENTS AND EXPECTATIONS

Our attachments can take many forms, from material possessions and relationships to intangible things like ideas, beliefs, and even the past. While these attachments can provide comfort and meaning, clinging to them too tightly creates an unnecessary opening to the pain of loss and the accompanying anxiety. Perhaps you've already experienced the constant worry of losing a prized possession, the stress of imagining your partner will leave you, or the bitterness of clinging to past pain and abuse. But it's a waste of precious time.

Many people have attachments to beliefs. Even when faced with concrete evidence proving them wrong, they continue to believe as they do. Flat Earthers are the perfect example. Our planet is unquestionably a globe, yet they insist it's not and produce altered data as fact. The question to ask is: Why do they have such an attachment to that belief? Why do they need for that falsehood to be true? Why do others hold attachments to religious beliefs or that we should all be vegans?

Clinging to nonsensical beliefs can be linked to underlying unresolved trauma responses, such as anxiety, paranoia, or magical thinking. These conditions distort an individual's perception of reality and make them more susceptible to believing in conspiracy theories. They're simply out of touch with reality. But why?

Firstly, a lack of trust in authority. If someone grew up with caretakers constantly breaking their trust, the need to create an alternate reality to survive can carry over to adulthood.

Secondly, the need for identity and community. Feeling like part of a unique group with special knowledge can be appealing. The Flat Earth community, while fringe, offers a sense of belonging and identity, especially for individuals who might feel marginalized or isolated in mainstream society.

And finally, fear of the unknown. Accepting the vastness and complexity of the universe can be daunting. The Flat Earth model, while unquestionably false, offers a simpler and more readily understandable explanation, providing a false sense of security and control.

In the 2008 housing crisis, I not only lost my house, but most of my savings. I was made painfully aware of not only my attachment to money, but also how tightly I clung to it to define my identity. During that time, I realized I had too much meaningless "stuff," and liquidated a three-bedroom house full of art, furniture, and objects down to a mere seven boxes. To this day, I live a rather minimalist life in a one-bedroom apartment, constantly eliminating things because of that experience.

Attachments to Expectations

One of the most common forms of attachments is to expectations. They're like mental blueprints, dictating how we "should" experience life. We expect vacations to be Instagram-worthy, relationships to be fairy tales with our partners able to anticipate our every need, and ourselves to be flawless. We expect the lights to go on when we flick the switch. We may have an expectation to be married by a certain age, have 2.5 kids, and live in a four-bedroom house with a swimming pool.

But we may also be subject to expectations placed upon us by others. Parents may expect their children to get perfect grades in school, become a doctor and marry well, and supply them with a house full of grandchildren. We're expected to attend every Sunday dinner and holiday and give gifts to everyone at Christmas, even if we don't want to. Trying to live up to expectations like those can be traumatizing.

We may have all sorts of expectations of our significant others based on nothing but our desires, rather than actual discussions with them. We believe everyone has the same upbringing as us and that our expectations are simply common sense. But that's far from true, and the inability to discuss expectations with a partner is a major reason why many relationships fail.

The character of Sheldon on the popular TV show *Big Bang Theory* comes off as neurotic, with his need for contracts for everything like a Roommate Agreement or a Relationship Agreement (when he finally gets a girlfriend). But I'd argue there's quite a bit of wisdom in this practice because, with contracts, all his expectations are laid out with nothing left to chance.

Unmet expectations feel like broken promises, even betrayal, etching lines of disappointment on our hearts. When dating, you might have the expectation that your text messages will be immediately answered. But how often does that happen? The stronger the attachment to that expectation, the deeper the disappointment is. The reality is, the delay may have nothing to do with us.

When I was eight years old, my birthday party had to be canceled due to weather. Although I'm a spring baby, we had a surprising several inches of snow that day and my out-of-town family couldn't make the hour drive. Well into adulthood, I was easily triggered when plans were canceled last minute, until I learned to surrender.

A great metaphor for life happens on reality television. If you've ever watched a food or fashion competition show, you'll know that when something goes wrong, contestants must either start over or pivot to work towards a new outcome. Often, they are forced to create something extraordinary they never thought possible. The game of life is change. Those who cling to specific expectations can't pivot as the game changes in front of them. Instead of suffering over how we thought things should've been, we can learn to accept the reality of the present moment and cultivate gratitude for what is. Developing the ability to let go of expectations truly is a superpower.

You can go as far as to eliminate the word *should* completely from your vocabulary. When I find myself thinking of things I "should" do, I immediately insert the word "not" after, freeing myself from that judgment. When speaking to another person, I suggest something like, "You'd benefit by doing that task," or "You can learn something from watching that documentary." The same applies for inner self talk; I always look for the specific benefit that comes from *choosing* to do something.

Taking Steps to Freedom

The first step to freedom is—yes, you guessed it—gaining awareness. Many of us live our lives mindless of the causes of our suffering. But what if we start to observe our thoughts and emotions without judgment?

This requires practice and self-compassion. With each baby step, you'll shed a layer of burden, revealing a lighter, more resilient version of yourself. You can discover a deeper peace, a freedom that rests not on external things, but on the unshakeable foundation of your own inner being. Let's allow ourselves to be open to the surprise of a quiet evening bringing more joy than a canceled party. Appreciate the unexpected connection with a stranger instead of focusing on the failed date. Cultivate gratitude for the present moment, not for how it "should" be or could've been, but for how it simply is.

Difference Between Practicing Detachment and Apathy

You might be thinking, "If I'm detached from everything, doesn't that mean I don't care?"

We only need attachments to build families. Everything else is negotiable. Detachment is a spiritual practice where we acknowledge our desires and attachments but choose not to be controlled by them. Detachment is not about becoming cold and uncaring. It's about letting go of what we can't control or what no longer serves us.

Practicing detachment empowers us to act with intention. It allows us to appreciate the beauty of impermanence and find inner peace. When we are present, we can truly appreciate things without possessiveness. We're detached from the outcome—we're free.

Scientifically, detachment can be linked to emotional regulation. A June 2013 study by Shian-Ling Keng, Moria J Smoski, and Clive J Robins, published by the National Institutes of Health, shows that mindfulness practices that promote detachment activate brain regions associated with self-awareness, and reduce activity in areas linked to emotional reactivity. This allows for a more balanced perspective and wiser decision-making.

Apathy, on the other hand, is a state of indifference and lack of motivation. It's a passive withdrawal from life, often accompanied by a diminished ability to feel emotions. Unlike detachment, apathy isn't a conscious choice; it's often a symptom of depression, burnout, or trauma. Apathy can significantly impair a person's well-being, leaving us disconnected and uninterested, while detachment allows us to engage with the world from a place of inner peace.

Even the most enlightened of us can experience setbacks, as spiritual teacher Ram Dass explains in his movie, *Becoming Nobody*. Dass had a rider in his contract specifying that his hosting venues supply a certain type of microphone. Upon arriving at one location, he found they didn't have the required microphone and became angry. But possessing self-awareness, he was able to quickly catch himself and realize that the tests of attachments and expectations never end.

With each awareness and gentle release of an attachment, we discover a deeper freedom, a lightness of being that allows us to truly embrace the wonder of this fleeting, ever-changing life. When we're not wasting all that energy on suffering, there's more time for satisfaction in life. If we can open our hearts and accept the unknown, we'll discover the unburdened joy that awaits us.

DEEPER DIVES

1: Exploring Attachments to Your Identity

Allow yourself to experiment with the possibilities of your physical expression with a little makeover. This doesn't have to be drastic. It could be as simple as going to a different hair stylist or barber. I rarely go to the same barber twice, so as not to get in a rut with my appearance. Or if you don't style it, try that for a change. A few highlights or a streak of blue. Small changes in our appearance feel huge.

Journal about the horror and resistance you feel to everything I just suggested. Take special note of where and how you feel it in your body.

Looking beyond your hair, do you always wear the same style or color of clothes? Are you one of those people who only wears black? Does everything have to be designer or brand name? Do you know why you always dress the same (besides it being comfortable)? Get yourself a couple items new to you. Thrift shops are great for these types of experiments.

Journal about the panic or discomfort you're feeling right now about doing that and where you feel it comes from. Again, write about what's going on in your body.

2: Challenge Your Beliefs

List the people, institutions, or aspects of yourself you don't trust, and explore where you're lacking in identity or a sense of community.

3: Discover the Expectations Placed on You

Make a list of all the expectations you feel were placed on you by parents, siblings, teachers, society, coworkers, friends, and so on. Explore how each situation makes you feel. You can dig deeper by writing about how they might be connected to an unpleasant childhood experience.

4: Create an Expectation Inventory

You've made a list of expectations placed on you; now, try making an expectation inventory for each area of your life. Try to be as honest as possible. Consider all eight areas: career, home, love life, finances, leisure activities, spiritual development, friends/family, and health. Choose three and write about what you expect from them. Make this a daily exploration of expectations to continually explore all eight areas to gain deeper awareness. Is any of this in your control?

4: THE ILLUSION OF POLARITY

Why is the human experience framed by a sense of duality—good versus bad, light versus dark, joy versus sorrow? This binary lens is a construct of the ego, which thrives on control and separation. The ego needs that "otherness"—the good, the bad, the beautiful, the ugly—to define itself.

Spiritual teachers and psychologists alike agree that true reality, and a path to inner peace, lies beyond these perceived polarities. The truth is that absolutely nothing is inherently good or bad. As the Buddha said, "Everything is what is, and not what it seems."

When the mind sees things in duality, as pleasure and pain, good and bad, love and hate, it creates conflict and misery. To reduce the conflict and misery in our lives, we must reduce or eliminate that perception of duality.

Let's use temperature as an example. At one end of the spectrum, we have scorching heat, and on the other, biting cold. Yes, those are opposites, but only because we negate every degree between them that causes the separation. The same applies to love and hate, sorrow and joy, light and dark. The only difference is the space between them that we refuse to acknowledge unifies them.

Judging situations as good or bad is subjective and often based on temporary desires or ego-driven expectations. The good situations are satisfying, and the bad ones are challenging soul lessons in which our ego would rather not engage. Every moment simply is, without inherent meaning.

Does everything we first judge as good or bad stay that way? Once the fear is gone, the new can be judged as good. A new boss, moving, rejection of any kind. A missed opportunity can open a new door; a heartbreak might lead to profound self-discovery.

Before I moved to my current apartment, I was living in a part of the city where I could step outside and find a grocery store, Chinese food, and dry cleaner right across the street. Then I moved downtown by the river and had to walk a quarter mile to the nearest store. I absolutely hated it and walked with resentment to get a coffee. Now, six years later, I prefer the more relaxed nature of my neighborhood and can't see myself living in a super urban environment again.

The reverse is also true: things labeled good can turn bad. Every relationship that ended started out "good." If the label can change, then the perception of the event can change, too.

Ice cream is good until we want to lose weight. Is ice cream inherently "bad"? Absolutely not! It is what it is. But now it doesn't align with our current goals. And what happens the moment we label it as bad? Guilt and resistance rear their ugly heads, making that forbidden pint even more tempting, disconnecting us further from self-love.

Say we planned a major outdoor event, with caterers and equipment rentals, but on that day, it rains heavily, leading to cancellation and a significant financial loss. What if this became a learning opportunity? Instead of labeling the weather and the cancellation, what if we shift our perspective to an opportunity to learn about flexibility, crisis management, and releasing attachments to expectations? Maybe this experience will open doors to better planning and resilience in future projects. It could be the portal to a whole bunch of growth that wouldn't have been possible without the rain.

Why do we automatically make these ego judgments that don't serve our souls? Because unresolved childhood trauma has conditioned us to respond in a desperate effort to never relive those experiences. The good news is that this constant judgment and classifying of the world around us is something we can learn to control. **How we respond to something is always within our control.** But, again, we must first gain awareness of how it operates.

"But Steve," you might ask, "what about truly heinous acts? Abuse, violence, human atrocities—surely those are inherently bad, right?" And here's where it gets a little messy and where your ego might throw a tantrum. Because the truth is, even these seemingly "unforgivable" actions which cause immense suffering have no inherent meaning, only the meaning that we give them. Those feelings of sadness or anger are only the meaning we place on them. Spiritual growth is the ability to finally accept that they are what they are: challenging soul lessons. I recognize this is a controversial position that can take a while to fully comprehend.

Accepting the illusion of polarity doesn't mean we become emotionless robots or abandon ethical responsibility. This acceptance isn't about condoning harmful actions, but rather about recognizing that even darkness holds the potential for meaningful transformation.

When we choose to embrace the wholeness of an event or experience without judgment or need to control, we see the full spectrum of what's really happening, from light to shadow or from joy to sorrow, unlocking a deep well of inner peace. When we become mere observers of the reactive world around us, it's a clear sign we're living in 5D consciousness.

Happiness comes out of cultivating a deep understanding that everything is exactly as it is, perfect in its imperfection. **If blessings can become soul lessons, and soul lessons can become blessings, then everything that happens to us is a blessing.**

By heightening awareness of the illusion of polarity, we can break free from the cycle of judgment and suffering to cultivate the acceptance, balance, and compassion required to reconnect to self-love.

DEEPER DIVES

1: Reveal Your Good and Bad Labels

Open your journal, and on the top left side of the page write "Good Things." On the right, "Bad Things." List as many as you can for each of the eight areas of your life (home, family, finances, relationships/friends, work, leisure, health, spirituality) you've labeled good or bad. Then, describe how you came to that decision and how it makes you feel.

2: Finding the Blessing

Go back to your original list of good and bad and reflect to see how they are what they are, neither good nor bad. Find a challenging life lesson learned in the aftermath of a "bad" experience. Find a blessing in the good things to be grateful for every day which you may have forgotten about.

3: Imprinting Non-Duality onto the Subconscious

Mantras are a powerful way to manifest desired realities. In this instance, find a quiet moment and repeat phrases throughout the day like, "Everything is as it is," or "There is no good or bad, only cause and effect," or "Everything is a blessing." Allowing these mantras to seep into your awareness will begin to change your polar perceptions.

4: Catching the Judgment in the Act

Heightened awareness of your thought process quickens the acceptance of the truth that we live in a non-dual world. When something new happens, see if you can catch yourself before or in the act of labeling it good or bad.

5: FORGIVENESS

The transformative power of forgiveness may be one of the most difficult steps of the 11 Insights to master. I invite you to treat yourself kindly and with patience as we explore the controversial topic of not just forgiving others, but the all-crucial act of self-forgiveness. Both are required to pave the way to healing trauma and reclaiming self-love.

There are many misconceptions about what forgiveness is and isn't. Most people see forgiveness as weakness and a free pass that condones bad behavior. When we've been harmed in a way that disconnects us from self-love, it's difficult to let go, especially if the person hasn't been punished for their transgressions to our satisfaction. Holding onto the anger feels like the only punishment they'll receive. It's also difficult to let go if there's some type of unconsciously perceived benefit. A grudge can seem like armor that protects us against the offending person.

The Poison Pill

Holding a grudge is like taking poison and hoping it kills your enemies. When you hold a grudge or resentment, it becomes an energetic poison in the body beyond your control. Don't just take it from me; the power of forgiveness plays such a significant role in healthy physical well-being that the renowned Mayo Clinic addresses it on their website.

Holding onto anger and resentment causes anxiety and depression and can wreak havoc on your body. Anger triggers the fight-or-flight response, flooding our bodies with stress hormones like cortisol and adrenaline. This is helpful in short bursts, but chronic anger can lead to headaches, insomnia, and digestive issues.

Chronic stress also increases inflammation, which is linked to various health problems, such as heart disease and diabetes, not to mention enflaming the immune system, making us more susceptible to illness. Doctors gladly prescribe pills to ease the symptoms that will never cure these issues; hard spiritual work is necessary.

Reconciliation Not Required

Another misconception is that forgiveness requires reconciliation. That the people we forgive must be part of our lives. Because it's often family members who hurt us the deepest, a path to a happier life with them back in it can sometimes be terrifying. Rest assured, reconciliation is not necessary, but forgiveness is required for everyone who left us in the dust, dead or alive—friend or co-worker, ex-partner, or a toxic ex-spouse.

There's a reason eighteenth century poet Alexander Pope coined the phrase, "To err is human; to forgive divine." Forgiveness isn't simply letting someone off the hook for their wrongdoing, but a powerful spiritual shift of perspective of the situation: a conscious release of anger, resentment, and the desire for revenge, realizing your ever-loving soul is helpless to express its true self while trapped behind a grudge.

Forgiveness is a display of strength, opening doors to understanding, empathy, and even compassion for the ones who hurt you. Compassion for our lives' villains might sound impossible at this point in your journey. But because we know people treat others the way they feel about themselves, we can begin to break through our unresolved trauma by understanding the awful things that happened are rooted in the offender acting out their own unresolved trauma.

In my story in Part I, I talked about an abusive landlord. I felt a deep hate for her, but with time I healed to the point of loving and having compassion for the abusive childhood she must've experienced to become such a miserable person. Without her, I wouldn't have had such a strong need to grow spiritually. In a sense, she's a soulmate who helped me grow as a person.

Holding onto resentment means there's not yet closure, and without closure we can't move forward. This leaves us stuck in the past, rotting away from the inside out. The ability to forgive also helps us have healthier relationships, which in turn brings more happiness.

Why do we cling to all this anger and resentment? Because it's stored in energetic cords. People are connected by invisible threads of energy, formed through interactions and relationships, transmitting both positive and negative energy between people. Deep love, shared trauma, or even unresolved arguments can create lasting energetic attachments. While healthy cords nourish relationships by fostering empathy and understanding, unhealthy cords drain our energy, create emotional dependence, and prevent closure, thus hindering personal and spiritual growth.

Cutting that energetic chord greatly lessens its intensity and will help us gain a new perspective on the situation that can aid in the process of forgiveness. This cord-cutting process is described in the Deeper Dives.

Forgiving Yourself

While forgiving others is a crucial first step, the truly transformative act lies in self-forgiveness. For some of us this may be difficult but, if we can stay with it for at least a month, we'll see growth.

Our inherent self-criticism is an evolutionary trait rooted in the need for group survival. We're hardwired to be vigilant about mistakes, often exceeding healthy boundaries of critique. It's important to remember that this self-criticism isn't personal or a reflection of our flaws. Some of us are wired by trauma to be more sensitive and prone to catastrophic thinking that turns minor missteps into major dramas.

Your ego's now shouting, "I'm supposed to forgive myself for someone abusing *me*? Ridiculous! That'll never happen." But when *we* hurt someone, we can feel guilt, and when they hurt us, we feel shame. We might not even be conscious of the guilt and shame operating inside. The core of self-forgiveness addresses them both. For guilt, we must accept that making mistakes is part of being human. Mistakes are learning opportunities, not indictments. For shame, we must embrace the fact that negative feelings about ourselves are limiting beliefs not of our creation. We can learn to replace that self-judgment with acceptance of our entire imperfect selves. **Fundamentally, self-forgiveness is about nothing more than releasing the anger, guilt and shame operating subconsciously.**

A friend of mine struggled with self-forgiveness after distracted driving led to a serious accident. He was consumed by guilt and shame. Through a difficult yet transformative process, he learned to forgive himself, recognizing the accident as a tragic mistake but not a reflection of his entire character. This shift not only helped him heal emotionally but also inspired him to advocate for road safety, turning his pain into purpose.

A great way to start forgiving yourself is to start with something not so serious or painful. This will open the door to allowing your ego to forgive yourself for the most heinous things that happened to you.

Hopefully, you now have a clearer idea of what forgiveness is and how to reduce the intense feelings of resentment. It's all about reframing the pain by asking ourselves, "What have I learned from this experience?" When we can begin to see all negative life experiences as steps on our spiritual journey, we reframe them in ways our ego can surrender to more easily.

Forgiveness will be an ongoing challenge, but the rewards are immense. By forgiving others and ourselves, we shed burdens, embrace self-love, and open ourselves to a future filled with peace, acceptance, and the freedom to truly thrive.

DEEPER DIVES

1: Get in Touch with Your Body

Journal about physical and mental health issues you're currently dealing with and let your soul fill in details through automatic writing focusing on how they're connected to past toxic people, traumatic events, and questionable institutions.

2: Who Do We Hate?

Make a list of people you hold grudges against. Dead or alive. Past or present. Known or unknown. The third-grade bully or a celebrity you can't stand, or even your religious faith. As you compile the list, observe the feelings in your body and where you feel them. Once the list is compiled, meditate on each, one by one, and allow the feelings to leave your body, breathing deeply into those troubled areas. Repeat this as needed.

3: The Function of Your Grudges

Take another look at your list, and journal about the three strongest hurts in your life right now. Use the automatic writing technique to discover why you're holding on to these resentments and how you benefit from them.

4: Defining the Lesson

Since all the pain and suffering we experience in life are soul lessons, we can begin the healing process by reframing past events as such. Take out your journal and continue working with the three major hurts you're living with and ask your soul, through automatic writing, what the lesson is to be learned and how you've grown or can grow.

5: Cord Cutting Psychic Surgery

This is a meditative visualization. Close your eyes and take three deep breaths, holding a few seconds after inhaling. Let's start with one person you hold a grudge against. Visualize them standing in front of you. Ask to be shown the energetic cords between you. The dark ones are negative, and the light ones are positive—if they exist. They may appear as simple lines or an intricate web connecting to different parts of the body. Thank the person for the valuable lessons they've taught you, and share with them that holding this energy no longer serves you. Visualize golden scissors cutting the dark cord or cords, and watch the person float away. Since we don't want the possibility of reconnecting, visualize your half of the cord being pulled from your body, a beautiful white light coming in to fill the void and heal the wound. Repeat if there is more than one connection.

6: Write a Letter of Forgiveness

Write a letter, to yourself or someone else, acknowledging the hurt and offering the gift of forgiveness. If you're writing it to someone else, you don't have to send it, but can put it in an envelope and burn it in a safe place.

- Shame and guilt often involve distorted thinking, so include what facts are true about the situation. How are your feelings about it different from the facts? Who was responsible for the event? What were the circumstances beyond your influence? Reframe the narrative to place the blame appropriately, releasing yourself from the burden.

- List all the "should" statements about this situation. "I should've said or done something I didn't." Are these expectations fair or helpful? If not, what might be a more balanced perspective?

6: COMPARE AND DESPAIR

We've all been there. We compare our lives, our bodies, our achievements to an endless parade of others' highlight reels, real or imagined, and inevitably find ourselves falling short. This cycle of compare and despair is a soul-zapping thief, robbing us of joy, self-love, and connection.

This need for comparison is also an evolutionary trait rooted in our DNA. Early humans needed to assess their social standing within the group for survival and reproduction. Comparing hunting prowess, resourcefulness, and social skills would've helped individuals determine their place in the hierarchy. Since we learn through observation and comparison, comparing ourselves to others helps us gauge our own abilities to develop a sense of competence.

Knowing that comparison is hardwired into us, how can it also be the thief of joy? The pain arises from the childhood root of comparison, when we're made to feel that who we are wasn't enough to be loved. Whether a parent was emotionally abusive, asking, "Why can't you be more like the neighbor kid?" or when we wish we looked like the models in magazines, comparison leads to disastrous results, creating anxiety, depression, shame, envy, self-criticism, and lack of self-worth.

Everywhere we turn in our high-tech society, there are overwhelming opportunities for us to compare ourselves to others. For example, we might find ourselves scrolling through social media, noticing a friend's promotion at work while we feel stuck in our job. Or perhaps at a family gathering, we overhear relatives praising another's parenting style. Even leisure activities aren't immune; we notice how others spend their weekends traveling or pursuing hobbies, which can make our own choices seem mundane in comparison.

We may assume friends, or even fictional couples have relationships naturally easier and more harmonious than our own. However, some of the most unhappy people post on social media, putting up a front to fool the world. We may also fail to see the behind-the-scenes effort involved in sustaining a healthy bond, as all relationships require work, compromise, and navigating challenges.

We might even be comparing where we are on our spiritual journey with where others are. I've been doing this work for twenty years and still feel I've only scratched the surface because, as I grow and learn, I continuously discover other vast aspects of spirituality. In fact, science supports the notion that it's humanly possible to compare just about anything that someone else has with what we have.

We're each unique souls on Earth for specific lessons and missions that happen at different stages of life. What seems enviable in someone else's life might simply be a chapter in their book, not yours.

Ending Comparison

The path to freedom lies not in striving to be someone else, but in embracing the magnificent mess that is you. **Yes, you can be a masterpiece and work-in-progress simultaneously.** Believe it or not, you are as perfect today as you will be after going through massive growth. Self-acceptance is the antidote to the poison of comparison.

When you reconnect to self-love and develop self-acceptance, you'll find no one compares to your unique brand of wonderful. To discover your unique qualities is a superpower.

How do you begin to rewrite the narrative from "why can't I be more like..." to "I am enough, exactly as I am"? There are three steps to the process:

1. Gain self-awareness.
2. Reframe the thought.
3. Celebrate your uniqueness.

Comparison for Growth

Comparison doesn't have to be a dead end. When used wisely, it can be fuel for growth. It can be a tool to see our own potential, set goals, and appreciate the uniqueness you bring to the world.

For example, looking at people who have achieved your goals can be incredibly motivating. It shows us what's possible and can light a fire within us to strive for more. Research the steps they took to achieve the goal: where they went to school, how long they've been practicing, which habits, skills, or strategies they adopted and then adapt these to your own journey. How can we use the comparison to stretch and evolve to become the best versions of ourselves?

Pop singer Ed Sheeran is proud to let people know he was an awful singer and musician when he started playing on the streets in England. But he loved what he did and kept learning and training to become the chart topper he is today.

It's also important to embrace a vital resource on our journey to self-acceptance and freedom from comparison: the strength found in like-minded community support. While individual effort is crucial, being part of a supportive network—whether it's friends, family, specialized groups, or communities focused on personal growth—can significantly bolster our journey.

Remember, the goal in these spaces is not to find new grounds for comparison, but to build connections, share experiences, and uplift one another. The combined power of personal effort and community support can truly transform your relationship with yourself and others.

The most important takeaway is that **the only person we need to be better than is the person we were yesterday**. Instead of comparing our current self to others, we need to compare ourselves to our past selves. This allows us to appreciate how far we've come. Especially on a spiritual journey, we can find satisfaction in daily growth.

It's a journey, not a destination, and requires daily practice. There will be days when despair seeps back in, but with each step, with each conscious choice, we build the muscle of self-acceptance. We can see the beauty in others, not as a threat, but as a testament to the magnificent diversity of life.

DEEPER DIVES

1: Affirmation of Worthiness

This mantra is borrowed from the spiritual teachings of Bashar, a spiritual entity channeled by Daryl Anka. Say this three times when you wake and before going to bed: "I am who I am and that is enough."

2: Self-Worth Reflection

Think about one recent instance where you compared yourself to someone else. How did it make you feel about your own worth? Write down these feelings and then counter each negative thought with a positive affirmation about yourself. For instance, if you felt envious of a friend's new job, remind yourself of a professional achievement or skill you're proud of. This exercise is a step towards recognizing and reversing the narrative in your head.

3: Childhood Comparison Reflection

Reflect and journal on how comparison played a role in your childhood. Did you feel compared to others by family or teachers? How has that shaped your adult comparisons? Write down one childhood comparison experience and how it impacts you now.

4: Write a Love Letter to Your Younger Self

Write a letter to your younger self, offering compassion and understanding for what they went through, and affirming their worth just as they are. This can help you start healing those old wounds.

5: Identify Your Strengths

This exercise will help you not only catch yourself in the act of comparing and despairing but also reframe the comparison to help you understand how your uniqueness is a superpower.

In your journal, list what you're good at. What makes you smile? What challenges have you overcome? Then, list where in the eight life areas you believe you fall short (home, finance, spirituality, love, friends, leisure, etc.).

Now, challenge the comparison: Is it based on truth or illusion? Are you comparing your entire journey to someone else's carefully curated snapshot or an unrealistic social standard? Are you comparing your looks to photoshopped magazine models? Remind yourself that everyone has their own story, their own battles, their own path.

Shift your focus. Instead of comparing, celebrate your own unique strengths, talents, and experiences. What makes you, YOU? What gifts do you bring to the world? Write down these qualities. We're all good at something. Let them be a beacon of self-love in the stormy seas of comparison.

7: BOUNDARIES

A crucial, yet often difficult, aspect of well-being is personal boundaries. When they've been crossed, we feel a pit in our stomach, a wave of anxiety, or that inexplicable drain after being around someone. Where do those emotions go when we don't have the inner strength to express how we feel? They get trapped inside to disrupt our inner peace, and we may use drugs, alcohol, sex, and food to numb the pain.

Self-love and boundaries are two sides of the same coin. A heart brimming with self-worth naturally constructs strong, clear boundaries with people, protecting its precious space and time, only allowing in those who uplift and make them feel good. Conversely, a deficit of self-love leaves us vulnerable, desperate to be liked, and allowing weak or nonexistent boundaries that lead to negativity, people pleasing, and manipulation, all of which further disconnect us from self-love.

We can't escape all boundary-breakers. But that's only because we unconsciously allow their transgressions to avoid feeling unloved or abandoned.

Six Types of Boundaries

There are six different types of invisible boundaries to be fully conscious of to reconnect to self-love: physical, emotional, mental, spiritual, material, and time.

> **Physical boundaries** relate to our physical space and our bodies. They encompass how comfortable we are with physical touch, how much personal space we need, and even what we're comfortable wearing in different situations. Do you know people who stand too close? Do you feel uncomfortable around friends who are huggers?

Emotional boundaries are about protecting our emotional well-being. They prevent us from giving or accepting unsolicited advice, blaming or accepting blame, and giving or receiving criticism. They protect us from feeling guilty for someone else's negative feelings or problems and taking others' comments personally. Healthy emotional boundaries require a clear understanding of our feelings and our responsibilities to ourselves and others. A few examples include mothers-in-law who give unsolicited advice on how to raise the children, people who want you to feel bad because they're having a bad day, and people who regularly criticize your weight or appearance.

Mental boundaries are about protecting our thoughts and opinions. They protect personal beliefs, choices, ideas, and values, and help us respect one another's different viewpoints. Recall the people who think you're crazy for trying to improve yourself in any way, or who tell you your dreams in life aren't realistic, or who claim there's only one right way to do something.

Sexual boundaries are about protecting our sexual desires and safety around intimacy. They protect the right to consent, to communicate sexual preferences and limits, and to honest knowledge about a partner's sexual history. This also means respecting an intimate partner's boundaries. People who've experienced sexual harassment, abuse, and molestation have had these boundaries violated.

Material boundaries relate to possessions and finances. They involve not feeling pressured to lend money or belongings and protect the right to spend money as we choose. We don't have to lend the neighbor the lawn mower or a friend $100 til they get paid, knowing they'll never pay us back.

Time boundaries are about protecting our time from being wasted. They involve learning to say no to requests that overload us, and scheduling time for ourselves and our own priorities. There are only twenty-four hours in a day, so if picking a casual friend up at the airport isn't how we want to spend two of them, then we simply say no.

Relatable examples include if guests overstay their welcome at dinner or for the weekend (that's both a physical and time boundary violation) or lending the car to a friend who brings it back late (which violates material and time boundaries.)

Our time has value, just like we do, and when we connect to self-love, we can command respect for all our boundaries.

Why Boundaries May Be Weak

Many of us grow up learning that setting boundaries means being selfish or unkind. However, healthy boundaries are the highest form of self-respect and a foundation for strong relationships. Understanding this helps us see the importance of reevaluating the boundary lessons we learned as children.

Childhood is fertile ground for disrespected boundaries. Parents can violate our mental and emotional boundaries by being overly critical, demanding, or intrusive. Maybe they violated our time and physical boundaries, being absent and neglectful, forcing us to navigate a confusing world alone. These early violating experiences become blueprints for troubling adult interactions that hinder our self-esteem and ability to safeguard our personal space. We become desperate to maintain connections, even at the expense of our mental health.

This absence of healthy boundaries acts like a slow poison, seeping into every aspect of life. We become people-pleasers, sacrificing our needs for approval. We say "yes" when we scream "no" inside. Or we fear conflict and agree to anything simply to avoid it. Either way, the self-betrayal we feel fulfilling someone else's desires instead of our own creates more repressed emotions and can become the breeding ground for addictions to reduce the emotional impact.

This sets the stage for adult struggles, impacting our interactions and our self-worth. We will never realize without reflection; we allow toxic people in our lives because they subconsciously remind us of what we know. That's a trauma bond. It's familiar, and familiar is comfortable for the ego, despite it being toxic. Even in domestic abuse situations there are symbiotic, or balancing factors, where past traumas attract two people together. That's why learning to build and maintain healthy boundary walls is crucial.

TV and movies normalize boundary breaking. Jokes about weight, jobs, or sexuality are often made at the expense of a character who just takes the insults without rebuttal. When it happens to us in real life, we're supposed to accept abusive insults as harmless teasing. We're left without role models on how to effectively handle boundary breakers.

Creating and Enforcing New Boundaries

It probably comes as no surprise that the key to establishing new boundaries is first and foremost awareness. Power lies in first recognizing that our boundaries exist, even if they're currently blurry. There's likely no awareness of boundaries in a trauma bond relationship like domestic abuse or narcissism.

With all that painful self-awareness, we can begin the challenging task to construct healthy new boundaries. This requires patience and likely won't happen overnight. If you're worried about conflict, remember that setting boundaries is about protecting your well-being, not causing arguments. Conflict might arise, but it's often short-lived with those who truly belong in your life. It can even lead to healthier relationships. Feeling guilty? Recognize that this guilt is a conditioned response or a survival personality trait and not a reflection of doing something wrong. **The only people who will protest your new boundaries are those currently bene-fiting from your lack of them.**

Fear Is Normal

This process can be scary and painful, especially with loved ones. To over-come these fears, start small. Practice setting boundaries in low-stakes situations where the risk of conflict is minimal, to build your confidence. Next time you're at a restaurant and the food you're served is not as ordered, or simply tastes bad, try politely sending it back instead of sitting there pretending it's okay.

Daring to set boundaries is about having the courage to love ourselves, even when we risk disappointing others. It's natural to worry about others' reactions or feel guilty for saying no, but these feelings can't deter us from looking after our mental and emotional health.

Setting boundaries is responsible self-care. The clearer we can commu-nicate our boundaries, the more we respect ourselves and teach others to do the same.

Use Direct and Clear Communication

Focus on expressing feelings without guilt or blame. Simply and clearly explain the boundary that was crossed and how it made you feel. Using "I" statements—and never "you"—helps avoid accusations and conflict. For example, "I felt disrespected when..." Be specific about the behavior and the desired change, such as, "Going forward, I'd appreciate it if..." When some-one asks too much of your time, you can respond with, "Let me check my schedule and get back to you." This gives you space to evaluate whether you can commit. "I appreciate your request, but I can't do that because…" Adding "I don't want to" is perfectly acceptable, too. If they show no compassion, that tells you they're likely someone who doesn't belong in your life.

Consequences for Violations

Be clear about the consequences of boundary violations. This isn't a threat, but a statement of self-care. For example, "I feel disrespected when you call after 10 p.m. In the future, I won't be answering calls that late so I can get enough sleep." This could also involve limiting communication, ending the activity you were doing together, or taking a break from the relationship entirely. Again, emphasize that the consequences are meant to protect you, not punish them.

Prepare for Pushback

People who have violated boundaries in the past might try to guilt-trip, manipulate, or argue. Developing a calm and assertive response like, "I understand you're disappointed, but this boundary is important to me," greatly helps the process. If we give in when they push back, it weakens our resolve. This might be difficult initially, but consistency is key.

Prioritize Self-Care

Setting new boundaries can be emotionally draining. Make sure you're taking care of yourself throughout the process. This might involve relaxation techniques, spending time with supportive people by joining a support group, or seeking professional help if needed. Talking it through with someone you trust can provide valuable encouragement and perspective.

Goodbye, Boundary Breakers

Sometimes, the ultimate act of self-love is letting go. If someone repeatedly disregards our boundaries, despite our best efforts, it highlights a deeper incompatibility and it might be time to create distance. The last resort of going no-contact can be a heart-wrenching decision and doesn't mean we won't grieve or miss them. But after a grieving period, when we reap the rewards of living a life with healthy boundaries, all the difficult work will be worth it.

Staying in a toxic relationship, be it with family, friend or work, is like drowning in quicksand. **All the hard work and sleepless nights on the path to happiness is useless if we remain surrounded by the same toxic people.** Our happiness cannot be a casualty of another's disregard. If our saying no to someone gets a raging, or worse, violent, response, then the relationship is unfixable, and you might require professional help from a therapist to step away.

I had to let several family members go from my life because of how poorly they treated me. I couldn't do it until I reconnected to self-love, but then it was clear I had no choice, and I had absolutely nothing to lose. My life has truly blossomed since letting those people go. I get positive news on all fronts almost daily, but most importantly, I no longer have those repressed feelings of having to deal with their toxicity that I numbed with alcohol and marijuana. I don't have urges to imbibe in anything, because the pain the substances were masking is gone.

The people who really care about you won't have a problem as you set new boundaries, so consider adding positive reinforcement. When a person respects your new boundaries, acknowledge and appreciate it with a "thank you."

As we gain more self-love, feelings of guilt, conflict, and so on dissipate. Life will be different. We may find ourselves in a new job with supportive coworkers or making new friends who admire our strength.

The road to healthy boundaries is a journey of self-discovery. It's about reclaiming your power, honoring your needs, and saying "yes" only to your own well-being. With every new boundary we set, we pave the way for a life filled with respect, peace, and self-love. Step into your power, build your boundaries, and watch your life blossom within its sacred space. Boundaries are our superpower. Claim them, protect them, and watch life flourish.

DEEPER DIVES

1: Identify the Boundary Violators

In your journal, start listing people in your life who disrespect your boundaries and how that makes you feel. Who can you not say no to, or who doesn't take no for an answer? This includes those who tell you how to live your life, make derogatory statements about your appearance, demand your time to help them but offer nothing in return. That friend, family member, or co-worker who's always late; someone who's constantly guilt-tripping you into doing favors; a friend who's always borrowing your clothes or asking for money; and the boss who tells you at the last minute you have to stay late. These are all examples of violations of your boundaries. Identify which of the six types of boundaries they cross.

2: Childhood Reflection

Journal about childhood experiences where your input was dismissed or decisions were made without your involvement, such as being forced into an activity you disliked. How does this manifest in your current life?

3: Identifying Trauma Bonds

Trauma bond relationships are often chaotic, with no sound basis for their being. List some of the people you have chaotic relationships with, if any, and list the things you like about them, why you enjoy spending time with them, and how they improve your life. If you find yourself unable to make a positive list and feel you're together because of sexual attraction, or you can't quite put a finger on the feeling, it's likely a trauma bond and the relationship needs to be reconsidered to heal.

Accepting difficult self-truths is the hardest part of spiritual growth and another opportunity to practice self-forgiveness. As mentioned earlier, the unresolved trauma that makes someone a People Pleaser or Doormat can also make them unintentionally disrespect the boundaries of others. Remember, this isn't anyone's fault, but rather that behavior developed as part of a survival personality. Do any of the previously mentioned boundary violations relate to you?

4: Taking A Hard Look at Ourselves

Journal about the behaviors you have that possibly overstep someone else's boundaries. Do you overshare your life with strangers? What void might this be filling? What illusory benefit is there to this behavior?

5: Practice Makes Progress

Setting and enforcing new boundaries can take time and practice, so let's rehearse what you might say to the boundary breakers in your life. Above, I've offered a few examples. Look back at your list of violators and write a few boundary-reestablishing statements, and what the consequences of future violations might be. Say them out loud to a mirror. For those who demand your time, also practice saying "no" out loud in the mirror.

6: How Do You Mask the Pain?

Some of us soothe the pain of boundary violations with drugs or alcohol, binge eating, or other addictions. Some of us may withdraw or engage in reckless behaviors. In your journal, use automatic writing to explore how some of your most painful boundary violations you've written about contributed to any addictive or isolating behaviors.

8: POWER OF LOSS

Loss is a universal experience. From relationship breakups to deaths, loss takes us on a rollercoaster of emotions and leaves us questioning ourselves and our world.

We spend much of our lives striving to avoid loss, oblivious to the fact that loss happens as a means for us to learn and grow. In its own raw, painful way, it holds the key to unlocking stronger, more fulfilled versions of ourselves. Loss closes a door so another can open.

A stone sculptor doesn't begin with a masterpiece. They chisel away at a chunk of stone, revealing the hidden beauty within. Loss, too, can feel like the universe wielding a chisel on our very souls. Though loss strips away the familiar and the toxic, leaving us exposed and vulnerable, in the end, our spiritual growth can be the masterpiece that comes of it.

The main reason loss is excruciating is because of our deep attachments. Our egos are shattered. We feel sad and angry, off balance, and need to establish a new footing in life. These are the same unpleasant growing pains that happen on a spiritual growth journey and why times of great loss are the perfect opportunities to begin looking inward for solace. We've already discussed the important role of surrendering what we can't control to a higher power.

As I mentioned earlier, when my dog and soulmate, Mossi, crossed the rainbow bridge after thirteen years, my world collapsed. Waking up felt meaningless. I cried, I wailed and then, amidst the pain, I stumbled upon a phrase that became my mantra: "post-traumatic growth," and started my conscious grieving journey of transformation.

What Is Post-Traumatic Growth?

The concept of *post-traumatic growth* originates from psychological research and refers to the transformative change that individuals experience as a result of battling through the adversity of loss. But it's also analogous to spiritual growth and reconnecting to self-love.

This growth isn't about bouncing back to where we were before our world was turned upside down but about using the struggle as a springboard to learn how to reach new heights of personal development. It's not about "getting over" something, but creating a new, stronger version of ourselves.

The *Omaha World-Herald*, in their aptly titled October 2020 article "The Power of Grief: Finding the "New You" After Loss is Part of the Journey," echoes this sentiment. They remind us that grieving is not just about wallowing in pain, but the first step towards rebirth.

The article identifies five key areas where this growth often occurs:

- A greater appreciation of life.
- Deeper personal relationships.
- New perspectives on personal strength.
- Recognizing new possibilities for one's life path.
- Significant spiritual development.

Each person's journey through post-traumatic growth is unique, but the common thread is a fundamental change in how we view ourselves and our place in the world.

I experienced all five areas of growth, though embracing the pain of Mossi's absence didn't immediately reveal its gifts. However, through the process of grieving, I gradually began to see the contours of a new self emerging from the wreckage of my old life. With the help of a phenomenal therapist, we mapped the path to "Steve 2.0." Eighteen months later, loss became my light, leading me to become a life and spiritual coach, an author, and a man overflowing with newfound purpose to share my knowledge of self-love.

The transformation starts with a simple choice: to grow from the ashes to be the rising phoenix. Set the intention to learn, to evolve, and watch the universe orchestrate your metamorphosis.

The Role of Self-Love in Loss

Without self-love, we can wallow in the self-pity triggered by our past unresolved traumas. All those past feelings of lack and disappointment are now choking us like a raging fire. These intense feelings we never felt comfortable expressing—or even knew how to—can finally be set free.

Self-love in the context of loss isn't just about affirming our worth; it's about deeply acknowledging our right to grieve, to feel pain and express it, and to take the time we need to heal. Self-love means offering ourselves the same kindness, patience, and understanding that we would offer a dear friend in mourning. We grieve, yes, but we grieve consciously, allowing ourselves to feel the waves of hurt without getting swept away with judgment. We acknowledge the void, the hollowness left behind, and also recognize the space it creates for something new to blossom.

Post-Traumatic Growth in Action

The sudden absence of a loved one can make us cherish the relationships that remain, to prioritize, forgive, and connect on deeper levels with the living. After losing a job, we might rethink our career path and pursue our true passions. A natural disaster might rekindle our environmental activism. Loss can be the compass that redirects us towards a more authentic life.

There are so many examples of people who utilized post-traumatic growth and didn't even realize it. Many cancer survivors report a newfound appreciation for life, a deeper sense of purpose, and a strengthened sense of self after facing their mortality. Veterans who heal their PTSD often develop a greater sense of empathy for others, a newfound resilience, and a stronger sense of community through shared experiences.

I have a cousin who survived the 2018 Parkland School shooting in Florida. Unfortunately, his best friend didn't. His life became about speaking out on gun safety. The woman who founded the influential organization MADD (Mothers Against Drunk Driving) lost her son to a drunk driver.

Loss can strip away limitations, revealing dormant abilities. A recent contestant on the TV show *American Idol* was a twenty-four-year-old NFL player who sustained such a debilitating leg injury, doctors were fearful he would never walk again. Not only was he able to walk again, but the process ignited his passion for music and singing, for which he won over the judges with his incredible voice. Travis Rudolph, after losing his leg in the Boston Marathon bombing, went on to become a Paralympic athlete, utilizing his experience of loss as a catalyst for resilience and a newfound appreciation for life.

Loss Redefined as a Turning Point

Let loss not be the thief of joy, but the turning point for growth. Let's be the alchemists of our own stories, transforming the lead of grief into the gold of self-discovery. Remember, the updated version of you, the You 2.0, is waiting to be revealed.

The journey, of course, won't be linear. There'll be days when the pain feels insurmountable, when doubts whisper in your ears, and despair threatens to engulf you. Be kind to yourself especially on those days, and remember you're not alone. We all travel on this path. With each other's support and the unwavering anchor of self-love, we can navigate the rough seas and ultimately reach the shores of a brighter future. Seek support: Don't be afraid to reach out to compassionate loved ones, a therapist, or a support group. Sharing your story can be incredibly healing.

Go forth and unlock the hidden strength within. The world awaits your new beginning.

DEEPER DIVES

1: Finding Potential for Post-Traumatic Growth

In your journal, reflect on a significant loss in your life and if it contributed in any way to personal growth. A death may have left you lonely, a natural disaster may have left you homeless, a firing may have left you jobless. If nothing changed, write down why the pain has left you stagnant, and then list three ways you can use this painful experience to contribute to personal growth in one or more of the five areas listed above. Repeat as needed.

2: Self-Care During Grief

Each day, dedicate a few moments to perform a small act of kindness towards yourself. It could be allowing yourself an extra hour of sleep, writing down three things you forgive yourself for regarding your grief process, or even just sitting with your emotions without judgment for a few minutes. "I feel sad, and that's okay." Journal about these acts of self-love to reflect on how they make you feel. Over time, you'll notice how these small gestures can make a significant difference in your journey through loss.

3: Accepting Your Emotions

Stand in front of a mirror, look into your own eyes, and say, "I'm going through a tough time, but I'm not alone. It's okay to feel these feelings. I love myself, and I will get through this." These affirmations reinforce self-compassion that may not have been felt as a child and remind you of your new inner strength and resilience.

4: Self-Compassion Pause

Whenever you feel overwhelmed by grief, place your hands over your heart, breathe deeply, and call upon the Shin Zo Ho Go symbol (introduced in chapter 4). Then say aloud or in your mind, "May I be kind to myself in this moment. May I give myself the compassion I need." This simple practice can be a powerful tool for navigating through the storm of loss with kindness.

5: New Possibilities After Loss Brainstorm

Let's illuminate new directions that loss may be nudging you towards. List five interests or dreams you've put on hold or never pursued. Next to each, write one small step you could take toward exploring these interests. The first step might be as simple as researching online what that first step might be. Watch a video. Enroll in a class. Redraft your resumé focused on a different type of job.

6: Write a Letter to Your Future Self

Writing letters to ourselves is a powerful exercise for growth. This time, write to yourself from the perspective of you, one year from now, detailing all the growth and positive changes you've experienced. Describe how you've navigated your loss and what you've learned about yourself. This act of envisioning can be a powerful motivator for embracing the transformative journey ahead.

9: INTERNAL VALIDATION

Are you constantly posting on social media, craving those Instagram likes or chasing compliments on a new outfit, only to feel empty moments later? Do you let everyone know it's your birthday or often need to be the center of attention? These are all examples of *external validation*.

It's human nature to crave validation, that pat on the back saying "good job" or "you're good enough." External validation isn't inherently negative, but "likes" are fleeting and dependent on others, i.e., it's out of our control. We've already discussed how trying to control what's beyond our control is a source of suffering.

But what if there was a way to feel good about ourselves, independent of these external validations?

Internal validation is the process of recognizing, understanding, and accepting our own internal experiences—thoughts, emotions, and sensations—as valid and important, without needing confirmation or approval from others. It means being our own source of compassion, encouragement, and acknowledgment.

Imagine a scenario where you've worked hard on a project. Instead of immediately looking for others to praise the effort, take a moment to acknowledge to yourself the dedication and hard work you put in. This self-recognition and appreciation are the essence of internal validation.

The Pitfalls of External Validation

External validation can also present itself in multiple casual sex partners, "shop therapy," binge eating, and other addictions. People pleasers often do things for others they'd rather not do just so that they'll be liked.

Constantly seeking reassurance from others before making decisions is an unhealthy form of seeking external validation called *learned helplessness*. I see this a lot online, where someone posts on Facebook asking a question that a simple Google search would answer. These people don't trust themselves to make good decisions.

When we find ourselves changing opinions, interests, or even our appearance to fit in and be liked by others, even if it means not being true to ourselves; if we need to be popular and rate our worthiness by how many friends we have; if we don't enjoy being alone or need to always be with someone to distract us from ourselves, these are all forms of seeking external validation.

Childhood experiences play a huge role in the need for external validation. Parents and caregivers, consciously or unconsciously, shape our sense of worth through their words and actions. If we seldom or never experienced acknowledgement of our emotions and feelings, or even were not allowed to express them, chances are we don't have a healthy base of self-worth, leaving us craving validation.

On the other hand, developing strong *internal* validation is like building a rock-solid fortress with everything we need within its walls.

Healing for Increased Internal Validation

The good news is we can heal from past pain, enabling us to rewrite those negative internal narratives to reconnect to self-love. That's where internal validation comes in as our superpower. It unlocks a treasure trove of benefits like:

- **Increased self-esteem:** We'll believe in our worth, regardless of external validation.
- **Reduced anxiety and self-doubt:** We'll stop judging ourselves harshly and accept our imperfections.
- **Improved relationships:** We'll set healthy boundaries and attract genuine connections.
- **Personal growth:** We'll embrace challenges and bounce back from setbacks with grace.

It may be normal to feel rejected after a job interview gone awry. But internal validation allows us to say, "This doesn't reflect my entire worth. I did the best I could. What can I learn from this and keep going?" We can accept disappointment as a valid emotion. Allow ourselves to experience it and know we can handle it. Instead of wallowing in pain for days, we can move forward with strength and resilience in a matter of hours.

The first step, as always, is gaining awareness of the impulse behind every desire for external validation.

Journaling, and meditations like those below in Deeper Dive 2, are effective ways to independently facilitate this healing process. Accepting our emotions doesn't mean condoning those that ignored them, but confirming their validity allows us to move on.

Self-awareness is the first critical step, but transformation occurs when we integrate this awareness to foster change in our lives. This shift towards action begins with cultivating practices that anchor our sense of self-worth internally rather than externally. We start building this internal foundation of validation that's independent of others' opinions or societal expectations by taking action.

The next insight, Connecting with Ancestors, offers a proven method of increasing internal validation. You might also consider returning to the section on forgiveness, as learning to forgive yourself greatly helps.

External validation isn't all bad, but what we're looking to achieve is balance, so that the more powerful internal validation becomes our primary source. With daily practice of the exercises, and journaling, tempered with a new self-compassion, we can learn to become our own best cheerleaders and embrace our unique experiences to let our inner worth shine through.

DEEPER DIVES

1: Exploring the Dark Side of External Validation

Think about the last week, and journal about moments when you altered your behavior or made choices based on what you thought would make others approve of you. This could be as simple as agreeing with a popular opinion in a group despite having a different view, buying a gift for someone you don't really like, or going out of your way to do something for someone in hopes of being praised. Recognize these moments and jot them down. Reflect on how each instance made you feel and whether it aligned with your true self.

2: Breathing Away Your Trauma

This is a quick version of the aura cleanse, to not only transmute the trauma behind your behavior but also to gain body awareness. Go back to your journal and reread your responses for the previous Deeper Dive. Notice if anything changes in your body, like a tightness in your chest or abdomen. Maybe you feel an energetic crust on your shoulders or back. Which phrase brought this on? Close your eyes and focus on that phrase and the sensation in your body. Allow it to be strong and identify itself. Then start taking deep breaths into that area, with the intention of release. Continue until the sensation is gone. Work on two or three from your list every day.

3: Gaining Awareness of Negative Self Talk

How we treat and talk to ourselves is a crucial marker. Are you aware of the negative self-talk happening in your mind? Or perhaps you're blaming yourself for events that aren't your fault? Even if you trip on the sidewalk, the response "Oh, I'm such an idiot," is negative self-talk, because it's 100 percent not true. Write in your journal about all the times you called yourself names or had a negative thought about your abilities. Then rewrite those experiences with a kinder, more compassionate voice.

4: Write a Love Letter to Yourself

Write another love letter to yourself, including all your wonderful qualities and accomplishments you admire in yourself that others may not have acknowledged. Let's face it: so far, you've made it through 100 percent of your most difficult days, so you can start with your incredible resolve and staying power. Your desire to learn about yourself and grow is also one of your lovable qualities. Write without judging. After this first letter, try writing a weekly love letter to yourself to see what other wonderful aspects of yourself you uncover. Put the letter under your pillow when sleeping to help your loving words manifest in your psyche.

5: Mirror Work to Develop Internal Validation

Establish a daily affirmation practice in the mirror. Mirror work was first developed by Louise Hay and can be deeply transformational. Each morning, stand in front of a mirror and affirm your value with statements like, "I am worthy of love and respect, just as I am," or "My worth is intrinsic and not dependent on others' approval," or "I am beautiful (or handsome)." These affirmations may feel awkward at first and not resonate with your personal experiences, but with daily practice, they'll put a positive spin your current inner negative beliefs. Observe what feels false and write it down.

As you incorporate these affirmations into your routine, observe the shifts in your daily feelings and behaviors. Notice when the impulse for external validation arises and gently remind yourself of your affirmations. This practice is not about suppressing the desire for validation but transforming them so that validation comes from within.

10: CONNECTING WITH ANCESTORS

Connecting to ancestors is the single greatest way to create internal validation. Imagine a vast tapestry, woven with threads of memory, resilience, and love. Each thread represents a life that came before you, an ancestor who paved the way for your very existence. Reconnecting to this tapestry, the forgotten power of ancestral connection, can profoundly reconnect us to self-love.

In 2010, I became obsessed with researching my genealogy and began building a family tree on Ancestry.com. I felt so much excitement as people and names I never heard of came up, dating as far back as to 1792. And much sadness as well came up, discovering unknown aunts and uncles who died in the Holocaust. But it was a labor of love, and I found new connections with living relatives in England, Belgium, Sweden, and South Africa, who immigrated during the Jewish diaspora and before. But it was all the deceased ancestors who intrigued me. Did I look like any of them? Did they face similar emotional issues? Did I get mine from them?

Then one day I came to discover the need for a powerful connection to these ancestors: I was watching a live concert clip of pop singer Ricky Martin on YouTube. Ten thousand adoring fans sending their love his way warmed my heart. And I thought "Why can't we all feel the love of ten thousand adoring fans?" But that's external validation. The fans don't go home with Ricky or any pop star. I'm looking for ten thousand fans to give me internal validation all the time. Eureka! Those are my ancestors! By connecting to them daily and expressing gratitude, I can feel the love and confidence of a rock star on stage at an arena concert twenty-four hours a day, seven days a week.

Death Is an Illusion

I mentioned earlier that we are interdimensional beings currently having a 3D experience. When we "die," we transition into another vibration invisible to those in the third dimension, which means that everyone you've lost is actually still with us. And if we speak to them, they hear us and will try to communicate in various ways.

This can be a challenging notion to grasp, especially for those raised in certain religions. But when we understand that death is an illusion, we more easily see how the "loss" of a relationship is merely transformed into a new one. Though someone's presence may end physically, their energy is present in another dimension, yearning to maintain connection.

Quite a few TV programs show mediums connecting to people's departed loved ones. The truth is that all of us inherently possess the ability to maintain connection with those who've passed, despite being taught or believing otherwise.

Ancestral Misconception

There might be some common misconceptions swirling in your mind. Many fear that connecting with ancestors is about summoning spirits or engaging in dark practices. That's your religious trauma. Connecting with our ancestors is a deeply respectful and loving spiritual practice that's more about acknowledgment and gratitude than anything fearful. It's about recognizing the lives that led to ours, understanding our roots, and finding guidance in the wisdom passed down through generations.

Another misconception is that we need to have known our ancestors personally or feel only positive emotions towards them. Remember, this journey is also about healing which can involve acknowledging past hurts and working towards forgiveness and understanding.

It's okay to start this process with mixed feelings. If blood relatives were all toxic and abusive and only caused pain, the healing and forgiveness of ourselves heals them too, and creates a two-way path of gratitude which makes this even more crucial for happiness.

Connecting to our ancestors is a radical act of self-love and self-care, a way to step into our full power and rewrite those lingering narratives of pain. By acknowledging and honoring our lineage, we tap into a wellspring of internal validation, understanding that we're part of a vibrant tapestry woven over time. Why is this so important to reconnecting to self-love? Think about this: How many ancestors do you have, going back seven generations? Grandparents, aunts, uncles, and cousins? Literally thousands. Regardless of our current earthly feelings for them, our relationships with them can become our secret force of internal validation, knowing those thousands are cheering us on in this lifetime and wanting to help us heal and grow.

Connecting to Ancestors is Part of Our Humanity

Connecting to ancestors isn't a new concept. For millennia, in cultures around the globe—Eastern, African, Native American, ancient Latin American—honoring of the ancestors is woven into the very fabric of life. Ceremonies, rituals, and offerings honor their sacrifices and request guidance from their wisdom.

Renowned anthropologist Dr. Jane Goodall is quoted on her institute website summarizing how "In many cultures, ancestors are part of the family, actively involved in the lives of the living." In Eastern traditions, the connection with ancestors goes beyond mere memory to become a living relationship that influences everyday life and decisions.

In Japan, the Obon festival is a time when people believe the spirits of ancestors return to visit their families. Lanterns are hung outside homes to guide the spirits back, and families clean their ancestors' gravesites, offering food and prayers in a celebration that reconnects the living with those who have passed.

Among the Akan people of Ghana, ancestral veneration is practiced through ceremonies where water or alcohol is poured on the ground as an offering, while prayers and messages are spoken to the ancestors, seeking their guidance and blessings for the family.

Many Native American tribes hold powwows, ceremonies, and story-telling sessions to honor ancestors, ensuring that the wisdom and teachings of the past are passed down to new generations, keeping the connection alive and strong.

This link isn't just spiritual; it's a source of wisdom, guidance, and strength. Greek philosopher Socrates says, "Ancestors are the best earthly friends we have, for they are the makers of our bodies."

Yet, in the West, this practice has been lost, shrouded in an overwhelming fear of death and dismissed as mere superstition. Death became taboo, and the connection to our ancestors faded. We lost access to this potent daily source of support and empowerment. But learning about the struggles and triumphs of our ancestors can provide a sense of strength and resilience. It reminds us that we come from a long line of survivors who faced challenges and overcame obstacles.

Ancestral connection gives a sense of belonging to something bigger than ourselves. Honoring ancestors brings a sense of peace and purpose to life. Understanding their struggles helps us appreciate our own blessings and motivates us to leave a positive legacy for future generations.

Types of Ancestors

I already mentioned blood ancestors, the ones who not only directly birthed our lineage but also all their offspring, with their genes whispering their triumphs and struggles in all our DNA to form the bedrock of our being.

There are two more types of ancestors with whom to reconnect: spirit ancestors and place ancestors.

Spirit ancestors are the inspiring souls who ignite our passions, like artists, thinkers, and changemakers who paved the way for our dreams.

Place ancestors are the guardians of the land we walk on, with their energy woven into the very fabric of our surroundings. They tell stories of the past, guiding us toward sustainability and honoring the cycles of life and death. Because I live in New York City, which was once inhabited by the indigenous Lenape tribe, they are some of my place ancestors.

Our ancestors need only four things from us:

- Acknowledgement
- Validation
- Understanding
- Forgiveness

It's interesting that those are the same things we all need in life. When we take the time to offer them the four needs—or suffer through the painful healing journey first required to do so—we then give all four needs to ourselves each time we connect with our ancestors.

As we do, we're healing seven generations before us and seven in the future. We're the ones who can break the generational dysfunction that caused us so much suffering. That's why there's nothing selfish about reconnecting to self-love; we're doing it to help our lineage and heirs.

Cultivating Connection

Ancestral contact can be cultivated through ritual practices; however, communication may also happen spontaneously in the form of dream contact, waking encounters, and synchronicity, like seeing butterflies or other repeating symbols connected to our beloved. When we have a framework to receive their outreach, their work is made easier and we're open to the enjoyment of conscious, ongoing relationships.

We can also cultivate this connection through simple practices like reading ancestral myths and folktales, visiting ancestral burial sites or homelands, cooking traditional family recipes, learning our family's language, volunteering in our community, and honoring the spirit of place ancestors.

The Importance of an Ancestral Altar

Ancestral altars, a practice seen across the globe, are a dedicated space to honor and connect with those who came before us. Their history stretches back millennia, and their forms vary greatly depending on the culture.

Evidence of ancestral altars dates to prehistoric times. In Japan, the Jomon period (10,000–300 BCE) saw the placement of grave goods near burials, suggesting a belief in connecting with the deceased. Similarly, ancient Egyptians built elaborate tombs with offerings for the afterlife.

Ancestral altars continue to be a vibrant tradition in many cultures today. In Mexican culture, on the Day of the Dead, people colorfully decorate altars for their ancestors. In China, ancestral tablets inscribed with names and dates are placed on home altars and families burn incense and offer food or tea to honor their ancestors.

In Hinduism, a *puja* room or *mandir* often serves as a space for ancestral veneration, with portraits or statues of deceased family members, and offerings like food and flowers made during daily prayers.

An altar doesn't have to be an entire room, as is the case in India. It can be as big or as small as you see fit. A space on the wall with a few photos and mementos, a small side table, or even a shelf in a closet to make it a more private experience, are viable solutions. I created an ancestral altar on the top of a low bookshelf and filled the wall behind it with family photos, those of my pet, and those of deceased people I admire, as well as mementos of the Lenape that once lived where I do now. I burn candles and incense while I stand there in meditation, rallying their support.

What do you gain from connecting with your ancestors?

- Self-discovery: We understand our strengths, vulnerabilities, and hidden gifts, inheriting untold legacies from generations past.
- Healing: We forgive and release pain, allowing healthy ancestors to become invested in our success, breaking cycles of suffering.

- Guidance: We receive whispers of wisdom and feel their unseen support as we navigate life's challenges.
- Empowerment: We understand our place in the grand story of humanity, reclaiming our power and purpose.

As we reconnect to our ancestral roots, we tap into a reservoir of love, wisdom, and strength. We discover more of who we are, where we come from, and where we're headed. Quirks, talents, and even phobias can have ancestral roots. This journey paves the way for deeper self-love and belonging, a legacy we carry forward for generations to come. Our ancestors are waiting, eager to connect. Open your heart, listen, and embrace the power.

DEEPER DIVES

1: Building Your Family Tree

In your journal, create your family tree with the relatives and ancestors you're familiar with. Parents, siblings, aunts, uncles, cousins. Even if you were adopted and don't know your biological family, these people, present and past, are still energetically your ancestors. Don't concern yourself with the graphic beauty of it. Once completed, write about who you believe is missing. What would you like to know about those who've passed? How you feel about the tree you just completed? What emotions come up and where do you feel them in your body?

2: Speaking to Ancestors

Our departed loved ones, and maybe not-so-loved ones, are around us all the time. If you haven't spoken to them, sit in a quiet space and invite them to be with you. When I practice this in meditation, I feel an ancestor or ascended master's energy move through my body with a tingle in the left side of my body, my head, or down my spine. You may feel a similar sensation. Begin speaking out loud as if they're right there, expressing what you'd like them to know and how you feel. What would you like them to help you with? This is a great exercise for toxic ancestors, to finally express how they made you feel and begin to create closure to move forward. You can also reach out to ancestors you never met to discover more of who you are.

3: Creating Your Ancestral Rituals.

Write in your journal about the rituals you could create for your ancestors. Is it something you bake on a birthday or even weekly? Visiting grave sites? A daily meditation? Clothing or jewelry to wear? Pilgrimage to a homeland? Planting a fruiting tree in their memory? Singing songs? Making art? It can be almost anything since the intention is honor and remembrance.

4: Building Your Altar

Locate a space in your home to dedicate to the altar. As mentioned, it can be as simple as a wall or surface with a few photos and candles, or as elaborate as you like. This is a space where you can stand and meditate and set intentions of gratitude and connection.

11: NOTHINGNESS

All the things we believe about ourselves that cause great suffering aren't even us. If we can't control it, it isn't us.

This is the spiritual concept at the heart of Buddhism, Stoicism, and Hinduism, where a seemingly paradoxical concept illuminates the path to profound self-love. Called Anatta in Buddhism and often translated as "nothingness" or "not-self," anatta might sound like a negation, a denial of our existence, but it's a liberating key to understanding who we truly are and aren't.

To simplify the nothingness of anatta, imagine we're performing a role in a play, wearing costumes, makeup, and adopting characteristics that aren't our own. At the end of the play, we take off our costume and return to being ourselves. Anatta suggests that much like actors, the roles, labels, and identities we adopt in life are temporary costumes we wear and not who we are.

Just as an actor isn't defined by their performances on stage, our true essence isn't defined by these temporary labels that we cling to—names, roles, achievements. **It's the ego that needs to believe these define us.** But just as clouds morph in the sky, so too do all these aspects of our being. Our thoughts flicker, emotions ebb and flow, and even our bodies are a constant dance of cells. Therefore, how can something so impermanent we have no control over truly be us? Which means everything we may dislike about ourselves isn't even us.

But wait, if nothing is truly us or ours, aren't we left with an identity crisis, lost in the void? Surprisingly, the opposite is true, where this understanding of our "nothingness," becomes the gateway to everything.

Currently we likely define ourselves by our nationality, ethnicity, religion, job, height, weight, looks. If you were happy about all those labels you likely wouldn't be reading this book. Now you're asking, "if we're not those things, then who are we?" And I'll answer, "Why do we have to identify with being anything?" All that does is limit us from the infinite possibilities of being. Anatta is the state of acceptance of not needing to be labeled anything to exist, and because we are not defined, we become capable of infinite possibilities.

Our universe, with its infinite potential, whispers the secrets of anatta. In quantum physics, black holes, those mysterious cosmic vacuums, are the epitome of nothingness. The computer world is made up of 1's and 0's. Therefore, if we live in the world of "1" (something), then it's true we live in a world of "0" (nothing).

Anatta for Self-Love and Growth

Can you begin to see how this "nothingness," is not emptiness, but an infinite spaciousness disconnected from our ego? It's the fertile ground where true self-love takes root. When we release negative thoughts about things mistakenly believed to be part of us, we can reconnect to self-love and the flow of life.

By letting go of a fixed self, we become more open to new experiences. We're not limited by preconceived notions of our capabilities and who we believe we are. We connect with others based on shared experiences, not self-interest. We recognize the impermanent nature of suffering in ourselves and others, fostering empathy.

When we embrace our interconnectedness with everything, the boundaries between "self" and "other" dissolve, revealing our shared essence. If everything physical about us isn't us, then everything physical or imagined about the eight billion others on Earth isn't them.

Letting go of all that negative mental chatter allows for a clearer focus on the present moment, where daily activities become more intentional and enjoyable. Connecting to our nothingness weakens the hold of material desires and cravings, so daily life becomes less driven by lack and more by gratitude. Recognizing the ever-changing nature of all things, including oneself, leads to a more peaceful acceptance of life's ups and downs.

At work we might be less concerned with personal credit, and more focused on collaboration for the good of the team. In relationships, we might be less likely to take things personally and instead focus on understanding the other person's perspective. We might be more open to new experiences and less afraid of failure, as our sense of self isn't tied to specific outcomes.

I've mentioned spiritual teacher Ram Dass and his film *Becoming Nobody*. In it, he mentions that sometimes you must first become "somebody" before you can be nobody. Now you're screaming, "Steve, make up your mind!" How I interpret this statement is that the state of anatta can be achieved *after* restoring a significant connection to self-love. When we get to a place where we're not drowning in trauma and fear, no longer surrounded by toxic people, and have healed our shattered ego, we've done the work to be somebody. Only then can we successfully venture to become nobody.

Achieving the state of anatta doesn't happen overnight. In fact, even with daily practice it can take years to achieve, so be patient. The journey to understanding anatta is obviously complex and ongoing and will be unique for each of us. If we simply explore it with an open mind and a kind heart, we can loosen our grip on the false self to discover a deeper, more expansive sense of who we truly are: a love that transcends the limitations of the ego and embraces the infinite.

DEEPER DIVES

1: The Role-Playing Reflection

Journal and reflect on the various roles you play in your life: as a friend, professional, parent, or any other. Write down how these roles change depending on context, how you change in temperament, voice, attitude, and how they differ from the core you believe is "you." What remains when these roles are stripped away?

2: Exploring Labels

Open your journal and start exploring the labels you place on yourself, or that others placed on you and how they affect you. Which ones do you cling to, and why? Are there any labels that are painful, and why?

3: Discover Impermanence in Action

Choose a daily activity (cooking, walking, working) and observe the constant change within it. See how each moment is different from the previous one, highlighting the impermanent nature of the experience.

4: Sensory Deprivation

If you have the financial means, and there's one near you, experience floating in a sensory deprivation tank for an hour. There are different models, but all are a type of clamshell design large enough for one adult to fully recline and allow no light or sound to enter when closed. The water has a high concentration of dissolved salts to permit buoyancy and is heated close to internal body temperature.

Journal about the fear or joy that comes up at the thought of doing this. If you've done it, how did you feel? What were some of your thoughts while floating?

An alternative is to lie on your bed covered with a blanket and with eyes and ears covered for an hour, to get a taste of nothingness.

INTEGRATION FOR YOUR NEW EMOTIONAL INTELLIGENCE

After reading through these 11 Insights, you can now begin to see how negative childhood experiences affect our ability to understand, accept, and healthily express emotions in so many areas of life, and where to focus future personal growth work. Even simply being able to see where others in your life, such as family, friends and partners, are lacking similar levels of emotional maturity, is a sign of integration. You can also see how important having this ability to restore emotional mastery is to maintaining healthy relationships.

Having this clarity, we can now integrate what we've uncovered by choosing our responses rather than being ruled by negative, reactive emotions. We integrate as we become adept at navigating the complexities of human connection. We integrate as we can now listen with genuine empathy, as if stepping into another's shoes, to foster trust and a sense of connection that goes beyond surface interactions.

Although integrating all we've learned for emotional intelligence can take months in some case, ultimately, it empowers us with the tools to live a more fulfilling, authentic life. We can navigate challenges with resilience. We can set healthy boundaries and prioritize what matters most. By cultivating emotional intelligence through spiritual practices like Reiki, mindfulness, and self-reflection, we pave the way for a life rich in connection, purpose, and personal growth.

PART IV:
LIVING LIFEPRINT REIKI

CHAPTER 9:

Living Authentically

The only person you are destined to become
is the person you decide to be.

—RALPH WALDO EMERSON

THE PRINCIPLES OF LIFEPRINT REIKI point to the fact that
everyone in the entire world suffers from various levels of unresolved
trauma which are at the root of all human difficulties. Only by taking
action to gain awareness and acceptance of them can we begin the process
of transmutation to be able to reconnect to self-love.

The biggest takeaway from what you've read so far is the painful truth
that happiness is healing the trauma caused by toxic people. Eliminating
them from our lives allows us to live with emotional intelligence. Going
no contact with anyone, especially a family member, can be agonizing, and
may require a stronger reconnection to self-love in many other ways than
boundaries, before gaining the strength and confidence to enact it. We may

have to be pushed to our limit by these toxic people before we realize there's no other choice but to move forward without them.

Gaining this emotional intelligence and stripping away our survival personality leaves us with our authentic self. Being authentic means dropping the mask we usually wear to fit in. It's when our actions and words are congruent with our beliefs and values, and with our true essence as a human being. Part of that is knowing what we believe in. It's being able to express our needs and only surrounding ourselves with people who support those needs. To succeed in being authentic, we first must know our true selves. By now, you may be getting a clearer idea of who you are not, and who you could be.

When we're living authentically, we allow ourselves to feel whatever it is that we're feeling. All emotions are okay; they're a key part of our intelligence and the human experience. If we feel sad, we allow ourselves to feel that. If we're in a situation where it's an inappropriate emotion to display, we consider when we'll next be alone, and able to allow ourselves to express it. Carve out time for yourself to reflect on your emotions. Journaling, as mentioned previously, is a great way to do this.

Authentic people are more optimistic. Optimism is the belief in a positive future and the ability to find good, even in challenging circumstances. We already know that everything that happens to us, whether or not it's pleasant, is a blessing, so positivity is the only authentic point of view. The Dalai Lama reminds us, "If you think you can, you can. If you think you can't, you're right."

Psychologists have also explored the link between optimism and well-being and agree that optimism is a key factor in resilience. Optimists explain setbacks as temporary, specific, and external, whereas pessimists explain them as permanent, pervasive, and internal. This optimism allows authentic individuals to bounce back from challenges and persevere on their spiritual path.

Another benefit of living authentically is strengthening your intuition. Authenticity allows us to shed societal expectations, and connect with our truest selves, until intuition becomes the clearest inner voice that guides us. It's your intuition that will guide you towards those other spiritual practices that can be helpful on your specific spiritual journey.

Psychology offers a complementary perspective, viewing intuition as a form of unconscious processing, where past experiences and emotions are integrated to form a gut feeling. Intuition is a "psychic" function that allows us to make sense of the world beyond logic and which plays a crucial role in self-discovery. When we're authentic, we're more open to listening to our intuition, which can guide us towards our true potential. By embracing our true selves, we become more receptive to subtle intuitive nudges.

Self-confidence is the byproduct of trusting our gut feelings and intuition. By living authentically, we create an environment where our intuition can flourish, and in turn, guides us on our path towards spiritual growth and more opportunities for happiness in life.

Because authentic living means having greater facility to express ourselves verbally and emotionally, it throws the doors wide open to also express ourselves creatively. The human spirit yearns for expression. That isn't just a character quirk, but a vital part of connecting with something larger than ourselves. With our new-found reconnection to curiosity, this becomes even more possible.

Creativity isn't limited to painting, writing, or music. If you have any kind of creative curiosity and are at all interested in living a more interesting life, then you are an artist. Whether you're cooking a meal, gardening, or fixing a car, you can approach it with a creative spirit, finding joy and fulfillment in the process.

Finding our passions and expressing them creatively allows us to be fully present in the moment, lost in the flow of creation. Our creative passions are a core part of self-actualization, for as we create, we learn, grow, and discover hidden aspects of ourselves. This passion project doesn't have to be our job, but something we can find time to pursue. As Bashar, the entity channeled by Daryl Anka, tells us, pursuing our passions without expectations is the truest path to happiness.

The collective unconscious is a shared pool of human experiences and ideas, and when we create authentically, we tap into this wellspring of creativity, and our artistic expression resonates with others on a deeper level. By embracing our passions and expressing ourselves creatively, we connect to an authenticity that nourishes our souls and allows us to contribute something unique and beautiful to the world.

A POSSIBLE AUTHENTIC DAY

What's the daily life of a spiritual explorer like?

Perhaps when you wake in the morning and open your eyes, you take a moment to feel gratitude for another day and all you have accomplished so far.

On your way to make your morning beverage, you stop at your ancestral altar to acknowledge and ask for their support throughout the day. You place your breakfast on the altar as an offering, then consume it after meditation to take on the infused healing energy.

Or after enjoying your breakfast, you check in with your body aches and do some stretching or yoga to work out the trauma still held in those painful areas.

Or you sit to give yourself a Reiki treatment.

If you have a pet, or children, you take a moment to let them know how much you value them.

If you have the time, this is a great moment to journal about everything that's troubling you, to clear it out of your psyche for a more enjoyable day.

Or perhaps you take twenty minutes to meditate.

Bathing is an opportunity to create a cleansing ritual that starts by lighting a candle or incense, or simply taking a moment to set an intention or recite an affirmation of release. While bathing, you use products you love, scented with essential oils, to invigorate your senses. To close, you choose anything from snapping the towel as an energy clearing before drying, to simply having a moment of gratitude for the cleansing experience.

As you leave the house, you recite the five precepts of Reiki from chapter 4 to lock yourself into the present moment.

When out on the street, you carry single dollar bills to give to the homeless asking for assistance.

You find you no longer have the appetite for heavy and fried foods and start making healthier choices to fuel the body you love.

You will likely be listening to different music as you find vibrations to support your new soul frequency. There are lots of great supportive music streams everywhere.

Being in nature is how you feel connected to the divine. You become an avid fisher, camper, or join a hiking group to meet like-minded, nature-loving people to embrace the social spiritual possibilities. You feel generous with your time and volunteer in the community to connect to service spirituality, or travel the world on volunteer vacations.

You look for monthly Reiki circles in your area or online to help reinforce your energetic connections.

And lastly, you find yourself spending more time alone relishing in solitude, instead of feeling lonely. Your circle of friends may dwindle after you realize what kept you together wasn't very healthy, but new authentic supportive people come into your life, removing all the drama of the past.

All these things can happen daily, or several times a week. It takes four to six weeks to break a habit and the same to start a new one. Make a promise to try something new for a month to see if it works in your spiritual practice.

There's a partial list in the appendix under Spiritual Practices, as an entire list is not feasible in a book. Try one and see how it goes. Or mix it up. Maybe you don't do each of them daily, but weekly. Some monthly. Whatever you feel is right for you. There's no way to do this wrong.

"Self-care" has become a popular buzzword in the self-help world to deal with external life stressors that are a survival personality's reactions to triggers. But as we continue the desire to live more authentically, focusing on the inner work to free ourselves from those anxiety-creating reactions, massages, bubble baths and scented candles will play a very small role in the larger picture of reconnecting to self-love.

Staying home instead of fulfilling plans is now thought of as self-care, but avoidance isn't living authentically. That we have plans we don't want to fulfill is a demonstration of a lack of boundaries or holding on to relationships that no longer serve a purpose in our life.

Self-care is often judged as being selfish. **Remember, people who see self-love as selfish either have no idea of the degree of effort it entails, don't feel worthy of it themselves, or both.**

Living authentically and following true self-care guidelines means making dental, medical and mental health appointments, and making sure we eat healthy, nutritious food and get proper sleep, as a holistic approach to one's entire authentic well-being.

GAINING MINDFULNESS IN THE MUNDANE

Physical and spiritual tools can be employed to assist with our growth on a self-love journey, and I consider the following practices part of Lifeprint Reiki. Some may seem like common sense. Some readers may have already made them part of their lives and spiritual practices, and for some they will seem brand new. These practices can take on a whole new meaning when you understand their original spiritual intent. Since there's no right or wrong way to practice Lifeprint Reiki, the tools you're unfamiliar with are here when you need them. Not every tool must be applied on day one—or ever.

Health and Cleanliness

The human body is made up of tens of thousands of integrated and organized biological and neuro-chemical systems. Many of our cells operate on strict schedules or circadian rhythms. Even at the atomic level, we're well-regulated and well-organized. It wouldn't be surprising, then, if the reason we crave symmetry and cleanliness in ourselves and our homes is to mirror the organization within our very own bodies to support health and oppose chaos.

Showering or bathing regularly, washing hands regularly and especially before handling food, washing hair, keeping hair short or removing hair, wearing clean clothing, brushing teeth, and cutting fingernails, are a few hygiene practices we're all aware of.

The earliest written account of elaborate codes of hygiene can be found in several Hindu texts, like the *Charaka Samhita*, where bathing is one of the five daily duties. Many religions require or encourage ritual purification via bathing or immersing the hands in water. In Islam, washing of the hands and face prior to the prayers is required, with additional rules concerning proper hygiene after using the bathroom. Orthodox Judaism requires a ceremonial *mikveh* bath for women following menstruation and childbirth, while ceremonial washing of the hands is performed upon waking and before eating. The Ethiopian Orthodox Church also prescribes similar requirements.

Bathing culture in Chinese literature can be traced back to the Shang dynasty (1600–1046 BCE), where Oracle bone inscriptions describe people washing their hair and bodies in baths. In the Han dynasty, bathing became a regular activity, where government officials were required to bathe at least once every five days.

In Europe, regular bathing was a hallmark of Roman civilization. Elaborate baths were constructed in urban areas to serve the public, who required the infrastructure to maintain personal cleanliness. The bathing complexes consisted of large swimming pool-like baths, smaller cold and hot pools, saunas, and spa-like facilities where individuals could be depilated, oiled, and massaged.

The importance of hand washing for human health—particularly for people in vulnerable circumstances like mothers who have just given birth or wounded soldiers in hospitals—was first recognized in the mid-nineteenth century. At that time, most people still believed that infections were caused by foul odors.

Today, we know that poor hygiene or hyper-hygiene can be a result of unresolved trauma and a symptom of a disconnection from self-love. The unresolved trauma that affects personal hygiene can come from a host of factors, including poverty, inadequate social or emotional support, or having physical disabilities.

Excessive hygiene is often related to obsessive-compulsive behavior, which can be a type of perfectionism. But too clean is not better. The Hygiene Hypothesis arose as doctors are believing we may be too clean and it's making us sick as our immune systems have no practice fighting bacteria and disease.

Hygiene is a spiritual part of humanity, and occurs in the animal world as well. Pet lovers have watched their dogs or cats groom themselves. Birds are seen bathing in puddles. Elephants have a ritual of spraying themselves with dirt, and monkeys sit around and pick each other's fur. Proper hygiene is who we are as humans, too.

Personal grooming is an extension of personal hygiene as the maintenance of a good personal and public appearance, which need not necessarily be hygienic. It may involve, for example, using deodorants or perfume, shaving, or combing. Just like in animals, hygiene is genetically instinctual and can be affected by trauma and lack of self-love. If we don't feel good about ourselves, we may not bathe as often, dress flatteringly, or fuss over appearance. As we heal, our integration includes a reexamination of the habits of our survival personality to see where we can establish new behaviors in line with our new authentic selves.

Oral Health

Spiritually, oral health also holds deeper meaning beyond just a healthy smile; it reflects inner well-being and a connection to the self and others. Healthy teeth contribute to a healthy body, allowing for clear communication and mindful eating.

Yoga teaches the concept of *saucha*, inner and outer cleanliness. Brushing and flossing represent a commitment to saucha, fostering a sense of purity and respect for the body.

The National Institutes of Health have published several papers over the years referencing the link between good oral hygiene and self-esteem; a healthy smile boosts confidence, allowing for better social interaction and a more positive self-image. Other NIH studies suggest oral health can impact mental well-being, where poor oral hygiene can lead to anxiety and depression, while good hygiene promotes a sense of control and well-being.

By caring for our teeth, we not only maintain physical health but also cultivate self-respect, confidence, and a foundation for positive interactions to align with the core spiritual principles of self-care, mindfulness, and connection.

Sleep Health

Sleep hygiene was developed in the late 1970s as a method to help people with mild to moderate insomnia. You may already be experiencing sleepless nights, or soon will. It's a part of the journey we all go through.

Beyond the spiritual journey, stress, anxiety, and depression can contribute to insomnia. Irregular sleep schedules, exposure to excessive screen time before bed, and uncomfortable sleep environments can also play a role. Additionally, certain medical conditions, medications, and substances like caffeine and alcohol can disrupt sleep patterns.

While insomnia can be a persistent and frustrating issue, several self-care strategies can help improve sleep quality:

- Establish a consistent sleep schedule.
- Create a relaxing bedtime routine or ritual.
- Optimize the sleep environment to be dark, quiet, and comfortable.
- Incorporate relaxation techniques such as deep breathing, meditation, or progressive muscle relaxation.
- Get out of bed if sleep doesn't come.
- Limit caffeine, nicotine and alcohol intake, especially close to bedtime.
- Perform daily physical activity, but avoid intense workouts close to bedtime.

If insomnia persists despite self-care efforts, consult a healthcare professional to evaluate underlying medical conditions and provide appropriate treatment options. Acupuncture is a tremendously helpful modality to restore the imbalance behind the insomnia.

The world of sleep holds deep significance in many spiritual traditions who view sleep as a sacred practice, a time for the body and mind to restore themselves. Through sleep, we withdraw our interest from the external world and suspend our relation to it. This detachment allows for internal renewal, a concept echoed in the Hindu practice of Yoga Nidra, a form of yogic sleep designed to bring about a state of deep relaxation.

Quality sleep is essential for mental clarity and emotional stability, both of which are necessary for spiritual growth. Maintaining present-moment awareness is difficult to achieve with a foggy mind. Adequate sleep allows for a quieter mind, making spiritual practices and self-reflection more accessible.

Maintaining a consistent sleep schedule requires self-discipline, a cornerstone of many spiritual paths. By prioritizing healthy sleep habits, we cultivate the willpower necessary to resist distractions and prioritize our well-being. We not only enhance our spiritual development, but also improve our overall mental and emotional well-being.

Food and Cooking

Food or *culinary hygiene* relates to the practicality of sanitary food handling and cooking to prevent contamination, food poisoning, and to minimize the transmission of disease to other foods, humans, or animals. But food hygiene goes beyond preventing illness, as a practice that nourishes the spirit as well as the body.

In many spiritual traditions, food is a tool for aligning ourselves with a higher vibration, impacting our physical, emotional, and spiritual well-being. Other spiritual traditions view food as a gift from nature, imbued with life force (*prana* in Hinduism, *qi* in Chinese medicine). Proper handling shows respect for this life force and honors the sacrifice made for our sustenance.

Focusing on the process of preparing and consuming food with care fosters a sense of mindfulness and appreciation that can reduce stress and enhance the enjoyment of the meal. By combining these perspectives, we see food hygiene as not just a practical necessity, but also a way to cultivate respect, purity, and a mindful connection with ourselves and the world around us.

How can we best feed the body so that we can have a healthier mind, body, and spirit? Just as not one spiritual path suits everyone, there isn't a one-diet-suits-all for food either. I take the controversial stance that our blood type defines the foods required for healthy functioning. Many books have been written on the topic and some appear in the appendix of this book. However, the importance of fresh, whole foods cannot be disputed; the food you eat can either be the most powerful form of medicine or the slowest form of poison.

Looking at the world's Blue Zones—regions with exceptional concentrations of centenarians—offers valuable insights into this connection between food, spirituality, and longevity. These communities, located in Sardinia, Italy; Okinawa, Japan; Loma Linda, California; Nicoya, Costa Rica; and Ikaria, Greece, share some key dietary habits. Blue Zone diets are predominantly based on consuming meat, fish, vegetables, legumes, whole grains, and fruits grown within a ten-mile radius.

Note that food is not the only factor contributing to longevity, but that these centenarians also all have a strong spirituality—a clear purpose of being—with strong family and community ties. (Family isn't defined by those with whom we share DNA, but includes those we choose to have in our lives who believe in us.)

The concept of *mindful eating* is another cornerstone. When we eat mindfully, we're aware of the food we're putting into our bodies. We're aware of the taste, the texture, the smell. We're aware of the gratitude we feel for the food that nourishes us. By slowing down and appreciating our food, we connect with the source of our nourishment and cultivate a sense of gratitude.

Shifting to a healthier diet can be daunting, but the potential benefits are significant. like increased energy, improved mood, and a heightened sense of connection to yourself and the world around you. When we eat right, we feel vibrant, healthy, and connected to our spiritual nature.

About ten years ago, I saw an ad by an ayurvedic chef here in New York offering a week of meals delivered for a very reasonable price. I took them up on their offer, and I must admit that in only a week I felt a great positive change in my energy and well-being.

When we find giving up a certain food difficult, it means that we have an attachment to it, and we know attachments cause us suffering. Eating the same thing every day for breakfast, for example, is also an attachment. What can be most helpful is simply bringing awareness to what we eat, why, and when. Mindfulness is the first step to releasing attachments and becoming the healthy person you desire to be.

Some practical steps to initiate your journey towards a high-vibration diet:

- Start small: Introduce or eliminate one or two new healthy or unhealthy foods each week.
- Plan your meals: This reduces reliance on processed options.
- Cook more at home: This allows control over ingredients and energy.
- Practice gratitude: Thankfulness for your food enhances its energetic impact.
- Listen to your body: Pay attention to how different foods make you feel.

The journey toward an optimal spiritual diet is a personal exploration. By embracing fresh, whole foods, mindful eating practices, and aligning your diet with your beliefs, you can create a powerful tool for elevating your vibration and fostering a deeper connection to yourself and the world around you.

Alcohol

Many spiritual traditions acknowledge the complex role alcohol plays in the human experience. On the positive side, some view it as a facilitator for spiritual connection and joy. In Hinduism, the Rigveda, a collection of hymns, mentions Soma, an intoxicating beverage believed to connect drinkers to the divine, though it was only consumed during rituals.

However, I, like most spiritual paths, also caution against the misuse of alcohol. In Buddhism, the Buddha himself laid down the Five Precepts, one of which discourages intoxication. The idea is that alcohol can cloud judgment and hinder one's ability to walk the spiritual path, which requires mindfulness and clarity.

But in today's world, consuming alcohol daily or to excess is an accepted behavior, even though it's rooted in a trauma response. We know alcoholics use it to fill a void, and so its mindless use fills the same purpose. Perhaps you, too, have seen on social media, where mothers jokingly brag and flaunt their need for wine. People do what they need to get through the day to anesthetize their trigger responses, but its consumption does lower one's vibration.

Once I removed the toxic people from my life, I found I lost the urge to drink alcohol. I still partake at celebrations or dinners where wine is served, but I propose a toast, to invite a spiritual intention to the imbibing.

Ultimately, the decision of whether to consume alcohol is a personal one. However, the importance of moderation and mindful consumption is key.

Medicines and Remedies

Certain medical practices are better suited to the Lifeprint Reiki life. For millennia, humanity has sought solace and healing not just from physical remedies, but also from practices that touch the spirit. We know that many illnesses in the body are a result of unresolved trauma, as it affects the brain, which controls the nervous system and, if untreated, can begin to shut it down.

Modern medicine has made undeniable advancements, but it doesn't address all aspects of well-being. Many people seek complementary and alternative medicine (CAM) alongside traditional treatments. Techniques like meditation, yoga, and tai chi can promote relaxation, reduce stress, and potentially boost the immune system.

Ayurveda is a traditional Indian system of medicine that emphasizes a holistic approach to health and well-being. Originating over three thousand years ago, ayurveda is based on a similar belief to Traditional Chinese Medicine (TCM) that health is a balance between the mind, body, and spirit. Illness is viewed as an imbalance, or disharmony, within the individual. The exercise of aura cleansing is perfect to remove toxic energy from the body.

Ironically, Hippocrates, the father of Western medicine, himself acknowledged this connection, stating, "It is more important to know what sort of person has a disease than to know *what sort of disease* a person has."

It's a sad truth that Western medicine practices aren't all based in healing. The American Heart Association was founded in the 1950s with funding by Procter & Gamble, with the sole purpose to convince people that their hydrogenated vegetable fat shortening and margarine were healthier than fat from animals. Healthy cholesterol levels were lowered from 300 to 200 simply to help Big Pharma have more people stay on their lipid drugs for the rest of their lives.

That's why, as we begin our authentic life, it's important to no longer limit ourselves to outdated Western healing standards that merely treat physical symptoms, but to also include alternative holistic methods like TCM or acupuncture, ayurveda, homeopathy, or something as simple as changing your diet, to address the root causes of illness.

Renowned integrative medicine physician, Dr. Andrew Weil, states in his book *Integral Medicine*, "True health addresses the physical, mental, and spiritual dimensions of life," suggesting that healing can't be limited to treating just physical symptoms but must encompass a person's well-being in its entirety. Western medicine doesn't do that, but Traditional Chinese Medicine and Ayurveda do.

These different approaches have different remedies. While Western medicine relies heavily on chemical formulas, TCM and other alternative healing modalities use natural herbs, plants, and minerals proven effective for thousands of years. Western medical culture encourages doctors to reject them, because Big Pharma can't trademark natural products, which is where the money is.

One of the most helpful alternative products I discovered are Bach Flower Essences. This type of therapy uses diluted extracts from wildflowers to address emotional issues. Developed by Edward Bach in the 1930s, these essences work by harmonizing negative emotions. I've found Star of Bethlehem and Rock Rose formulas highly effective in relieving trauma symptoms. They're readily available at Whole Foods and other health food stores.

I'm not suggesting anyone adopt the extreme Christian Scientist approach to medicine that limits medical care to prayer. It's important to remember that spiritual practices are often complements, not replacements, for conventional medicine. But most people wait to see doctors until their condition has deteriorated to the point of needing the acute care that Western medicine addresses well. The ideal scenario combines traditional healthcare providers and those offering alternative wellness therapies.

Ultimately, the spirituality of medicines and remedies lies in acknowledging the interconnectedness of body, mind, and spirit. By nurturing all aspects of ourselves, we create fertile ground for healing and a more holistic approach to wellness.

Supplements

When your new authentic self becomes more conscious of healthcare options, the value of supplements to improving our trauma healing can't be ignored. The arena for supplements can at times be controversial. However, I'm a firm believer in healing with foods and have done so for decades visiting holistic doctors. The caveat is they're not a magic pill that can work overnight but can take several weeks to months for the body to properly respond. Patience is required.

Supplements for Trauma

There are references to books on supplements in the appendix, but here I'm listing seven supplements that I found greatly helpful in restoring the proper reregulation to my brain and nervous system from functioning in the trauma induced "fight or flight" mode.

Please consult a trained healthcare professional before taking any supplements to be certain they don't interfere with any medications you might be taking, or that you may be allergic to.

L-Theanine

L-Theanine, an amino acid found naturally in green and black tea, has gained popularity as a supplement for its brain-boosting effects. Research suggests L-theanine can alleviate trauma symptoms of anxiety, sleep issues, and brain fog by elevating levels of GABA, dopamine, and serotonin, promoting relaxation and lowering anxiety. A 2019 randomized trial at the Cleveland Clinic noted decreased stress-related symptoms in healthy adults taking L-theanine for four weeks.

The same 2019 study found it improved verbal fluency and focus in healthy adults, especially when combined with caffeine, which makes green tea a healthy addition to your diet if you can handle the caffeine.

Additionally, a study in *Pharmacology, Biochemistry, and Behavior* showed that 400mg of L-theanine one hour before bedtime significantly improved sleep quality in adults with chronic sleep problems.

Lion's Mane Mushroom

Lion's Mane mushroom (Hericium erinaceous), native to East Asia and used in traditional Chinese medicine for centuries, has been gaining traction in the West for its benefits on brain health.

A 2008 study published in *The International Journal of Medicinal Mushrooms* noted the mushrooms' compounds promote nerve cell growth

192 ⊕ YOUR TRAUMA HEALING JOURNEY

and function. A 2010 pilot study in *Nutritional Neuroscience* found that Lion's Mane extract improved cognitive function in older adults with mild cognitive impairment.

When I started taking a higher dose of Lion's Mane daily, I noticed a difference in my alertness and thought processes after just the first week.

Choline

Choline is an essential nutrient that plays a vital role in brain health; it's a precursor to acetylcholine, a key neurotransmitter involved in memory, mood, and muscle control. Optimum levels can become out of whack due to trauma, and this supplement can be helpful in relieving the 'fight or flight' sensation.

It is found in small amounts in eggs, liver, fish, nuts, beans, and cruciferous vegetables like broccoli and cauliflower. But Choline supplements are also available in various forms like choline bitartrate, alpha-GPC, and citicoline, with doses typically ranging from 1-3 grams daily.

Astaxanthin

Astaxanthin improves brain and nervous system function through its antioxidant and anti-inflammatory properties. It's a powerful antioxidant, even surpassing vitamin E in its ability to neutralize free radicals that damage cells. And unlike many antioxidants, Astaxanthin can cross the blood-brain barrier, allowing it to directly target and protect brain cells.

Astaxanthin's anti-inflammatory properties help reduce inflammation in the nervous system, offering protection against brain degeneration. Additional studies suggest it can promote nerve cell regeneration and increase the production of proteins crucial for brain health, which play a role in memory, learning, and overall cognitive function.

12mg a day is all that's needed.

Ashwagandha

Ashwagandha is an herb with a long history of use in Ayurvedic medicine, and it's gaining traction for its benefits on the brain and nervous systems. Its potential lies in its adaptogenic properties. Adaptogens help the body adapt to stress, both physical and mental. Chronically high stress can disrupt the nervous system, particularly the sympathetic nervous system (fight or flight response). Ashwagandha can help regulate the stress hormone cortisol, promoting a calmer state and nervous system balance.

A study published on *Healthline* found that 60 people taking 240 mg of ashwagandha daily for two months showed significant reductions in anxiety compared to a placebo group. By regulating stress hormones and promoting nervous system balance, ashwagandha may indirectly improve sleep quality. Studies suggest it might help with falling asleep and overall sleep quality, which can positively impact cognitive function.

This isn't something I used daily but had on hand for the occasional times of fleeting overwhelming emotions. It comes in various dosages and I would take 3000mg in the morning and the serenity lasted all day.

Omega-3

A recent study into ADHD, showed that all participants were lacking in Omega-3 fatty acids. These compounds, particularly EPA and DHA, are crucial components of the brain and nervous system functions. Our brain cells rely on healthy membranes for communication and function. Omega-3s help build and maintain the fluidity of these membranes, allowing for efficient functioning of the cells and transmission of signals between them.

"Omega-3s and Brain Health" by the Brain Health Education Institute elaborates on this, stating, "DHA plays a particularly important role in development of the brain and nervous system in infants, protection and repair of brain and nervous tissue from age-associated damage, and improving mental function."

Additionally, omega-3s have neuroprotective qualities, potentially slowing down age-related cognitive decline and protecting against degenerative brain diseases like Alzheimer's. Omega-3 may offer benefits in a variety of psychiatric and neurological disorders, and in particular neurodegenerative conditions.

While omega-3 supplements offer a concentrated dose, incorporating these fatty acids into your diet is a great way to boost your intake. Fatty fish, like salmon, mackerel, tuna, sardines, and herring are a great source. A vegan alternative is algae oil. Also, flaxseeds and chia seeds are rich in ALA, a plant-based omega-3 that the body can convert to EPA and DHA.

Of course, consult a qualified healthcare professional before starting any supplements, but a general guideline for omega-3 intake is 1,000–2,000 mg of omega-3 fatty acids from fish oil per day. Be aware that excess of 3,000 mg daily can increase bleeding risk.

Probiotics

The link between the health of our gut microbiome and our brain function is called the gut-brain axis. Probiotics can help restore a balanced gut environment, potentially reducing inflammation and promoting the production of beneficial neurotransmitters.

Studies show probiotics influence the production of mood-regulating chemicals like serotonin and GABA in the gut, which then communicate with the brain. Also, chronic inflammation has been linked to various neurological conditions, and probiotics help reduce inflammation throughout the body, including the brain.

Foods with Probiotics:

- Yogurt with live and active cultures
- Kefir (fermented milk drink)
- Kimchi (fermented vegetables)

- Kombucha (fermented tea)
- Sauerkraut (fermented cabbage)
- Miso (fermented soybean paste)
- Tempeh (fermented soybeans)

There's no one-size-fits-all dosage for probiotic supplements. Different strains offer varying benefits, and the appropriate dose depends on the specific strain and one's individual needs. The capsule supplements that will be the most beneficial are labeled "enteric coated," which means they won't be dissolved until they can do their intended work in the small and large intestines.

Clothing and Fabrics

Beyond its basic function of providing warmth and protection, clothing has long held deep spiritual meaning across various cultures. The materials we choose to put next to our skin can influence our well-being and connect us to something larger than ourselves.

In 2003, Israeli doctor Heidi Yellen, published study findings in *Hebrews Today* on the frequencies of fabric titled *Healing Flax*. She utilized a digital instrument called the Ag-Environ machine, to show that the human body has a signature frequency of 100, and organic cotton is the same.

The study showed that if the number is lower than 100, it puts a strain on the body. A diseased, nearly dead person has a frequency of about 15, and that's where polyester, rayon, and silk register. Non-organic cotton registers a signature frequency of about 70. However, if the fabric has a higher frequency, it gives energy to the body. This is where linen comes in as a super-fabric, with a frequency of 5,000.

Linen, derived from the flax plant, holds a unique place in the history of spirituality. Prized for its natural qualities, linen transcends its physical properties to become a fabric imbued with meaning and potential for healing, which is why it was used to make healing bandages.

Across cultures, linen's remarkable strength and resistance to decay have earned it a prominent place through history. In ancient Egypt, the dead were wrapped in linen shrouds, symbolizing a healing path to the afterlife. Similarly, in Judaism, priestly garments were traditionally made of linen, signifying purity and righteousness.

Linen's breathability isn't just a practical benefit. Freely circulating air allows for a sense of lightness and ease, mirroring the pursuit of inner peace and spiritual clarity. Even sleeping on linen sheets can promote a more restful and spiritually receptive state due to its cooling properties.

Wool is also 5,000, but when blended with linen, the frequencies cancel each other out and fall to zero. Even wearing a wool sweater on top of a linen outfit collapsed the electrical field in Yellen's findings. The reason for this could be that the energy field of wool flows from left to right, while that of linen flows from right to left. This may be why in the bible chapter of Leviticus it's stated not to blend the two fibers.

Therefore, if polyester and synthetic fabrics have the same resonance as death and disease, it would behoove us to eliminate polyester and blended fabrics from our wardrobes and replace them with linen. This is important, as Reiki attunements raise our vibration, and fabric choice in our clothing can maintain the highest level. Plus, the production of synthetic fibers is often resource-intensive and pollutes the environment, which misaligns with the spiritual principle of living in harmony with nature.

Linen is quite a bit more expensive than cotton and polyester fabrics, and those economic factors may be a barrier for some to make the switch. My pants were already 100 percent cotton, but I discarded my polyester-blended fabric shirts and replaced them with 100 percent linen ones purchased used on eBay. It's a practical way to not only save money but help the environment by recycling clothing. (Garments purchased used need to be machine washed with a 1 / 2 cup of salt to neutralize the previous owner's energy.)

I also splurged and purchased 100 percent linen bedding and sleepwear. While it's not a guarantee of a perfect night's sleep, it has been a helpful tool simply by reinforcing my intent to keep my energies at a higher vibration.

Replacing one's wardrobe is a big expense, so I suggest that, before selling or donating your polyester fabric clothing, you try an experiment. Put your 100 percent cotton or linen garments at the front of your closet and drawers and try wearing only those every day for a week to a month and document any changes to your energy. If you sleep on polyester or microfiber sheets, switching to 100 percent cotton ones is not usually an expensive replacement.

It will be impossible to completely avoid synthetic fabrics, as some have elastin for stretch, like socks and underwear. Many brands of underwear have an elastic band at the top But since we don't want that next to our skin, look for styles that have the 100 percent cotton enveloping it. Athletic wear especially has become high-tech, with synthetic sweat-wicking properties, so sporty folks have limitations on fashionable styles that can be worn at the gym or on the field. But, by using your creativity from your clearer sense of curiosity, you'll find a solution that works for you.

Media and Music

We face a constant barrage of stimuli from television, music, news, and social media. As you transform into your authentic self, the information you take in may change to support your new vibration. While these media can be enriching, they have potential downsides. Unchecked consumption can create a mental and emotional static that drowns out our inner voices and hinders our personal connection to the divine. Try watching television only for programs that uplift you. Otherwise, turn it off. That goes for anything that'll create agitation or anxiety in your mind.

Everything we choose to listen to, watch, or read can affect us in unhelpful ways we may not be aware of. Especially if we watch the news. Nightly, daily, or even all-day news, if we have cable, are all best avoided. Unplug from that world, because those are all issues beyond your control. Try avoiding any news for a week to feel like you've been on vacation.

I also suggest the authentic you may no longer dwell on politics. It's currently a polarizing pit of hate you can't get yourself out of. Avoid listening to actual radio. Radio is tuned to 440 Hz, which is a tremendously unbalancing frequency. There's an app called "432 Player" that plays all your stored music at 432 Hz, which is one of the nine Solfeggio frequencies. Listening to more music on Solfeggio frequencies brings peace and relaxation.

Social media posts try to obtain engagement to boost their algorithm and are often negative in nature to induce a trigger response. If someone's post triggers you, it's not a content creator to follow, at least until you figure out why you're triggered.

We know what we're keeping out. What information are we allowing in for our spiritual growth?

Many spiritual teachers have emphasized the transformative power of music when listened to mindfully. When you listen to music and listen to it consciously, the music flows through you, and resonates on a deeper level, fostering a sense of peace and presence. Listen to the sounds of nature— wind blowing through the trees or rain falling—to be in touch with the present moment and to find peace.

Bashar tells us that the first three minutes of the second movement to Beethoven's seventh symphony hold all the vibrations required for healing.

Some of this will become second nature as you awake to the painful toxicity behind the lyrics of popular music, where the artists share expressions of unresolved trauma. By choosing to listen to positive love songs, for example, we can bring more love into our lives. Because music by indigenous people from around the globe already incorporates the importance of nature and grounding, listening to it can offer a greater benefit than entertainment.

Ten popular songs scientifically proven to create a sense of happiness as reported in MediMusic.co are:

1. Don't Stop Me Now (Queen)
2. Dancing Queen (ABBA)
3. Good Vibrations (The Beach Boys)
4. Uptown Girl (Billy Joel)
5. Eye of the Tiger (Survivor)
6. I'm a Believer (The Monkees)
7. Girls Just Want to Have Fun (Cyndi Lauper)
8. Livin' on a Prayer (Bon Jovi)
9. I Will Survive (Gloria Gaynor)
10. Walking on Sunshine (Katrina & The Waves)

A Google search will help you discover more helpful songs that may better suit your musical tastes. Creating a playlist of these songs to enjoy throughout the day can boost your feelings of happiness.

Understandably, we all have listening habits, want to stay up to date on the latest music crazes, or simply find calming music boring. Since we may choose to listen to certain music out of habit, switching to a more mindful approach can take time. Our taste in music can change if there's a desire to give it effort for our spiritual growth.

Visual entertainment can also be a vehicle for spiritual exploration. Works that depict beauty, compassion, and the interconnectedness of life can elevate our perspective. Films and documentaries that explore profound themes or showcase the wonders of the universe can cultivate this sense of wonder and appreciation for the world around us. They can easily be found on almost any streaming platform.

Horror films, thrillers, and other dramatic genres induce a sense of fear, which disconnects us from self-love. Remember, you can't feel love and fear at the same time. Over time, you'll gain a greater consciousness of how certain programs make you feel.

I've found myself watching more low-angst reality programs of cooking or home renovation, as there's little toxic behavior. Characters in our sitcoms are often toxic without consequences. I used to love watching *Will & Grace*, but now all I see are traumatized people making everyone around them feel bad, and no longer find that entertaining. *The Real Housewives* series are sad to watch for me, as all I saw were women displaying painful ego dramas of past unresolved traumas.

My list of ten popular TV Shows and Movies that can be uplifting are:

1. All Creatures Great and Small (PBS)
2. Anne with an E (Netflix)
3. *Ted Lasso* (Apple TV)
4. Somebody Somewhere (HBO MAX)
5. Abbot Elementary (Hulu)
6. The Other Two (HBO MAX)
7. The Wonder Years (ABC / Disney+)
8. *Groundhog Day* (Various outlets)
9. Heartstopper (Netflix)
10. *Julia* (HBO MAX)

Ultimately, the most spiritually enriching forms of music and visual entertainment are those that resonate with your unique path, prompting introspection, fostering connection, and leaving you feeling more aligned with your inner self. I discuss more on how to get the most spiritual benefit from watching TV in the section below on rituals.

Designing Your Physical Space: Feng Shui and Vastu Shastra
As mentioned in chapter 5, our homes are a mirror of our lives. The Chinese

have had a spiritual understanding of the placement of objects for four thousand years called feng shui. It's an important part of self-empowerment with Lifeprint Reiki. Translated as "wind-water," feng shui has roots in Taoist philosophy, which emphasizes balance and interconnectedness in nature. It's a system for creating a sacred harmony between people and their surroundings with the core belief that energy, or *qi* (pronounced chee), flows through all living things and spaces. By arranging a space in a particular way, you can improve the flow of qi and create positive influences in your life.

There are several key concepts to grasp in feng shui. One is the importance of creating clean, uncluttered spaces. Clutter is believed to stagnate the flow of qi. Another concept is the five elements: wood, fire, earth, metal, and water. Each element is associated with different colors, shapes, and energies, and can be used to balance the energy in a specific area of your home.

The *bagua* is a nine-square grid used to map different areas of your life onto specific sections of your home. For example, the wealth and prosperity area is typically in the southeast section of a home. Placing objects that symbolize wealth and prosperity in this area, or using wealth-associated colors on the walls, like violet, can potentially strengthen that aspect of your life. The entrance to the home is an important area, as it's considered the "mouth of qi" where energy enters. It needs to be kept clean and well-lit with the door able to open freely and fully.

Start by decluttering. You know that feeling of satisfaction when you clean out a drawer or closet? That's the feeling of stagnant energy moving again. Decluttering needs to be done regularly, as things pile up. For instance, I'm in the practice of throwing away magazines when the new issue arrives.

Everything must work properly, including all doors, windows, plumbing fixtures, electric lighting, and switches. Colors and materials need to be thoughtful, deliberate, and beautiful. Even the art we hang on the walls can affect this harmony. Most people hang art too high on the wall, and feng shui tells us that can lead to feelings of not being enough.

Sofas, desks, and beds should all be placed in commanding positions. Placement of the bed is most important. It's recommended to have the bed opposite the door, but not in line with it. Positioning the bed on the same wall as the door is considered inauspicious, as well as having the head of the bed in line with the door. However, if something inauspicious can't be altered, there's always an auspicious cure. (If you wish to further investigate feng shui, there are books and videos listed in the appendix.)

Even older than feng shui is the Hindu Vastu Shastra, which utilizes directional alignment and energy flow (like qi in feng shui) to create a positive influence. Vastu Shastra prescribes ideal placements for rooms, furniture, and even common objects within a dwelling. The Taj Mahal is considered the epitome of perfect Vastu Shastra, a form which also made its way to the Middle East in Islamic architecture.

Basic Vastu principles include locating the kitchen in the southeast for good digestion, the master bedroom in the southwest for stability, and the main entrance in the northeast for positive energy flow. However, it's important to remember that Vastu Shastra, like feng shui, is a guideline, not a rigid rulebook. Adaptations can be made for modern floor plans. Focusing on the core principles of functionality and creating a positive atmosphere is key.

By making some small changes based on either set of principles, you can create a more harmonious and balanced home. Even if you don't have extra money to spend on decor, with either practice, intention is key.

Creating New Spiritual Practices

The new authentic you will be seeking ways to deepen your Lifeprint of personal divine connection and healing. There's a list of possibilities in the appendix to see if anything resonates with you. It bears repeating that implementing additional spiritual tools are not required to heighten your divine connection. Despite the fact they can be helpful, they're only worth incorporating into your practice if they resonate with you. Hopefully your self-empowerment to discover other effective spiritual tools on your own will prove fruitful. Just like your physical being needs daily care and attention, so does your spirit.

Everyone needs to spend time awake and alone daily, which may require an adjustment to your sleep schedule if you don't live alone. This time can be used for fulfilling anything on your practice list, but the importance is for it to be spent alone.

We don't usually think of fun as something spiritual, but that feeling is us connecting to a higher power. Spiritual practices don't have to all be serious, so finding fun daily practices goes a long way to shifting our reality to one we prefer.

Creating Rituals

In chapter 5, I mentioned the importance of discipline. One of the most powerful ways to enforce our spiritual discipline is with the creation of daily rituals. Gurus and psychologists alike have recognized the power of rituals in infusing everyday activities with divine significance. They can be as simple as a cup of tea in the morning or as elaborate as a traditional wedding ceremony. The way we brush our teeth, the way we eat our breakfast, the way we walk in the garden—everything can become a spiritual practice. Regardless of form, rituals offer a powerful tool for fostering reconnection.

Rituals play an important role in creating structure and fostering a sense of security. By transforming routines into rituals, we cultivate mindfulness, connect with deeper aspects of ourselves, and create a sense of grounding in our often-chaotic lives.

Like life, rituals have a beginning, middle, and end. Making a routine activity a ritual minimally requires creating that beginning and ending moment. A moment of gratitude or stillness, or lighting a candle or incense, are such possible moments. Only your creativity to make the moments personally unique matters.

The present moment is the only place where life ever happens. Rituals, by their very nature, take us out of the frenetic energy of daily life and place us in the current moment. This focused attention allows us to reconnect with our inner selves and quiet the mental chatter that often obscures our true feelings and desires.

Rituals can also be a bridge to reconnect us to the vast tapestry of humanity. Many cultures have ancient rites of passage that mark significant life transitions, from birth to death. The cycles of the moon have inspired countless rituals throughout history, associating the full moon with heightened intuition, and the new moon with fresh starts. Moon rituals can be as simple as setting intentions under the new moon or practicing gratitude under the full moon.

Rituals can be bolstered by the power of personal affirmations and mantras. By incorporating affirmations into our rituals, we can amplify their reconnective power.

Now think of all the activities and routines throughout the day which you perform mindlessly and out of habit. Imagine giving one of them spiritual intention to make it more ceremonial, adding affirmations to amplify the intent. Perhaps at the start of your day, instead of rushing through your coffee routine, light a candle, savor the aroma of the beans, and focus on the present moment as you grind and brew. Ending with a thought of gratitude for this exquisite moment sets a mindful tone for the day ahead.

You can elevate your lunch break from a mindless scroll-fest to a nourishing ritual. Disconnect from technology, find a quiet spot in nature, and savor your food, focusing on its taste and texture. To end, take a few deep breaths to appreciate the simple pleasure of sustenance.

Commuting can become a ritual, even if you travel by public transport, by dedicating this time to self-care. Read a book, listen to calming music, or practice mindfulness meditations to create a spiritual buffer zone between work and personal life. Even if you drive yourself to work, sitting in traffic can be the perfect time to surrender and know you'll arrive at precisely the time you need to be there.

At night, before bed, perhaps safely light a small candle or incense and spend a few minutes reflecting on three things you're grateful for that day. This simple ritual fosters a positive mindset and promotes better sleep and dreams.

Your family might already employ a Sunday dinner ritual. That may be the reason you've been reading this book. If not, try turning a regular meal into a gathering ritual, by inviting closest friends, cooking together, and sharing stories, to foster connection and create cherished memories.

Even the habit of watching TV can be transformed into a mindful spiritual ritual! By approaching TV with intention and mindfulness, you can transform it from a passive activity into a tool for exploration, reflection, and spiritual growth.

Before turning on the screen, take a moment to set an intention for your viewing experience. When you find yourself bored or looking to escape the reality of life, ask yourself what you want to gain from this time. Is it seeking inspiration, exploring different cultures, or simply find a moment of peace? With a focused mind, you'll be more receptive to the messages that resonate with your spirit.

Then, instead of mindless channel surfing, choose programs with intention, like documentaries about awe-inspiring natural wonders, films that explore profound themes, or shows that celebrate the human spirit. Even animated movies can hold deep messages about compassion, courage, and self-discovery. If you desire to watch dramatic programs of people displaying toxic human behaviors like violence, betrayal, or hatred, ask yourself how this serves your higher good and how it can be healing. For example, police procedurals are popular because they offer a sense of justice. If you need to watch an episode of *Law & Order*, first ask yourself where justice is missing from your life.

Avoid multitasking and focus on the visuals, sounds, and narratives. Notice how the story unfolds, how characters grapple with challenges, and how emotions are evoked. Ask yourself how these elements connect to your own life or spiritual journey.

After watching, take a moment to reflect. What resonated? Did the program spark any insights or questions? Express gratitude for the experience and how it enriched your perspective by journaling these thoughts.

The mundane task of walking the dog can become a spiritual act and meditation if given that intention. Before clipping on the leash, take a few deep breaths. Set your mind on connecting with your furry companion and appreciating the present moment by letting go of worries to focus on the simple act of being together.

When outside, embrace the details of the sensory world you might otherwise miss—the dappled sunlight filtering through leaves, the cool morning air on your skin, the symphony of birdsong. Observe your dog's enthusiastic exploration through their sniffing and playful detours and allow their joy to be contagious.

Be present in each step, feeling the ground beneath your feet. Notice the rhythm of your breath and the way your dog's gait mirrors or contrasts yours. Consider the walk as a form of gratitude by appreciating the companionship, unconditional love, and zest for life your dog offers. Be thankful for the opportunity to move your body and be outdoors in nature.

Using the restroom can be ritualized for spiritual growth and divine connection. Our bodies have natural rhythms, and attuning ourselves to them can be a powerful spiritual practice of release and renewal.

Begin by taking a few deep breaths before entering, acknowledging this as a time to cleanse and let go without any distractions. As you go, offer a silent gratitude for your body's natural ability to eliminate waste, and visualize the elimination process as a form of internal purification. Imagine negativity or burdens leaving your body with the waste.

After finishing, take a moment to appreciate the feeling of lightness and release. Wash your hands mindfully, focusing on the cleansing water. Re-enter the world feeling refreshed and ready to tackle the rest of the day with renewed energy.

If turning going to the bathroom into a ritual is possible, then anything you do can also benefit from that intention.

Smudging

Smudging is a spiritual cleansing practice I utilize that's deeply rooted in indigenous cultures and which involves the burning of sacred plants. This smoke purifies individuals, spaces, and objects, dispelling negative energies and creating a sacred atmosphere. It's also used for personal purification and healing, as well as blessing.

Commonly used plants for smudging include sage, cedar, sweetgrass, and tobacco. Each plant carries its own unique properties and energetic qualities. For instance, sage is often associated with purification and protection, while sweetgrass is linked to prayer and positive energy. The choice of herbs depends on the individual's intention. Many people find that the act of smudging, accompanied by intention and mindfulness, creates a sense of peace and clarity.

The most common smudge is dried sage, or *Salvia officinalis*. It's a plant rich in essential oils, including thujone, camphor, and pinene. These compounds contribute to sage's distinctive aroma and flavor, but they also possess antimicrobial and antioxidant properties. When dried sage is burned, these compounds are released into the air in the form of smoke with therapeutic effects. This antimicrobial action could contribute to a sense of purification and renewal often associated with sage smudging.

Whichever plant or plants you choose, it's important to know its origin and if it has been sustainably grown. Because of the New Age popularity of smudging, what was once a product gifted to shamans for limited sacred use, is now obtainable for purchase by anyone. To meet the commercial needs, overharvesting is common, which damages future growth potential.

Before meditation, incense works in a similar way to smudging. The mechanics behind incense's spiritual efficacy are rooted in symbolism, intention, and the power of suggestion. The act of lighting incense can be a ritual, a moment of conscious dedication to a spiritual practice. The choice of incense often holds significance, with different scents associated with various intentions or goals. As the incense burns, its tantalizing fragrance fills the air, creating an atmosphere that supports the desired spiritual state. Whether it's relaxation, focus, or connection to the divine, the mind is subtly guided by the sensory experience.

Both methods are often performed before meditation, ceremonies, or important life events to create a sacred and focused environment. As I mentioned, our homes are as sacred as any house of worship, and smudging or burning incense can help remind us of that fact.

Crystals

Crystals, formed over millennia within the earth, are conduits of various potent, earth-bound energy. These natural formations are revered for their metaphysical properties, acting as tools for spiritual growth, healing, and manifestation, which is why they're part of Lifeprint Reiki. Each crystal carries a unique vibrational frequency, corresponding to specific energies and intentions.

The mechanics behind crystal power are rooted in the concept of energy exchange. Humans are intricate energy fields, constantly interacting with the environment. Crystals, with their stable and concentrated energy, can influence and harmonize personal energy patterns. When a crystal aligns with a specific intention, it acts as an amplifier, focusing and directing energy towards the desired outcome. This energetic interaction stimulates the body's natural healing processes.

There are countless ways to incorporate crystals into your spiritual practice. Here are a few common methods:

Meditation: Holding a crystal during meditation can focus your attention and enhance your meditative state. Its energy can be used to ground, balance, or uplift your spirit.

Healing: Placing crystals on specific chakra points of the body is a popular practice. Each crystal is believed to correspond to a different chakra.

Carrying: Wearing crystal jewelry or carrying crystals in your pocket allows you to benefit from their energy throughout the day.

Some of the most popular crystals are mentioned in the appendix.

When shopping for crystals, the best way to choose which one is right for you now, is to simply choose the ones you're drawn to.

Working with Archangels

While archangels are prominent figures in many religions, their essence transcends specific doctrines or labels. Throughout history, these powerful energies served as bridges between the seen and unseen, offering guidance and support. The archangels' assistance is available to all, but they only help if asked. This is why a deeper understanding of these energies, and how to incorporate them into daily meditation, can play a crucial role in our healing journey.

Most people will recognize archangels as part of Christianity, or more specifically, Catholicism, but the fact that they all have Hebrew names, tells us knowledge of their existence predates that. "El" in Hebrew means "God." Names like Michael are built from the separate Hebrew words "Mi" ("who"), "cha" ("like"), and "el." The name translates to "One Who is like God."

The Jewish Talmud offers glimpses into angelic figures, with the concept of *Malachim* (messengers) that appear throughout the text, often associated with specific tasks or natural phenomena, just like the archangels.

While archangels are historically depicted in human form, they are truly forms of interdimensional energy, and are available to assist us in our earthly incarnations in various, but specific, ways. They are energies that can assist on your healing journey. A list of eleven popular archangel energies is included in the appendix for you to invite them to join you while in meditation.

Connecting with these energies can involve meditation or visualization. During meditation, focus your intention on the quality you wish to cultivate or the question you wish to have answered. Visualize that radiant energy surrounding you as your guide. As you become more attuned to their presence, you may receive intuitive guidance or simply a sense of peace and support. Remember, these archangel energies are pure expressions of divine energy that are a part of all of us, waiting to enhance the lives of those who seek their assistance.

Ascended Masters

The concept of Ascended Masters originates from the Theosophical Society, founded by Helena Blavatsky in the late nineteenth century. They're considered to be enlightened beings who once lived on Earth as ordinary humans, but transcended the limitations of the physical world through spiritual evolution.

Having achieved a state of perfect wisdom and mastery over their emotions and desires, they reside in higher dimensions to watch over humanity, offering guidance and support to those who seek it. Because they were once human, they can be added to our list of spirit ancestors for increased internal validation. Calling upon them in meditation assists in not only acquiring the spiritual knowledge they possess, but also in gaining empowerment for our own abilities.

There's no one definitive list of Ascended Masters, but some of the most well-known include Jesus Christ; his mother, Mary; the Buddha, a prince who achieved enlightenment through meditation and self-denial; Krishna; Quan Yin, who is the embodiment of compassion and mercy; and Lao Tzu, the founder of Taoism, who is credited with writing the foundational text of the religion, *the Tao Te Ching*.

We don't need to know their names for them to be helpful in mediation. I simply call upon "all known Ascended Masters" to assist in my daily meditations. Since they were once living, I feel them move through me like spiritual ancestors, bringing a tingly feeling to my body. I may ask "Who is that?" Most recently, it's been Krishna who's appeared during meditation to help me.

Ascended Masters offer a model for our own spiritual growth. They serve as reminders that enlightenment is possible and that even ordinary people can achieve extraordinary things.

CHAPTER 10:

Applying Lifeprint Reiki to a New Society

Compassion is a manifestation of the relationality
that binds people together in community and that
constitutes the very essence of their humanity.

—CHRISTOPHER D. MARSHALL

WHAT IF WE COULD LIVE IN A WORLD made up entirely of compassionate people practicing compassionate ideas? What would a compassionate society look like?

We can become more than just a compassionate society; we can become a spiritually compassionate one as well. That means simply understanding that everything we do is spiritual and all of us are looking to continually heal on the inside, without controlling anything or anyone beyond ourselves.

It is important to find like-minded or open-minded people to surround ourselves with and to choose for our partners and spouses. Having someone who supports our personal growth is crucial to the process.

If we understood that people who break laws are acting out unresolved trauma, could we create a justice system not based on revenge, but on rehabilitating, to help offenders reconnect to self-love?

PARENTING AND RELATIONSHIPS

Through raising emotional intelligence, I hope that Lifeprint Reiki will help make you the last stop for ancestral dysfunction. This starts with raising more confident, healthy, and emotionally stable children who become confident, healthy and emotionally stable adults.

I've written a lot about trauma, but the truth of the matter is, you can't raise a child free from trauma, because they are born carrying ancestral trauma, soul trauma, and past life trauma. And not all children react the same way to the same stimuli during their present incarnation. Seemingly innocuous situations or benign treatment can create trauma. So, how you interact with them carries tremendous weight. When kids believe your first goal is to empathize and understand rather than to admonish and correct, you leave the door open for future healthy conversations.

Trying to protect a child from trauma, or emotions a parent feels they're not ready to handle, can be further traumatizing. Remember how emotional intelligence relies on a parent openly, yet appropriately, expressing their feelings? The child always knows something isn't right and covering up what's really going on puts a wrench in the desire to build a close relationship. It's important to honor the child's need for your emotional truth because you now have tools to help them learn to resolve that trauma before it becomes ingrained in their psyche and causes unnecessary difficulties in life.

CHOOSING A SPOUSE OR PARTNER

To avoid passing inherited and personal life trauma to a child, both parents need to have evolved high levels of emotional intelligence. This makes finding an emotionally compatible spouse or partner a cornerstone of fulfilling, happy relationships. Compatibility goes beyond initial attraction, and includes shared values, communication styles, and the ability to connect on a deeper level. True intimacy is when you can be seen by somebody and not be judged. This vulnerability and acceptance form the bedrock of emotional compatibility.

Before seeking a partner, the introspection of the 11 Insights is key. We need to know what our emotional geography is like before we can even begin to navigate someone else's. Gaining the self-awareness to identify our core values, communication preferences (direct, indirect), and emotional needs (affection, independence) lays the groundwork for finding someone who compliments us by understanding us.

Part of our core values is our love language. The term and concept originally developed by Dr. Gary Chapman, is another behavior our trauma unconsciously creates to seek and demonstrate love to fill the love gap. The concept suggests that understanding and speaking your partner's love language is crucial for a fulfilling relationship. There are five primary love languages:

1. Words of affirmation
2. Acts of service
3. Giving/receiving gifts
4. Quality time
5. Physical touch

Those who value words of affirmation feel loved through compliments and verbal appreciation. Acts of service-oriented individuals express and feel love through helpful deeds. Receiving gifts signifies love through tangible presents. Quality time lovers cherish undivided attention, while physical touch emphasizes the importance of non-sexual touch.

When couples are unaware they possess differing love languages, communication and emotional fulfillment can be challenging. For instance, a partner who primarily expresses love through acts of service might consistently perform chores and favors, expecting their partner to feel loved. However, if the recipient's love language is words of affirmation, they might feel unappreciated despite the partner's efforts. This discrepancy can lead to feelings of resentment, neglect, and misunderstanding. Conversely, a partner who expresses love through gifts might shower their loved one with presents, only to find their partner longing for quality time. This disconnect can create a sense of emotional distance and frustration. Understanding our preferred love language, and that of our partner, enables us to truly connect with them.

When we begin healing past trauma, there's no desperation to be in a relationship or have children to satisfy an external social expectation. When we're on a healing journey, the only appropriate partner is someone who also can dive deep into their emotional past, heal, and openly communicate with us.

When we're empowered by self-love, the red flags wave high and loudly at the appearance of a narcissist—covert or overt—because we don't feel good around them. We can wish them well and send them away, regardless of a strong physical attraction.

Finding someone who's willing to participate in some of the deeper dives is a good start. Be wary of someone telling you what you "should" do, and have the awareness if you find yourself having that impulse to "fix" someone.

Emotional and spiritual growth continues in relationships, and even if we're vulnerable to some of our past pains, some areas may take more time and patience to address. Therefore, neither you nor your partner can be forced to face those painful self-truths within any timeframe.

HEALING BEFORE CONCEIVING

It's best if you've gone through the self-love journey of healing some of your childhood traumas before having kids. If both you and your children understand the principles of Lifeprint Reiki, then your grandchildren will be at a much better starting place in the world.

We know from epigenetic studies that trauma is passed down to our children through the DNA of both parents. In an ideal situation, if we transmute as much of the trauma as possible before conceiving children, less of that trauma will affect them. Using the modalities mentioned in chapter 3 and working through the 11 Insights in chapter 8 can lead to improved mental and emotional well-being in parents, allowing them to be more present and responsive to their children's needs, fostering a secure and nurturing environment.

The same holds true for parents who choose to adopt. While there's obviously no personal trauma that's been passed down to an adopted child, they still hold trauma from their biological parents, and healing ourselves before becoming their parent helps us raise them in a more emotionally secure environment.

Perhaps you've heard stories of adopted children who become angry and violent as they grow older. Trapped in the fight or flight response from their trauma, they consistently choose to fight. How different their life would be with adoptive parents who understood the possible cause of their behavior, and knew to provide Reiki sessions as a baby, to help clear the trauma energy.

Gaining the self-awareness of the 11 Insights will help you identify their emotional pains as they grow and take action to help them heal from the challenging experience.

REIKI AND YOUR CHILD

What types of traumas can you heal in a child with Reiki? When trauma manifests in physical symptoms like frequent headaches or stomachaches, energy work can ease physical discomfort and promote relaxation. The sense of isolation and fear associated with emotional neglect and abuse can also be soothed by Reiki. While Reiki alone is not a cure for the trauma itself, it can soothe the nervous system overwhelmed by energetic aftereffects of anxiety, depression, or sleep disturbances. It can also help soothe fear and anger, which are fight or flight responses. Reiki helps to release these trapped emotions, allowing the child to feel a sense of peace and safety.

Open communication is key. Parents must first explain the process in an age-appropriate way to ensure the child feels comfortable and safe. You want to create a supportive environment where the child feels loved and empowered to heal. They must understand they're not broken nor in need of "fixing"; you simply want to help them feel better.

As mentioned earlier, children over the age of five have been successfully attuned to Reiki, empowered to heal themselves of some uncomfortable symptoms. This has been effective on some levels of autistic children, so can be helpful on neurotypical children in calming rumination or catastrophic thoughts and reducing anxiety.

Distant Reiki can be effective for infants and toddlers, by familiarizing youngsters with the advantages of Reiki from an early age. However, it's important to manage expectations.

If you suspect your child has experienced external trauma and exhibits severe behaviors, consult a pediatrician or mental health professional who specializes in childhood trauma. Integrating Reiki with established treatments, like play therapy or cognitive behavioral therapy (CBT), creates a holistic healing environment that addresses both the emotional and energetic aspects of trauma.

EMOTIONALLY INTELLIGENT CHILDREN

Raising children with emotional intelligence is about nurturing their ability to understand and manage their own emotions, as well as recognizing and responding to the emotions of others. It's a journey that starts from infancy and continues throughout childhood. I've included resources in the appendix for further study. Here, I offer an overview.

Key aspects include:

Validation and empathy: Creating a safe space for your child to express their feelings, both positive and negative, is crucial. Listen attentively and validate their emotions, letting them know it's okay to feel sad, angry, or frustrated. Use phrases like "I see you're upset," or "It sounds like you're feeling left out." This builds trust and helps them understand their inner world.

Emotional vocabulary: Help your child develop an emotional vocabulary by labeling their feelings. When they're frustrated, say, "It sounds like you're feeling frustrated because you can't reach that toy." This bridges the gap between emotions and words, allowing them to express themselves more effectively.

Coping mechanisms: Teach your child healthy ways to manage their emotions. This might involve deep breathing exercises, taking a quiet break, or engaging in calming activities. Role-playing social situations can also help them navigate tricky emotions.

Leading by example: Children are constantly absorbing the hidden emotions behind certain behaviors around them. Be mindful of how you *don't* express your own feelings. Model healthy coping mechanisms and open communication about emotions. By prioritizing emotional intelligence in your own life, you become a role model for your child.

CREATING A COMPASSIONATE SOCIETY

Emotionally intelligent children grow into emotionally intelligent adults brimming with self-love, but in the United States, we don't seem to be living in an emotionally intelligent society. Though many have awakened to the past injustices inflicted on non-white people and those of various faiths, sexual orientations, and genders, we still have a long way to go to create a compassionate culture. This seems like an impossibility in the United States.

A compassionate and inclusive society demonstrates empathy, understanding, and a sense of shared humanity. Inclusion goes beyond merely tolerating diversity. Everyone is valued and respected, regardless of their differences. Until we grasp the fact that racism and bigotry are in fact mental illnesses suffered by millions, progress towards a compassionate society in every state of America will be slow.

In reading this book and working towards being a more compassionate and empathetic human, it follows that you want those conditions you live and interact with to be equally compassionate in maintaining proper boundaries. Wouldn't it be wonderful to have supportive, like-minded people as our new friends and neighbors, and government policies that support a compassionate agenda?

In broad strokes, here are five conditions needed to achieve an inclusive, compassionate society:

- **Universal mental health care access:** As quoted at the top of chapter 3, *"Trauma in a people, decontextualized over time, looks like culture."* The path to world peace is a mental health one. We need to acknowledge toxic behaviors like racism, addiction, and what were previously believed to be personality traits, as the trauma responses they are, and provide the needed help for those willing to heal and grow.

- **Legislation and inclusive policies:** While there are anti-discrimination laws and protections against hate crimes in some states, the challenge in America is that diversity is so politically charged. Fearful lawmakers won't support measures that benefit a minority group because, as stated earlier, if they feel they're not better than someone, then who are they?

- **Inclusive education:** When we foster an educational system that not only values and respects diversity, we can also encourage development of an individual's curiosity, unique talents and abilities.

- **Empowerment:** Spiritual empowerment leads to physical empowerment. Offering empowering healing and non-religious divine connecting tools to marginalized communities provides them with the means to fully participate in a compassionate society.

- **Reducing income inequality:** While money doesn't buy happiness, the perception of one's financial standing in relation to others plays a substantial role in overall well-being. Income inequality also limits opportunities for individuals with lower incomes.

Income inequality is the most important of the above conditions because of its positive effects on lowering crime rates. The world's safest countries, like Iceland, Denmark, and New Zealand, share one key factor: greater income equity. With greater access to opportunity and a stronger social safety net, citizens feel a sense of security and are less likely to turn to illegal means to obtain money or fulfill any desire. This translates into better overall health outcomes, higher levels of trust within society, and a greater sense of fairness.

COMPASSIONATE JUSTICE

A youth pastor is found to have molested several children. An accountant embezzled from his clients. A vengeful justice is cried out for by the offended. But what if there was a way to understand and treat justice with the spiritual compassion you've gained from reading this book? As Victor Hugo said, "The purpose of punishment is not revenge but to correct."

The current penal system is ineffective at reducing crime, and only serves to create a cycle of violence. We can all agree that incarcerated individuals experience high rates of potentially traumatic events within prison walls. These events, which can include violence, witnessing violence, and harsh treatment by guards, contribute significantly to the development of post-traumatic stress disorder that contribute to the parolee reoffending. Furthermore, in his book *Why They Kill*, Dr. James Gilligan, a violence reduction expert, reiterates my point that many violent offenders have experienced significant trauma in their past, often stemming from abuse or neglect. Placing these individuals in a hyper-vigilant, dehumanizing environment like a maximum-security prison may simply re-traumatize them, hindering their ability to develop empathy, remorse, and the skills necessary for successful reintegration into society.

This focus on punishment over rehabilitation creates a vicious cycle as high-security prisons often fail to provide the necessary mental health and spiritual growth resources and rehabilitation programs. It's a perfect recipe to keep inmates disconnected from self-love.

A compassionate justice system aims to break the cycle by addressing its underlying socioeconomic and mental health factors. It strives for a more humane and restorative approach, prioritizing rehabilitation and healing alongside accountability and retribution, and moves away from the archaic "eye for an eye" punitive model, to embrace empathy for all parties involved.

Rather than solely relying on incarceration, compassionate justice reevaluates sentencing practices by exploring alternatives like drug courts, mental health courts, and community service programs. These programs offer therapeutic solutions by addressing some of the root causes of criminal behavior and addiction or mental illness that start in the offender's childhood development. The end goal is much more positive: reintegrating healed and rehabilitated individuals into society as productive members.

However, preconceived ideas keep us clinging to the Hammurabi code of justice. People erroneously believe that the criminal didn't need to perpetrate that crime; that somehow all criminals can simply decide not to commit the crime.

A great metaphor for understanding the broken ego's overwhelming strength for void-filling is looking at one's uncontrollable desire towards foods.

Mindless consumption of foods like cake, cookies, ice cream, and fast food fill the void of love. We don't want to eat the whole package of cookies or the whole pint of ice cream; common sense says that this goes against our health concerns. But saying no becomes impossible against an overwhelming desire. While this isn't a crime against humanity, it's a violation of our self-love, in not providing ourselves with proper nutrition.

We can look at any criminal activity and trace the impulse back to an unmet childhood need that broke the ego. A vandalizing graffiti-tagger feels disenfranchised from society and needs to show the world not only how meaningless they've been made to feel by making someone else's prized property their canvas, but also that they are somebody by writing their name all over town.

The premeditated murderer seeks ultimate control. The entitlement felt by racketeers and gangsters also stems from a desperate need for control and validation. Someone who scams people out of millions with a Ponzi scheme likely does so to appear successful and valuable, which they never felt as a child.

Doctors commit insurance fraud. Judges accept bribes. Priests molest children. Scammers take advantage of the elderly and immigrants. Many of these people don't believe they're doing anything wrong and sleep well at night.

Perhaps this is the first you're hearing about the concept of compassionate justice, but it's been studied and implemented for decades. The Eglinton St. George's (ESG) United Church of Toronto, Canada has been hosting a free speaker series called *Compassionate Justice* several times each year since 2009. Their 2024 speakers included a Canadian Supreme Court Justice and Benjamin Perrin, a Law Professor at University of British Columbia, discussing how Canada can move beyond "tough on crime" policies to compassionate, evidence-based approaches. Perrin's new transformative justice vision is laid out in his book, *Indictment: The Criminal Justice System on Trial*.

In the USA, recent decades have seen a modicum of compassionate progress in our justice system in several areas:

- **Sentencing:** Mandatory minimum sentences, once widely used, are being re-evaluated. Judges now often have more discretion in considering factors like a defendant's background and potential for rehabilitation. Some states have even passed laws allowing for resentencing in certain drug cases.
- **Drug courts:** These specialized courts offer non-violent drug offenders treatment programs instead of incarceration. This approach aims to address the root causes of addiction and reduce recidivism rates, and is now widely implemented across the country.

- **Mental health:** Courts are increasingly recognizing the role of mental health issues in criminal behavior, but not yet that it's the main issue. Programs for diversion and mental health treatment are being established, but they're not effective at addressing the unresolved trauma at the core of these behaviors.
- **Family law:** The focus in family court is shifting towards solutions that prioritize the well-being of children. Mediation and collaborative divorce processes are becoming more common, aiming to minimize conflict and create workable co-parenting arrangements.

Nowhere is a compassionate approach needed more than in juvenile courts. Understanding how our unresolved trauma causes all sorts of acting-out behavior in children makes it clear that putting juveniles who desperately lack emotional connection and validation in stark block cells, where they're treated like meaningless humans, does not provide the help they need, but exacerbates their disconnect from self-love.

With all the policies and infrastructure required for a compassionate justice system, what matters most is the ability to apply the truths discussed in the 11 Insights. There's actually a spiritual connection between offender and victim worthy of mediating in a restorative justice process. There's great room for spiritual growth by both. The victim can use the incident to deepen their self-awareness, and find the blessing in the loss, that is, by asking, "What lesson have I learned, and what is the path to build on it?" A profound growth occurs when the offender finds self-awareness and spiritual connection through service to the victim and the community.

Changing Building Laws

It's difficult to be truly happy if you find yourself in an intolerable housing situation. For instance, having a slumlord or a landlord who doesn't honor their contractual obligations to maintain habitability. Through the volunteer healing efforts I do with clients at various organizations, I've discovered a majority have tumultuous relationships with their landlords. This lack of safety in your own home is traumatic. And as I've mentioned, it's impossible to heal from a trauma if constantly exposed to the trigger.

If one opens a restaurant, the Board of Health sets standards on running a safe and hygienic establishment to prevent the spread of illness. If the establishment fails an inspection, they are closed. I therefore propose applying this same common-sense approach to the laws regarding multi-family housing ownership.

When a landlord traumatizes their tenants with toxic behavior that debilitates their mental health, there are almost no repercussions. That needs to change. The law I propose would make slum lordship a felony, where the property in question would become the property of the local government and be auctioned to qualified buyers who have no record of building violations.

Yes, it's an extreme step, but a law like this already exists in New York City, though it's rarely enforced. Since 2018, the law was not enforced, until an April 2025 execution on a slumlord owing nearly $30 million dollars in taxes and fines. The Worst Landlords List of over 100 violators maintained by the city's Public Advocates office is simply ignored. This lack of enforcement is likely because New York City's most abusive landlord is New York City Public Housing itself, and keeping bureaucrats out of jail is the priority.

We no longer live in a feudal system where those who own real estate can treat tenants as they please. We're in the Age of Aquarius, which means tenants' rights to live in an emotionally stable environment outweigh those of greedy landlords. Building owners without empathy or compassion, who don't care about people, have no right to own buildings, just like toxic restauranteurs cannot own restaurants.

As a greater portion of the population heals and grows to become authentic compassionate people, we'll be electing a larger number of lawmakers who reflect our compassionate values to effect the needed change in laws. In the meantime, we can work on our inner selves to be the change we want to see in the world.

ROAD TO
RECONNECTION

It's not about how slowly you go,
as long as you never stop.

—CONFUCIUS

ARE YOU THE SAME PERSON YOU WERE before reading this book? By now, you've gained a lot of awareness about how you may not have loved yourself as much as you thought. Can you better see that the world is not how you see it, but rather is how it is? Are you thinking about boundaries as never before, with the realization that some people close to you might be toxic and draining your energy?

Can you see how your personal spiritual growth makes the world a better place? Are you motivated to do the work to fully reconnect to self-love? Do you know the lessons you're here on Earth to learn? Do you better understand the significance of the changing spiritual energy brought on by the Age of Aquarius?

We're living in a time that supports freedom to develop and practice the independent divine connection of self-love. We're awakened to the fact that we're souls having human experiences to learn and grow from the suffering and adversity of the past. Our disconnection wounded our egos, making us always want what's comfortable and familiar to avoid painful triggers.

We're not comparing ourselves and our lives to anyone else's. And we're opening our hearts to forgiveness, simply to release the lingering energies of guilt and shame, without needing an apology. Most importantly, we feel empathy, knowing everyone is on an equally painful journey. We also now know spiritual growth lies outside our comfort zone, and is why we must be uncomfortably off balance for a while as we develop a strong new footing in a more authentic sense of reality.

As compassionate and authentic people, we have the awareness to recognize that everyone has unresolved trauma, and that some peoples' actions harm others or break laws. We know that happens because a broken ego's desperate needs are stronger than common sense or willpower. Whether the offense was criminal or civil, violent or victimless, the perpetrator didn't see any way to control the behavior and still achieve their overwhelming desire.

An attunement to Reiki can not only be a shortcut to a heightened spiritual awakening, but also helps heal us and our families, by deeply connecting to the intrinsic divine energy that flows through us all.

The 11 Insights are powerful, and I'm sure just reading them without the Deeper Dives brought a rumbling and cracking to many a dysfunctional foundation. We can see how so much of the way we behave today is a result of surviving our upbringing, and not of our personal doing. There's nothing wrong with us, but something wrong may have happened to us. We're not broken, only disconnected, and now we know what thoughts need to change to reduce the suffering and anxiety which stands in the way of our desired happiness. Releasing the need to control to a higher power will assure us of living in the abundant flow of the universe.

When you get your head above the rocky waters of trauma, the full expanse of your intrinsically divine humanity will be revealed, leading to a happier life experience in the school called Earth.

THE DIVINE IS ONLY WITHIN.

STAY IN TOUCH

WRITING THIS BOOK was a labor of love. Hopefully, you've gained insights to improve your own life. This work isn't easy and I don't want you to ever feel you're alone working towards a more peaceful life.

To that end, I offer a free online support group for those dealing with the unpleasantness of spiritual growth. For coping tools, lifestyle tips, and a community of folks who've been where you are, check out Lifeprint Reiki's Self-Love Journey Support on Facebook. Simply use this link and answer a few questions for entry: https://www.facebook.com/groups/selflovejourneysupport.

If you'd like to stay connected to continue learning more about yourself, as well as to receive moral support, I offer a few ways:

- @lifeprint_reiki on Instagram
- My website, www.lifeprintreiki.org, offers classes, videos, live webinars, and a store with curated products and services to enhance your life-long journey.

ACKNOWLEDGMENTS

I WOULD LIKE TO THANK all the people in my past who made my life a living hell. Without their toxic behavior, I never would've had the grave need to look within for a healing journey of self-discovery that led me to being the strong, authentic person I am today. I appreciate their past presence in my life and relish in the fact they're no longer part of it.

There are many positive people to acknowledge without whom this book and my happier life would not be possible. Firstly, my Reiki teachers, Jean-Phillippe Schmitt of *Unstruck Sound NYC*, with whom I completed my level two training, and Geordie Numata of *Deer Spirit Reiki*, with whom I completed my level 3 and master training. Their shared wisdom and continued support allowed me to bring transformational healing to myself and others and they encouraged me to discover my own path of Reiki.

Much gratitude to Fern Gorin, founder of *Life Purpose Institute*, who was my spiritual coaching teacher. It was starting as a spiritual coach that I began assembling the initial concept of *The Self Love Journey* to assist my early clients.

I was so fortunate to find Katya Fishman to hold my hand through the professional publishing process. She was my guiding light as an invaluable coach, providing deadlines throughout the year it took to write this book, and then step-by-step instructions over the following six months of editing, design and publication. Katya helped me assemble my core team of industry experts. Alexandra O'Connell performed editor duties, teaching me to love *The Chicago Manual of Style* and guiding me in creating a coherent flow of complex ideas. Victoria Wolf created an engaging cover and interior design that set the perfect spiritual tone. There might be an unneeded comma, dangling participle or run-on sentence without the brilliant line editing of Romy Sommer and detailed proofreading abilities of Eva Fox Mate. It really takes a village to publish a book, and I was surrounded by true talent.

And lastly, but perhaps most importantly, I hold a depth of gratitude for all my groups of ancestors. Starting with my blood ancestor parents, Tama and Jules Fogelman, who set the stage for me to reap the rewards of my healing journey, to my grandparents, to every level of great-grandparent and every relation in between, I give daily thanks for their eternal love and earthly sacrifices inscribed on my soul. My influential spirit ancestors are too many to list, but at the top are Mikao Usui, Krishna, and Grandmother Ayahuasca, who offer invaluable advice. The indigenous tribes of the Lenape are place ancestors who bring me great understanding of my connection to nature at home, and those of the Shipibo people in Peru and the Borucas in Costa Rica, when I travel.

APPENDIX

WELCOME SERIOUS JOURNEY-GOERS! That you're reading this in search of more information is a clear affirmation of your ability to find success on this spiritual growth journey. Here, in this appendix, discover additional resources to further explore the topics and themes discussed in this book, plus listings for various spiritual and wellness practices not mentioned. Think of Lifeprint Reiki as a Christmas tree, and other spiritual practices as the ornaments and lights. Everyone's tree is different, though there may be similarities.

Also included are lists of archangels and crystals, as well as books and a variety of online resources. Investigating even one is an expression of curiosity, a step on the path of curating your own, unique collection of spiritual practices. What you gravitate towards forms the beginning of your very own lifeprint.

The additional spiritual practices you can incorporate into your life are limitless. There are hundreds of different meditation practices alone. There are also many types of healing breathwork, including Mantak Chia, Prana Breathing, Hindu Mudras, or hand gestures.

Learning new practices is another opportunity to meet like-minded people, virtually or in-person, with whom you may begin to repopulate your life. These other practices may or may not remain throughout your journey to happiness, as many need only weeks, months, or a year to offer up their benefits.

CHAPTER 9: FURTHER EXPLORATION

Popular Archangels

- **Barachiel**: Meaning "God's blessing," this energy embodies the essence of divine favor and positive energy, to serve as a universal archetype for abundance, prosperity, and guidance. This energy can assist in finding gratitude for what we already have in life and optimism for the future. Inner peace and a positive outlook act as magnets for opportunities and personal growth.
- **Gabriel:** Gabriel, said to bring news and insights, is associated with communication, creativity, and new beginnings. This energy is the one that helps restore creativity, inspires you to journal, and offers insights into a healed life reconnected to self-love.
- **Haniel**: This name itself translates to "grace of God," hinting at their core function: to guide us towards a life filled with joy and inner peace. Unlike a fleeting emotional state, this energy influence cultivates a deeper sense of contentment. It's a beacon of intuition, gently nudging us towards paths that align with our soul's purpose, and can help reawaken the joy inherent in the journey of life.
- **Jophiel:** When seeking clarity, inspiration, or a boost to your creativity, Jophiel can be a valuable resource. This energy assists answering our most persistent questions. Ask the energy to illuminate your path and open your mind to new possibilities.

- **Metatron:** The Hebrew root of this name is "keeper of the watch" or "one who guides." This energy's functions are multifaceted: keeping a record of our deeds, guarding esoteric knowledge, and acting as a bridge between humanity and the divine. Metatron's Cube, a geometric form said to embody the building blocks of creation, can assist in creating balance and guide understanding of the universe's esoteric fundamental structure.

- **Michael:** Michael provides the energy of protection and defense. He's associated with courage, strength, and standing up for what's right. To connect with his energy, focus on your own inner strength and call upon him during times when you need to make difficult decisions or overcome challenges.

- **Raphael:** The energy of Raphael is associated with physical, emotional, and spiritual well-being, and is said to watch over travelers and those seeking healing. Bring that energy into your meditations to assist in helping transmute trauma and its physical embodiment. Feel that glow of energy surrounding you and focus on releasing trauma from your DNA.

- **Raziel:** Meaning "Secret of God," this energy acts as a keeper of divine knowledge and esoteric wisdom, and is seen as a guide, helping those on spiritual paths to understand cryptic knowledge and unlock their own inner wisdom. Those seeking deeper spiritual understanding, or those engaged in creative pursuits, can call upon Raziel for inspiration and illumination.

- **Sandalphon:** This energy is said to bridge the gap between Heaven and Earth. This physical immensity reflects Sandalphon's role as a conduit—they gather prayers from humanity and weave them into a celestial crown, offering them to the divine. Sandalphon energy is also connected to music, with its presence likened to the harmonious blending of notes. In this sense, Sandalphon represents the unification of earthly aspirations and the divine realm, a bridge built of both melody and meaning.

- **St. Germain:** Although technically not an archangel but an ascended master, this energy, associated with the Violet Flame, can assist in transmuting negativity into positive energy. Meditations on this Violet Flame energy can help individuals release their own negative thoughts and emotions to achieve greater freedom and spiritual connection.

- **Uriel:** Uriel is said to illuminate the mind and bring clarity. This energy is associated with knowledge, learning, and problem-solving, and can be asked to assist with gaining the wisdom of the 11 Insights, gaining self-awareness, and bringing clarity to your self-love journey.

- **Zadkiel**: The name translates to "Righteousness of God" in Hebrew, and holds special significance for those interested in the non-religious spiritual realm. As a guiding force towards mercy, forgiveness, and compassion, this energy offers support in letting go of judgment, guilt, and fear, to help cultivate more compassion, understanding, and release in your life.

Popular Crystals

- **Amethyst** is a purple crystal associated with the crown chakra. It is thought to promote spiritual growth, intuition, and wisdom. This crystal is often used in meditation, dream work, and to alleviate stress and anxiety.

- **Black Tourmaline** is a grounding stone that is believed to protect against negative energy and electromagnetic fields. It is thought to promote stability, courage, and willpower. Black Tourmaline can be carried as a protective amulet, placed near electronic devices, or used in grounding rituals.

- **Citrine** is a golden crystal associated with abundance, prosperity, and joy. It is believed to stimulate creativity, motivation, and personal power. Citrine can be placed in wealth areas of the home, carried in a wallet to attract abundance, or used in meditation for manifesting desires.
- **Clear Quartz** is often referred to as the "master healer" due to its ability to amplify energy and thought. It is believed to enhance clarity, focus, and spiritual awareness. Clear Quartz can be used in meditation, grid work, and energy cleansing.
- **Rose Quartz** is the stone of love and compassion. It is believed to foster self-love, romantic relationships, and emotional healing. Rose Quartz can be carried as a talisman, placed in the bedroom to attract love, or used in heart chakra healing.
- **Selenite** is a white crystal known for its cleansing and purifying properties. It is believed to clear away negative energy, promote peace, and enhance spiritual connection. Selenite can be used to cleanse other crystals, be placed in spaces to purify the environment, or be held during meditation for spiritual cleansing.

SPIRITUAL AND WELLNESS PRACTICES: FURTHER EXPLORATION

Emotional Intelligence

- Justin Bariso, *EQ Applied: The Real-World Guide to Emotional Intelligence*, 2018
- Alyssa Blask Campbell and Lauren Elizabeth Stauble, *Tiny Humans, Big Emotions*, 2023

- Maurice J. Elias, PhD, Steven E. Tobias, PsyD, and Brian S. Friedlander, PhD, *Emotionally Intelligent Parenting: How to Raise a Self-Disciplined, Responsible, Socially Skilled Child*, 2000
- Daniel Goleman, *Emotional Intelligence: Why it Can Matter More Than IQ*, 2005
- Philippa Perry, *The Book You Wish Your Parents Had Read*, 2020

Healing

Books

- Dr. Laura E. Anderson, *When Religion Hurts You: Healing from Religious Trauma and the Impact of High-Control Religion*, 2023
- John Bradshaw, *Family Secrets: The Path from Shame to Healing*, 1996
- John Bradshaw, *Healing the Shame That Binds You*, 2005
- Julia Cameron, *The Artist's Way: A Spiritual Path to Higher Creativity*, 2002
- Pema Chödrön, *When Things Fall Apart*, 2016
- Paul Conti, MD, *Trauma: The Invisible Epidemic*, 2021
- Natalie Gutiérrez, *The Pain We Carry: Healing from Complex PTSD for People of Color*, 2022
- Leonard G. Horowitz, Joseph Puleo, *Healing Codes for the Biological Apocalypse*, 2021
- D.D. David Hulce, *A Fork in the Road: An Inspiring Journey of How Ancient Solfeggio Frequencies Are Empowering Personal and Planetary Transformation*, 2009
- Monique Joiner Siedlak, *Connecting with Your Ancestors*, 2020
- Amy Eden Jollymore, *The Kind Self-Healing Book: Raise Yourself Up with Curiosity and Compassion*, 2015
- Shelley A Kaehr, *Heal Your Ancestors to Heal Your Life*, 2021
- Patrick King, *The Art of Self-Awareness*, 2022

- Katherine Morgan Schafler, *The Perfectionist's Guide to Losing Control: A Path to Peace and Power*, 2023
- Chris Niebauer, *No Self, No Problem: How Neuropsychology Is Catching Up to Buddhism*, 2019
- Bessel Van der Kolk, MD, *The Body Keeps the Score: Brain, Mind, and Body in the Healing of Trauma*, 2015
- John Purkiss, *The Power of Letting Go*, 2020
- Colin Tipping, *Radical Self-Forgiveness: The Direct Path to True Self-Acceptance*, 2011
- Hitendra Wadhwa, *Inner Mastery, Outer Impact*, 2023
- Andrew Weil, MD, *Breathing: The Master Key to Self-Healing*, 1999
- Marlene Winell, *Leaving the Fold: A Guide for Former Fundamentalists and Others Leaving Their Religion*, 2024

Digital Sources
- *Belief It or Not* podcast, Trevor Poelman, host, https://www.youtube.com/c/BeliefItOrNot
- *MythVision* podcast, Derek Lambert, host, https://www.youtube.com/@MythVisionPodcast

Independent Spiritual Philosophy

- The Dalai Lama, *The Art of Happiness*, 2020
- The Dalai Lama, *How to See Yourself as You Really Are*, 2007
- Neville Goddard, *The Power of Awareness*, 2020
- Neville Goddard, *The Power of Imagination*, 2015
- Thich Nhat Hanh, *The Art of Living: Peace and Freedom in the Here and Now*, 2023
- Thich Nhat Hanh, *No Mud, No Lotus: The Art of Transforming Suffering*, 2014
- Sam Harris, *Waking Up: A Guide to Spirituality Without Religion*, 2015

- Linda A. Mercadante, *Belief Without Borders*, 2014
- John O'Donohue, *Anam Cara*, 1997
- Eckhart Tolle, *A New Earth: Awakening to Your Life's Purpose*, 2008
- Eckhart Tolle, *The Power of Now: A Guide to Spiritual Enlightenment*, 2004

Physical Spiritual Practices

- Lynda Bunnell and Ra Uru Hu, *The Definitive Book of Human Design*, 1981
- Adele Ahlberg Calhoun, *Spiritual Disciplines Handbook: Practices That Transform Us*, 2015
- Mantak Chia and William U. Wei, *Basic Practices of the Universal Healing Tao*, 2013
- Mantak Chia, *The Six Healing Sounds: Taoist Techniques for Balancing Chi*, 2009
- Deepak Chopra, *The Seven Spiritual Laws of Yoga*, 2005
- Alison DeNicola, *Mudras for Awakening the Five Elements*, 2017
- Karen Fraser, *Crystals for Beginners*, 2017
- Robert Gass, *Chanting: Discovering Spirit in Sound*, 1999
- Dr. Hillary L. McBride, *The Wisdom of Your Body: Finding Healing, Wholeness, and Connection through Embodied Living*, 2021
- Leah Middleton, *The Beginner Witch's Handbook: Essential Spells, Folk Traditions and Lore for Crafting Your Magickal Practice*, 2023
- Dr Michael Norton, *The Ritual Effect: From Habit to Ritual, Harness the Surprising Power of Everyday Actions*, 2024
- Linda Star Wolf, PhD, *Shamanic Breathwork: Journeying Beyond the Limits of the Self*, 2009
- Swami Sivapriyananda, *Secret Power of Tantrik Breathing: Techniques for Attaining Health, Harmony, and Liberation*, 2009

Reiki
Books

- Mark Hosak and Walter Lubeck, *The Big Book of Reiki Symbols*, 2006
- Sandra Ramos, *Karuna: One of the Most Beautiful Branches of Reiki*, 2014
- William Lee Rand, *Reiki for a New Millenium*, 1998
- Penelope Quest and Kathy Roberts, *The Reiki Manual: A Training Guide for Reiki Students, Practitioners, and Masters*, 2010

Digital Sources

- Divine White Light, YouTube Channel, https://www.youtube.com/@DivineWhiteLight
- Mainstream Reiki, YouTube Channel, https://www.youtube.com/@MainstreamReiki

Self-Evaluation
A great way to discover our strengths is the free website, VIA Character Strengths Assessment (www.viacharacter.org).

Social Change
Books

- Daniel Borstein, *How to Change the World: Social Entrepreneurs and the Power of New Ideas*, 2007
- Katherine J. MacLachlan, *Trauma Informed Criminal Justice Towards a More Compassionate Criminal Justice System*, 2024

Digital Sources

- *Revolution Now* podcast, https://revolutionnow.podbean.com

Wellness

- Peter J. D'Adamo and Catherine Whitney, *Eat Right 4 Your Type: The Individualized Blood Type Diet Solution*, 2016

- Barbara O'Neill, *Sustain Me: The Comprehensive Natural Remedies Book Guide*, 2024
- Paul Pritchford, *Healing with Whole Foods*, 2002
- Andrew Weil, MD, *Natural Health, Natural Medicine: The Complete Guide to Wellness and Self-Care for Optimum Health*, 2004

ABOUT THE AUTHOR

STEVE FOGELMAN is the founder of Lifeprint Reiki, a non-religious spiritual path of healing to reconnect to self-love. He first became a certified spiritual coach through Life Purpose Institute, before accepting the journey to become a Reiki Master with teacher Geordie Numata.

His innovative methods for ridding trauma from the body have proven effective for all of his students, due in part to his discovery of a new Reiki symbol he calls Shin Zo Ho Go. Steve's Facebook group, Lifeprint Reiki's *Self-Love Journey Support*, has become a helpful meeting place for those dealing with the pains of spiritual growth and shifting mindset to gain new insights, understandings and compassion.

Steve is reaching out to those with reading difficulties by creating visual educational courses based on this book as well as exclusive content for his website, www.lifeprintreiki.org. Steve, who is also a published playwright, professional actor and painter, is relocating to Costa Rica with his four-year old rescue, Zelli, to lead attunement and healing retreats.